HUMANITY IN CRISIS

SELECTED TITLES FROM THE MORAL TRADITIONS SERIES
David Cloutier, Kristin E. Heyer, Andrea Vicini, SJ, Editors

All God's Animals: A Catholic Theological Framework for Animal Ethics
   Christopher Steck, SJ

A Culture of Engagement: Law, Religion, and Morality
   Cathleen Kaveny

Diverse Voices in Modern US Moral Theology
   Charles E. Curran

Family Ethics: Practices for Christians
   Julie Hanlon Rubio

Hope for Common Ground: Mediating the Personal and the Political in a Divided Church
   Julie Hanlon Rubio

Keeping Faith with Human Rights
   Linda Hogan

Kinship across Borders: A Christian Ethic of Immigration
   Kristin E. Heyer

Love and Christian Ethics: Tradition, Theory, and Society
   Frederick V. Simmons, Editor

Moral Evil
   Andrew Michael Flescher

The Origins of War: A Catholic Perspective
   Matthew A. Shadle

Prophetic and Public: The Social Witness of US Catholicism
   Kristin E. Heyer

Reconsidering Intellectual Ability: L'ARCHE, Medical Ethics, and Christian Friendship
   Jason Reimer Greig

The Social Mission of the US Catholic Church: A Theological Perspective
   Charles E. Curran

The Vice of Luxury: Economic Excess in a Consumer Age
   David Cloutier

HUMANITY IN CRISIS
Ethical and Religious Response to Refugees

DAVID HOLLENBACH, SJ

Georgetown University Press / Washington, DC

© 2019 Georgetown University Press. All rights reserved. No part of this book may be reproduced or utilized in any form or by any means, electronic or mechanical, including photocopying and recording, or by any information storage and retrieval system, without permission in writing from the publisher.

The publisher is not responsible for third-party websites or their content. URL links were active at time of publication.

Library of Congress Cataloging-in-Publication Data

Names: Hollenbach, David, 1942– author.
Title: Humanity in Crisis : Ethical and Religious Response to Refugees / David Hollenbach, S.J.
Description: Washington, DC : Georgetown University Press, 2020. | Series: Moral traditions series | Includes bibliographical references and index. |
Identifiers: LCCN 2019003698 (print) | LCCN 2019018028 (ebook) | ISBN 9781626167193 (ebook) | ISBN 9781626167179 (hardcover : alk. paper) | ISBN 9781626167186 (pbk.: alk. paper)
Subjects: LCSH: Refugees—International cooperation—Moral and ethical aspects. | Emigration and immigration—Moral and ethical aspects. | Emigration and immigration—Religious aspects—Catholic Church. | Forced migration—Moral and ethical aspects. | Forced migration—Religious aspects—Catholic Church. | Asylum, Right of—Religious aspects—Catholic Church. | Humanitarian assistance—Moral and ethical aspects. | Humanitarian assistance—Religious aspects—Catholic Church.
Classification: LCC JV6346 (ebook) | LCC JV6346 .H65 2020 (print) | DDC 261.8/328—dc23
LC record available at https://lccn.loc.gov/2019003698

∞ This book is printed on acid-free paper meeting the requirements of the American National Standard for Permanence in Paper for Printed Library Materials.

20 19   9 8 7 6 5 4 3 2   First printing

Printed in the United States of America.

The illustration on the cover is *Jesus Comforts the Women of Jerusalem* by Engelbert Mveng, SJ, from his Stations of the Cross and Resurrection in the chapel of Hekima University College, Nairobi, Kenya. Mveng was assassinated by an unknown assailant on the night of April 22, 1995, in Yaounde, Cameroon, because of his defense of poor people against political oppression.

Cover design by Martha Madrid.

*For my friends at Jesuit Refugee Service,
and for the displaced people they accompany.*

CONTENTS

Acknowledgments   ix

1   Threats to Humanity   1

2   Humanity as Moral Standard   12

3   Religious Traditions and Humanitarian Response   25

4   Religious Action Today   46

5   Borders and Shared Humanity   63

6   Rights and Negative Duties   79

7   Positive Duties and Shared Responsibility   96

8   Acting across Borders   114

9   Justice and Root Causes   130

Endnotes   155

Bibliography   175

Index   189

About the Author   197

ACKNOWLEDGMENTS

The inspiration for this book began when John Guiney, the regional director of Jesuit Refugee Service in Eastern Africa, invited me to travel with him from Hekima University College in Nairobi, where I was teaching as a visiting professor, to Kakuma Refugee Camp near Kenya's northwest border with Sudan and Ethiopia. There were over a hundred thousand refugees from Sudan, Somalia, and many other African nations effectively confined at Kakuma. Being with them as part of a weeklong workshop on peace building wakened me to the needs of displaced people. It launched me on a journey, an ongoing attempt to understand what could be done to respond. Since that initial encounter with the realities faced by people forced from their homes by war, I have been aided by many other people in the work that has led to this book. Collaboration with the Jesuit Refugee Service has taken me to a number of places where many have faced crisis: Rwanda and Burundi, Kampala and the north of Uganda, southern Sudan and the camps for Burundian refugees in Tanzania. I thank Augustine Karakezi and Tony Wach for welcoming me and helping me begin to see what was happening. Bernard Arputhasamy hosted me in Bangkok and encouraged me to visit the camps on the Thai-Myanmar border. Collaboration with Catholic Relief Services, especially Luc Picard and Dan Griffin, and with the Solidarity with South Sudan movement, especially Cathy Arata, gave me the privilege of being in Juba, the capital of the new nation of South Sudan, as it achieved independence and, a bit later, as it was falling into its current chaos.

Numerous intellectual exchanges in more academic contexts have contributed much to this book. My former colleagues at Boston College's Center for Human Rights and International Justice, Daniel Kanstroom, M. Brinton Lykes, and Maryanne Loughry, taught me about both the legal and psychosocial challenges of forced migration. During a number of stays as visiting professor at Hekima University College, my friends Agbonkhianmeghe Orobator, Aquiline Tarimo, Laurenti Magesa, Elias Opongo, and Elisée Rutagambwa have helped me learn about both the achievements and the struggles of Africa. I am most grateful to all at Hekima. At Georgetown University, where I am now working, I have learned much from Elizabeth Ferris of the Institute for the Study of International Migration and from Georgetown faculty connected with the Berkley Center for Religion, Peace, and World Affairs. I am grateful to Donald Kerwin, director of the Center for Migration Studies of New York for inviting me to events sponsored by the center. An earlier version of some of the ideas in chapter 6 of this book were presented at a conference sponsored by that center and published in its *Journal on Migration and Human Security*. I have also benefited from events at the Refugee Studies Centre at the University of Oxford, and from their invitation to write an essay, "Religion and Forced Migration," for *The Oxford Handbook of Refugee and Forced Migration Studies* (2016), which contains some ideas treated here in chapters 3 and 4.

I have special gratitude to the John W. Kluge Center at the Library of Congress, where I was honored to hold the Cary and Ann Maguire Chair in Ethics and American History in the fall of 2015. Early research for this book was done there, with much support from the staff of both the Kluge Center and the Library. I am especially indebted to Jane McAuliffe. As the director of the Kluge Center, she invited me to come to the Library and hold the Maguire Chair. I thank her in a special way.

Above all, I thank the many refugees and displaced people I have interacted with as this book was being developed. To the extent the book makes some small contribution, it is due to what they have shared with me. I hope and pray that this effort will be of some help to them.

CHAPTER 1

THREATS TO HUMANITY

Today millions of men, women, and children live amid severe humanitarian crises. Dire social, political, and environmental conditions menace their well-being, their lives, their very humanity. Many people face these dangers because of the violence of war and civil conflict. Brutal strife puts large numbers of people in grave danger, undermining the stability of whole countries and regions and putting future generations at risk. Mere mention of some of the recent and continuing conflicts indicates the magnitude of the challenge: Syria, South Sudan, Central African Republic, eastern Democratic Republic of Congo (DRC), Colombia, Yemen, Myanmar, and others. Civilians continue to die by the millions. In addition, these conflicts are displacing millions more people from their homes. Fragile states are unable or unwilling to protect their citizens from the perils that force them to migrate in pursuit of safety and survival. Many are displaced as refugees move across the borders of their home country. Many more become internally displaced within their homeland. Oppressive states persecute their own people because of ethnic identity, religious belief, or political conviction, causing them to flee. Terrorism menaces others with indiscriminate acts of violence or with fear that such attacks may occur. Severe poverty, which is itself often exacerbated by war, puts the well-being and even the lives of many more in grave danger. This poverty increases the risks posed by natural disaster or pandemic disease. Climate change is a growing threat to both the environment itself and to the people dependent on it. It also increases the dangers to human well-being that arise from conflict, poverty, and lack of food.[1]

These perils are commonly called humanitarian crises. They are humanitarian threats because the very humanity of the people affected is on the line.

In these crises, the human life and human dignity of large numbers of people are in peril. A recent study defined a humanitarian crisis as "any situation in which there is widespread threat to life, physical safety, health or basic subsistence that is beyond the coping capacity of individuals and the communities in which they reside."[2] There is no doubt that many of the people affected by the wars in Syria, South Sudan, Yemen, and elsewhere today face threats that go well beyond their "coping capacity." Nor is there any question that the fragility of the states governing Somalia, Central African Republic, and a growing number of other weak countries leaves their citizens facing dangers that go beyond their capacities.

THE CHALLENGE OF CRISIS

Several of the particularly disturbing crises that occurred in the 1990s have increased public awareness of the tragic effects of humanitarian emergencies, including those brought about by war and conflict. The 1994 genocide in Rwanda and the 1995 massacre in the Bosnian city of Srebrenica are perhaps the most widely known of the recent tragedies. These atrocities wakened many to the barbarous abuses that have been taking place in our time. In Rwanda, the Hutu-controlled government and its affiliated militias killed—in three short months—at least eight hundred thousand Tutsi people because of their ethnicity. The other nations of the world, including the former colonial power in Rwanda, Belgium, did virtually nothing to stop this massive tragedy. In addition, the United Kingdom, France, and the United States took action in the UN Security Council to prevent the United Nations from acting to halt the killing. The memory of this moral failure has made the reality of genocide a matter of urgent concern in recent discussions of the ethics of international affairs and policymaking.

Adding to the Rwandan tragedy was the fact that when the Tutsi-led Rwandan Patriotic Front came to power following their overthrow of the Hutu regime that committed the genocide, many Hutu fled to the eastern part of neighboring Zaire, now the DRC. The presence of these Rwandan refugees contributed to the emergence of conflict in the eastern DRC, which has led to the deaths of many millions since 2005, chiefly from the disease and malnutrition brought about by the fighting. In addition, more than 6 million Congolese remain in severe need today because of the continuing strife. The repression and instability of the Joseph Kabila regime in the DRC has contributed to the fighting that has done so much harm.[3]

In a similar way, as the multiethnic, multireligious Yugoslavia was disintegrating at the end of the Cold War, Serbian Orthodox Christian forces massacred seven thousand to eight thousand Bosnian Muslim men and boys in Srebrenica, a Bosnian town that the United Nations had designated a safe haven that would supposedly protect those who fled there. Many of those not killed, mostly women and children, were driven away in an "ethnic cleansing" of the region, and many women and girls were raped. Although the numbers massacred in Srebrenica were relatively few compared to losses in Rwanda, the fact that the victims were murdered precisely because they were Bosnian Muslims means this slaughter also meets the legal definition of genocide.[4] The atrocities in Rwanda and at Srebrenica led the leaders of several major Western nations and of the United Nations to ask how the international community could have failed to fulfill its promise that, after the Holocaust, the crime of genocide would "never again" be tolerated. These failures generated intense reflection on how to prevent tragedies like Rwanda and Srebrenica in the future.[5]

The human suffering and loss brought by humanitarian crises caused by war have continued to reach tragic levels in the years since Rwanda and Srebrenica. The civil war in Sri Lanka came to a very bloody end in May 2009, when up to seventy thousand civilians perished and several hundred thousand Tamils and other minorities were held captive under brutal conditions. The leadership of the United Nations once again asked how they could have allowed this to happen and concluded that a much more vigorous international response should have occurred.[6]

The crisis in Syria, which brutally continues at the time of this writing, has been even more severe. As of mid-2018, more than 5.6 million Syrians have been compelled to flee their country as refugees and more than 6.6 million have been internally displaced within Syria, the biggest single displacement crisis in over a generation.[7] This dislocation of people, combined with over three hundred thousand deaths, means that virtually the entire population of Syria is facing severe violations of their humanity. Overall, 13 million people in Syria are in need of assistance. This is well more than half of Syria's total population. The crisis in Syria has become so severe that the UN Human Rights Council's Independent International Commission of Inquiry on Syria has concluded that the Syrian reality should "shock the conscience of humanity."[8]

The civil war that began in South Sudan in December 2013 is a further example of how conflict continues to bring massive human suffering. The two sides in the conflict are the government of Salva Kiir and his supporters, who are mostly from the Dinka people, and the chief opposition group loyal to former vice president Riek Machar, who are largely of Nuer ethnicity. These opponents have turned their new country, which achieved independence in 2011, into a land where both the rights and the lives of most of the population are threatened. A panel of experts appointed by the UN Security Council judged that both sides to the conflict were directly targeting civilians.[9] Adding to the chaos, the conflict has led to famine, widespread hunger, and the malnourishment of hundreds of thousands of children.[10] In the face of this mayhem, it is not surprising that many South Sudanese have fled from their homes. As of June 2018 the number of refugees from South Sudan had reached 2.6 million, a half million more than a year earlier, and there were 1.75 million internally displaced people within South Sudan.[11] The strategies and tactics used by both sides have turned the situation into a grave humanitarian emergency. Alleviating the crisis will require significant initiatives to reestablish at least rudimentary respect for basic rights.

The very large number of people displaced by war indicates the human cost of humanitarian crises. In recent decades, the forced migration of refugees and internally displaced persons across the world has been rising markedly, reaching extraordinarily high levels by historical standards. In 2018 the UN High Commissioner for Refugees reported that persecution, conflict, and generalized violence had forcibly displaced 68.5 million individuals worldwide. This was 2.9 million more displaced people than the previous year, a record high, and 50 percent higher today than ten years ago. Today, 1 out of every 110 people in the world is displaced, compared with 1 out of 157 a decade ago.[12] The Syrian civil war has been the most dramatic cause for this rise.

Upheavals in nature also take lives and drive people from their homes. For example, in January 2010 a major earthquake struck Haiti, severely affecting 3.5 million people, killing 220,000, injuring 300,000, and forcing 1.5 million people to live in tent cities at the height of the displacement.[13] Increased climate change and environmental degradation also contribute to the stresses that are forcing people to leave their homes. When those facing negative consequences from environmental change lack the resources to move, they can become trapped in conditions that slowly but inexorably threaten their humanity.[14] Poverty multiplies the effects of natural disaster or environmental degradation since poor people have fewer resources to manage these threats and the very poor lack all the resources needed to protect themselves.

These crises threaten humanity by putting the life and well-being of large numbers of people in grave danger. Humanity is at risk when persons are not treated with the respect their human dignity requires. Thus, the title of this book—*Humanity in Crisis*—points to the fact that far too many people are being denied their human dignity by conflicts and by being forcefully displaced from their homes. Their very humanity is threatened by such events, and sometimes it is taken from them by death. Humanity in crisis can also refer to the way conflict fractures the links that join persons together in a community that is often called the human family. War and conflict break the bonds that link persons together as brothers and sisters that share a common humanity. When persons are displaced as refugees, they fall through the cracks of a world shattered by war or injustice. Thus, the common humanity that should tie them together in mutual support is torn apart by crisis. The crisis facing humanity today threatens both individual persons and the communities upon which they depend. The moral challenge of humanity in crisis therefore calls for increased respect for each person who is threatened and for an effort to restore the communal support all humanity requires. Both of these challenges are moral, and both have religious dimensions. The discussion to follow addresses both the individual and the social dimensions of the crisis that humanity faces. It does so from both a moral and religious perspective.

THE DUTY TO RESPOND

The growing number and intensity of these humanitarian crises suggests that something has gone wrong in our conduct of international affairs. The journal *Foreign Affairs* bluntly suggests in the title of a recent issue that today's international system is "Out of Order."[15] Many of the international institutions developed after World War II to secure peace and justice are today under threat. These threats include challenges to the political institutions created to protect peace and human rights, such as the United Nations and its regional counterparts. They also call into question the importance of transnational economic cooperation through the Bretton Woods institutions, regional development banks, and treaties that enhance trade and positive forms of economic integration. The European Union became the fullest realization of this political and economic collaboration, and some are calling it into question. Challenges to the European Union such as Brexit in the United Kingdom and the rise of populist nationalisms in other European countries are symptoms of the contemporary weakening of institutions created to promote global justice and peace, including the justice and peace needed to prevent war and humanitarian crises.

The weakening of the tools needed to protect people from these crises is not occurring just in the North Atlantic region. The dangers are also rising in the Global South, as the UN High Commissioner for Human Rights, Zeid Ra'ad Al Hussein, stated forcefully:

> We find ourselves in a political earthquake zone. . . . Fresh shocks are opening up unsuspected fault-lines, weight-bearing pillars are in danger of collapse. Our humanitarian colleagues are being asked to do the impossible, as the number and scale of raging conflicts continue to cause immense suffering and force unprecedented numbers of people to flee their homes. Violent groups of inconceivable brutality are still emerging from this furnace of wars. And countries in southern Africa are struggling with catastrophic drought. It is difficult to overstate the gravity of these and other crises, which we currently face.
>
> Yet rather than dealing with them, we seem to be turning away and looking inwards.[16]

High Commissioner Al Hussein is right that nations and peoples are turning inward. The resulting lack of transborder collaboration leads to growing disorder and brings increased threats to humanity. Brexit in the UK, the election of Donald Trump in the US, and the rise of nationalist political movements in a number of European societies are vivid examples of this turn inward by countries of the Global North.[17] In the Global South, the dynamic is different, but a turn inward is present there also. The spread of intrastate conflicts between ethnic or religious groups is weakening national citizenship and transnational commitments to peace and justice, as in the Central African Republic, Myanmar, and Yemen. It is also evident in claims that transcultural norms such as universal human rights threaten indigenous cultures, and in the charge raised in some African countries that the International Criminal Court's efforts to create accountability for mass atrocity are really efforts to revive European colonial domination.[18]

These turns inward can be called nationalist, ethnocentric, anticosmopolitan, antiliberal, or populist. The term "populist" captures a key element of most of them. They claim to support "the people" over against elites who are seen as ignoring or exploiting the common person. The anti-elitist impulse was vividly clear when Donald Trump declared that his inauguration as US president was not a transfer of power from one administration or one party to another but a transfer of power back to "the American People."[19] Trump's anti-elitism also has ethnic and religious dimensions, evident in his opposition to Mexican immigration and Muslim refugees. The same is true of Marine Le Pen, who conducted her strongly anti-immigrant and antirefugee campaign for the presidency of France *au nom du people*.

The causes of these movements can be analyzed in several ways. Some see them as caused by "cultural backlash" against the unfamiliar languages, lifestyles, and religions brought by immigrants and against new values embraced by more cosmopolitan youth, such as gender equality and same-sex marriage.[20] Others argue that the turning inward is more a response to economic challenges and suffering. For example, the "America first" nationalism of Donald Trump has been traced by some to economic causes. It can be argued that insufficient market regulation in the US brought on the 2008 financial crisis, leading to declining living standards for many workers, loss of jobs and pensions for others, and reduced economic prospects for their children. Dramatic rise in the incomes of financial- and high-tech-sector billionaires accompanied these declines for middle- and working-class people.[21] For our purposes, however, it is not necessary to determine whether cultural pressure or economic pressure is the chief source of the current upheaval. The key point is that sizable numbers of people in the rich countries of the Global North feel sufficiently threatened that they support political approaches directed against those in greater need who live outside the borders of their own countries and cultures. Their response is leading to a declining sense of transnational responsibility and to reduced assistance to those facing humanitarian crisis.

These declines in the sense of global responsibility are just what the world does not need. New forms of global integration and interdependence have dramatically increased transborder interaction, including the movement of people, information, dollars, weapons, viruses, and greenhouse gases. These new interactions will require positive responses, not inward-turning flight. The need for a positive response through new forms of global interaction has led the president of the Council on Foreign Relations, Richard Haass, to call for a stronger appreciation that political responsibilities reach across boundaries of sovereign states. Haass is a good political realist who continues to affirm the importance of respect for national borders and the need to avoid the use of military force across these borders. In our increasingly interconnected world, however, he also insists that realism requires that we recognize obligations that reach across borders toward those in other countries and regions.[22] Since our interdependence on one another reaches across national borders, our responsibilities must reach across borders as well. States therefore have duties to other countries that go beyond avoiding military aggression or intervention.

Climate change is a quintessential illustration of how countries are deeply affected by what goes on inside other nations. The movement of refugees is another, as the political upheavals in Europe due to the arrival on the continent of large numbers of Syrian refugees has shown. Thus, each country has an obligation to work with others to address the interconnected, transborder challenges that face all people on the planet.

Haass calls these obligations across borders "sovereign duties"—the duties of peoples that reach across their borders even though their sovereignty remains important.[23] Haass uses the moral language of duty because today's rising nationalist impulses carry considerable moral danger. Nationalist movements are threatening to undermine the institutions of world order created to support peace and justice after World War II. This book argues that these transborder duties include responsibilities to help alleviate the suffering of people caught up in humanitarian crises more effectively and to provide more effective assistance to the refugees that these crises create.

The international humanitarian system is severely challenged today. In recent decades, the human suffering occurring amid humanitarian crises has increased substantially, and the number of such crises has risen dramatically as well. The humanitarian movement that has arisen over the past several centuries has done much to assist suffering people. Many humanitarian organizations, numerous governments, and specialized international agencies have developed programs of relief as well as political and economic initiatives that have significantly improved the lives of many. We should be grateful for these humanitarian accomplishments. Nevertheless, the ongoing crises of recent decades show that the response is falling short of what people affected by conflict really need—in some cases far short. War and disaster continue to pose severe threats to the humanity of many. The dehumanization and suffering brought about by these crises remains scandalously pervasive. Adequate protection of people from the harms brought by these crises remains a distant goal.

This book proposes some ways we might work to overcome some of this suffering. It does so by drawing on ethical and religious resources that can help shape a more adequate response to humanity in crisis. The responsibility to develop more adequate ways of protecting the humanity of those threatened by these crises is a moral one. The moral challenges, of course, are deeply embedded in the political, military, economic, environmental, and other conditions that lead to wars or disasters. Examining the ethical questions therefore requires paying close attention to these contextual conditions. Although this book takes these contextual issues into account, its central goal is to address the distinctively ethical questions that arise in humanitarian crises. It shows the relevance of moral values and traditions developed over the centuries to the crises of today. It does not seek to invent a new ethic from scratch. Of course, these values and traditions may sometimes need to be revised, and I will not hesitate to propose revision when it is called for. The chief goal, however, is to explore how existing ethical wisdom can shed light on our moral responsibilities to people who are suffering because of war and disaster.

The UN General Assembly approved a new Global Compact on Refugees on December 17, 2018. The Global Compact sets forth an agenda that requires ethical support. The compact seeks more effective international response to major humanitarian crises and to the needs of the people these crises displace. The compact has four major goals: (1) to ease pressures on countries that host refugees; (2) to enhance the self-reliance of refugees; (3) to expand refugees' access to third countries through resettlement; and (4) to support conditions that enable refugees to return to their home countries.[24] These are ambitious goals, and pursing them will call for significant change in contemporary ways of responding to crises. The fundamental principles of humanity and human solidarity, including human rights, humanitarian law, and refugee law, are at the basis of all that the compact calls for, though it is not legally binding in the way a formal treaty would be.[25] Regrettably, one of the world's most important political actors, the United States, was one of two countries that voted against the compact in the General Assembly. The Global Compact's success will be heavily dependent on the voluntary commitments of governments, their citizens, and the many humanitarian agencies that work with and for refugees. The exercise of ethical responsibility by these groups will be especially important. This book provides ethical and religious support for all four of the compact's goals. It aims to carry us closer to the important goals of Global Compact on Refugees by focusing direct attention on ethical responsibilities toward those whose human dignity is threatened by displacement.

The religious traditions of the world are important sources of the ethical wisdom that can help clarify these responsibilities. I draw upon these religious traditions to suggest ethical ways to respond to humanitarian crisis. I pay particular attention to the Christian tradition, especially Roman Catholicism because Catholic Christianity is my own tradition. It is also because the Christian church has played a central role in the development of the humanitarian movement and because Christian agencies continue to be strongly engaged in efforts to help those facing crises. Christianity, however, is not the sole religious focus. Other religious communities are also deeply involved in the humanitarian movement, and I attend to their contributions. In addition, when Christian faith-based organizations respond to war and disaster, many of those they assist are from traditions other than Christianity. Christian agencies frequently rely on local staff from other religious traditions. For example, in its work assisting internally displaced persons in Syria, the Jesuit Refugee Service not only aids a population that is largely Muslim, but more than half of the local staff that Jesuit Refugee Service has recruited for its work in Syria are themselves Muslim. Thus, commitment to interfaith understanding and cooperation is essential to the success of the work of Christian humanitarian agencies and to efforts by agencies rooted in other religious traditions. I therefore approach the moral dimensions of humanitarian responsibility in a way that is attentive to Christian and Catholic traditions, to the understandings of other religious communities, and to the importance of interreligious collaboration. I also draw upon rich secular philosophical and social scientific reflection on issues raised by humanitarian crises. These secular traditions contain wisdom that is indispensable in developing a well-informed understanding of our ethical responsibilities toward people in crises. Clarifying the relation between religious and secular approaches to the ethics of humanitarian response is needed because secular and religious humanitarian agencies routinely work together. Mutual understanding among secular and religious agencies enhances their collaboration in responding to the ethical challenges they jointly face.

Sadly, there is a significant gap between the protection of people facing conflict today and what is required to protect their humanity effectively. This gap is an ethical one—the painfully evident distance between the *is* of the conditions faced by people caught in humanitarian crisis and the *ought* of what their human dignity requires. Addressing this gap calls for the development of new forms of response by governments, intergovernmental agencies, and nongovernmental organizations. What these new kinds of response should be is in part a normative question—a question of the moral values, principles, and virtues that shape response. These values, duties, and virtues—as well as the religious and secular traditions that form them—can contribute to reducing the level of crisis so many people face. They can help bring the *is* of existing crisis situations a bit closer to the *ought* of what humanity and human well-being require. This book seeks to move current humanitarian efforts further along that path by shedding some light on the moral and religious dimensions of the task.

CHAPTER 2

HUMANITY AS MORAL STANDARD

Humanitarian crises can inflict massive harm on those they affect. They frequently violate human rights and damage human dignity. They undermine the justice of the social institutions that support people's life together. These negative effects call for moral assessment. Not all of the harms brought by humanitarian crises, of course, are due to moral fault on the part of other persons. Earthquakes and tornadoes, for example, can inflict grave harm, but since they are not the result of human actions, they are not due to human moral fault. When aggressive war kills innocent people, however, or when xenophobic action toward those of another culture creates large numbers of refugees, moral fault is involved. And when those with the capacity to aid people who lack water, shelter, or other basic needs because of a crisis fail to do so, moral fault may well have occurred. Ethical values are thus central to our response to humanitarian crisis. These crises are called humanitarian because they threaten or violate the moral value of humanity. Humanity is itself the central moral standard relevant in such crises. The moral standard of humanity is spelled out with greater specificity in the human rights that protect human dignity. Thus, an increasing number of humanitarian agencies see their work as based on human rights rather than on philanthropic commitment alone. Since the standard of humanity should be respected equally for all, it makes moral requirements that reach across borders. This chapter sketches some dimensions of humanity as a moral norm relevant to emergency situations. It pays particular attention to moral obligations toward refugees and other displaced people.

WHAT "HUMANITARIAN" MEANS

We can begin by clarifying the meaning of the term "humanitarian." The word is occasionally used in a deprecating way. For example, in the *Communist Manifesto*, Karl Marx and Friedrich Engels saw humanitarianism as synonymous with moralistic sentimentalism. They lumped humanitarian action together with the activities of "temperance fanatics" who thought they could improve society by prohibiting the drinking of alcohol. In their view, humanitarian work would leave serious social abuses untouched and relieve pressure for more significant political and economic changes.[1] "Humanitarian" is also sometimes used in contrast with religious activity, as a quasi-synonym for "secular." In this vein, G. K. Chesterton suggested that the term could describe action expurgated of all religious dimensions and of anything divine.[2] In fact, neither of these uses of the term gives an adequate sense of what goes on in humanitarian crises or in humanitarian response to war and displacement. To use the term "humanitarian" to suggest that the activity described is sentimental or supportive of political complacency misrepresents reality. These crises often cause deep suffering for those who must face them. Efforts to alleviate this suffering can require action that is courageous and based on tough-minded analysis. Humanitarian relief can also be far from secular in its motivation. Much relief work is carried out by religious people joined together in religious agencies and acting for religious reasons. Religious responses are considered in the next two chapters. Of course, many who struggle to survive the suffering caused by conflict or natural disaster and many who come to their aid do not have religious motives for their action. Identifying "humanitarian" with "secular," however, overlooks the importance of religious faith for many of the victims of crises and for many who seek to alleviate their suffering.

We can avoid these unhelpful interpretations of "humanitarian" by noting several historical moments in the development of the humanitarian movement. The International Committee of the Red Cross (ICRC) is generally seen as the organization that stimulated the rise of this movement in its current form. The ICRC has been called the "gold standard" for humanitarian action.[3] The Red Cross began in 1859 when the Swiss businessperson Henri Dunant encountered the suffering of many soldiers left wounded on the frontlines at the Battle of Solferino. This battle took place at the small village of Solferino in northern Italy on June 24, 1859, between the Franco-Piedmontese army under Napoleon III of France and Victor Emmanuel II of Sardinia-Piedmont, on one side, and the army of Austria under Franz Joseph I, on the other. This conflict led to the annexation of most of Lombardy by Sardinia-Piedmont, and it contributed to the unification of Italy. At Solferino, more than forty thousand were killed or injured. Dunant's book, *A Memory of Solferino*, published in 1862, described the bloody aftermath of the fighting and vividly portrayed the suffering of the soldiers left to die on the battlefield. The book was widely read and had a significant influence on public opinion toward the suffering caused by war. Its strong influence led a group of Swiss to found the ICRC as a relief organization dedicated to aiding soldiers wounded in battle. Their organization gradually broadened its goals to include the development of international standards for the regulation of conflict and for the protection of civilians in wartime. These standards developed into the Geneva Conventions that have become central to the contemporary law of armed conflict and of international humanitarian law.

Through reflection on the experience of assisting those affected by conflict, the ICRC gradually came to formulate a set of principles to govern its activity. These principles are often taken as defining what should count as humanitarian action, although alternative definitions certainly exist. Former Red Cross vice president Jean Pictet gave these principles the form approved by the ICRC in 1965. In shorthand form, these principles are humanity, impartiality, neutrality, independence, voluntary service, unity, and universality.[4] The first two of these specify the central aims of humanitarian endeavor: it should support the *humanity* of those suffering and should do so in a way that is *impartial* among national, religious, and cultural groups. The other principles spell out these two central values in greater detail. Assistance should be provided in ways that are *neutral* among the parties in conflict, *independent* of political or ideological commitments, and *voluntary* for those assisting in ways that support *unity* among responding agencies that have their home bases in different countries and that seek to provide *universal* assistance to all in need.[5] Here we consider the first principle of "humanity."

Pictet wrote that the principle of "humanity" is the very center of the value system governing the work of the Red Cross. In his view, if the Red Cross were to have just one principle, it would be this principle of humanity.[6] What, then, does this principle mean? First, it refers to the entirety of humankind. To be concerned with humanity is to be concerned with *all* members of the human race and the conditions that *all* are facing. To act in accord with humanity, therefore, is to act with inclusive concern toward all men and women. It is to respond to all members of the human family based on their need, not because of their nationality, race, religion, class, or political opinion.[7] Such differences, of course, can be legitimate grounds for treating some people differently from others in particular areas of life. For example, one can have special duties to members of one's family that one does not have to those outside the family. Similarly, one can have a patriotic duty to fellow citizens in promoting the common good of one's country or a religious duty to help the members of one's own faith community in the practice of their belief. When it comes to the protection of the most basic requirements of human well-being such as life and safety, however, the demands of respect for humanity take on an inclusive quality. The principle of humanity means that the duty toward people whose life or safety is jeopardized by war or natural disaster reaches across boundaries. As Pictet put it, "Blood is the same color everywhere."[8] The conviction that there is a responsibility to provide care whenever members of the human family are gravely threatened is a central theme of the humanitarian movement. The principle of humanity means that national interest should not be the sole normative determinant of the foreign policies of the government of one's country. Nor should loyalty to one's religious or cultural community override the respect due to all men and women if they face grave suffering. Duties to humanity thus challenge the nationalist and populist movements that have been growing in influence of late. Respect for humanity means that when the lives and basic well-being of human beings are in serious danger, moral responsibilities reach across the borders of national, cultural, and religious communities. Later chapters consider some practical implications of this commitment and how it relates to religious and cultural loyalties and to the national interests of one's country.

Second, the principle of "humanity" refers to an affective spirit of concern for others that could be described as being humane.[9] In this sense, to act with humanity is to show an active spirit of care toward others, responding with compassionate assistance to those who are suffering. Pictet suggests that humanity understood this way is similar to Christian love or charity. When people encounter others who are suffering, their humanity leads them to take action aimed at alleviating the distress. This humane spirit was the moral impulse that led to the founding of the ICRC: a desire to bring assistance without discrimination to those wounded and suffering on the battlefield.

The Red Cross gradually broadened the goal of aiding wounded soldiers to include efforts to alleviate suffering brought about by causes other than war, such as natural disasters like hurricanes and earthquakes, and by the epidemic spread of disease. It also came to have the more encompassing goal of preventing suffering over the long term. Such prevention requires action that addresses the root causes of suffering and seeks to overcome them.[10] It calls for efforts to shape social institutions and structures, challenging those institutions that lead to suffering and supporting those that reduce it. Activity of this sort can have significant political dimensions or can become forthrightly political through the use of power and influence. This raises challenges concerning the ways that humanitarian agencies should relate to political actors such as states or armies. It can call into question ICRC's principle of neutrality, which insists that humanitarian action should avoid entanglement with politics. These institutional and political dimensions are treated in what follows. Here it is important to note that the principle of humanity can lead to action that goes beyond compassionate response by individuals to larger corporate efforts to prevent suffering by shaping social institutions.

HUMAN DIGNITY AND HUMAN RIGHTS

There is a significant overlap of the goals of the humanitarian movement and recent efforts to promote human rights. The *humanity* at the heart of the first principle of the Red Cross and the *human dignity* at the basis of the contemporary human rights movement are markedly similar notions. Pictet affirmed that the principle of humanity seeks to "insure respect for the human being." It demands that "everyone shall be treated as a human being and not as an object, as an end in himself and not as a mere means to an end."[11] This echoes a major philosophical understanding of human worth or human dignity, namely, that of Immanuel Kant. The core principle of Kant's moral philosophy is that persons must always be treated as ends in themselves and never simply as means.[12] To treat a person as an end is to treat her with the respect her humanity requires, not using her as simply a tool that is useful for obtaining other objectives that are more highly valued. Since the middle of the twentieth century, this call to respect the dignity of persons has increasingly been expressed in human rights terms. Showing a person due respect means securing her rights to the basic requirements of human dignity. Thus, the preamble of the United Nations' 1948 Universal Declaration of Human Rights links recognition of the "inherent dignity" of all persons with protection of "the equal and inalienable rights of all members of the human family."[13]

Humanity, human dignity, and human rights are ideas that share much in common on the level of moral theory, even though they are not identical in meaning. They also have overlapping practical implications for the movements that promote them. For example, both the humanitarian and human rights movements seek to reduce the harms caused by warfare and displacement in practical ways. The humanitarian law to which the work of the Red Cross has made important contributions appeals to the principle of humanity and to an understanding of human dignity in its efforts to prevent the abuses to which humans are often subject in war. For example, the third article that all four Geneva Conventions share requires that civilians and soldiers hors de combat "shall in all circumstances be treated humanely." This requirement of humane treatment is directly linked with respect for human dignity when article 3 of the conventions goes on to prohibit subjecting war prisoners, the wounded, and noncombatants to violence, cruel treatment, torture or other "outrages upon personal dignity."[14] In a similar way, the Universal Declaration of Human Rights sees respect for human dignity and rights as linked with the avoidance of war and the abuses that occur in war. The preamble to the Universal Declaration affirms that respect for human dignity and rights contributes in important ways to sustaining "peace in the world." It also states that when rights are not protected by the rule of law, people may have to use force to rid themselves of tyranny and oppression.[15] The protection of humanity, respect for human rights, and the limitation of war are closely interconnected.

RIGHTS-BASED HUMANITARIANISM

The parallels between the principle of humanity central to the humanitarian movement and the idea of human dignity at the heart of the contemporary human rights movement help explain how some humanitarian agencies have come to understand their actions as "rights-based." For example, one of today's major international humanitarian agencies, Oxfam International, now bases its work on the Universal Declaration of Human Rights and on the major international human rights covenants that translate the declaration into action. For Oxfam, both emergency relief and work for development should seek to secure people's basic rights: the right to life and security, to a sustainable livelihood, to be heard, to have an identity, and to have access to basic social services.[16] Actions aimed at relief and development are therefore genuine obligations, not simply the expression of an overflow of generosity on the part of those providing it. If assistance amid crisis is a right, then there is a corresponding duty to provide it.

This rights-based understanding of assistance helps to avoid two dangers that can arise when aid is seen as the result of compassion. First, action based on compassion is sometimes understood as beyond the obligations of duty, a kind of supererogation that is praiseworthy but not strictly required. Although such compassionate response is highly desirable, seeing it as beyond the call of duty could well leave people facing crisis unassisted. Rights-based approaches seek to avoid this lack of assistance for people in crisis by insisting that there are real duties to provide aid that correspond to their rights. Second, since people who carry out voluntary acts of compassion toward those in need are often regarded as especially admirable precisely because their actions go beyond the call of duty, there can be a risk that the assistance will be provided in a condescending or paternalistic way. I discuss below why religiously motivated acts of compassion can be required rather than optional and why faith-based assistance must avoid such paternalism. Here I simply note that rights-based approaches have come to the fore because of the desire to stress the genuine duty to assist people in crisis and to assist without a condescension that can be humiliating to recipients. The duty to assist in a nonpaternalistic way arises from the equality of providers and recipients. This equal dignity grounds the recipient's right to assistance, the provider's duty to provide it, and the need to avoid condescension and paternalism.[17]

In recent years, Catholic Relief Services (CRS) has developed a working philosophy that is notably similar to Oxfam's rights-based approach to crises. CRS declares that the first "guiding principle" of its work is the "Sacredness and Dignity of the Human Person."[18] CRS sees the protection and promotion of the dignity of the person as central to all of its work, both in responding to major emergencies and in promoting human development. CRS's stress on human dignity means that human rights have become the central norms that should guide all its activity. CRS's guiding principles affirm that "every person has basic rights and responsibilities that flow from our human dignity and that belong to us as human beings regardless of any social or political structures. . . . Corresponding to our rights are duties and responsibilities to respect the rights of others and to work for the common good of all."[19] CRS therefore joins Oxfam and many other humanitarian agencies in affirming that human dignity and human rights are the central moral norms that should guide its work. It understands these norms as rooted in the central religious convictions that shape its Catholic identity. Human dignity is grounded in the biblical conviction shared by Jews and Christians that the human person is created in the image and likeness of God, an affirmation that provides religious warrant for all the work of CRS and religious guidance for how its work should be carried out. I discuss this more fully in the next chapter. At the same time, CRS also holds that its principles can be appreciated and affirmed by all, not just by Christians or Catholics. Thus, CRS affirms that the values that guide its work can be shared across religious and cultural boundaries, with all people who are working for justice and lasting peace, and to provide help to the displaced.[20]

This rights-based approach to humanitarian crisis is thus both universalist and egalitarian. The principle of humanity developed by ICRC and the standard of human dignity at the foundation of human rights affirm that *all* persons deserve *equal* protection from grave threats to their worth as persons. Each person threatened by crisis should count equally, and protection should be extended to all who need it. Both the Geneva Conventions and the Universal Declaration of Human Rights insist on the universal and equal worth of every person. The same is true of the work of organizations like ICRC, Oxfam, and CRS.

This means that the efforts of agencies seeking to aid persons confronted by emergency conditions should not be restricted by nationality, race, religion, or gender. To the fullest extent possible, protection should be provided wherever human beings face crisis-level threats to their humanity and dignity. In the face of such threats to their humanity, *all* persons have an *equal* claim on the concern of the larger human community. All persons belong to the "we" who are due respect and support. The scope of concern should include the entire human family, especially those whose humanity is under threat. In grave crises like war, earthquake, or epidemic, all human beings deserve to be treated in a way that takes account of their common humanity and that seeks to provide them with at least the basic requirements of dignified living.

This is evident in the way terms such as "all," "everyone," and "no one" are used throughout the Universal Declaration of Human Rights. The declaration affirms that all persons possess human rights without distinctions based on "race, color, sex, language, religion, political or other opinion, national or social origin."[21] This relativizes all in-group/out-group boundaries. It challenges understandings of religious, national, or cultural identities that suggest only those people with a particular identity deserve respect. The human rights ethos seeks to tear down the walls dividing people into those who count and those who do not count when the most basic requirements of humanity are at stake. No white rule over nonwhite; no Aryan over Jew; no European colonist over non-European colonized; no male superiority to female. Although religious convictions are deeply important to those who hold them, such convictions must never be used to deny the humanity or human rights of others in the name of God. Ethnic or national identities are never legitimate grounds for excluding people from the most basic requirements of their human dignity. Respect for human dignity also calls for solidarity across economic divisions. It calls for the provision of basic economic goods such as food, work, education, and health care by affirming a set of social or economic rights to these goods.[22] Securing such rights for all thus becomes a goal of humanitarian efforts that see themselves as "rights-based."

The principle of humanity at the heart of the humanitarian movement thus defines responsibilities to people in distress in an inclusive way. As the ICRC puts it, wherever people are being harmed by conflict or disaster, humanitarian concern gives rise to "a desire to bring assistance without discrimination . . . to alleviate human suffering wherever it may be found."[23] Similarly, the declaration proclaiming human rights is called the *Universal* Declaration because it calls for respect for the dignity of *all* people, independent of their nationality, ethnicity, religion, gender, or politics. This universality of concern is perhaps the single most challenging aspect of the humanitarian and human rights movements today. The power of the challenge is evident when the universalism of the humanitarian ethic confronts loyalty to a community whose scope is defined by a particular cultural or religious identity or by commitment to one's homeland and its citizens. When cultural, religious, or national loyalties supersede commitment to one's duties to all humans precisely because they are human, the ethos of humanitarian movement will be in danger. Conversely, the normative values of the humanitarian and human rights movements question forms of politics that effectively make the borders between cultural, religious, or national communities into absolutes.

EQUAL ACROSS BORDERS

The emergence of this universally inclusive understanding of humanity, human dignity, and human rights as a standard for the action of nation-states and of their citizens has been a dramatic, even revolutionary, development in the political and moral consciousness of humanity. Until the modern era in the West, few held that all human beings possessed equal dignity or that all persons should be treated equally. It was not until the American and French revolutions and the emergence of the democratic philosophies inspired by these revolutions that the pursuit of equal dignity for all became a widespread political aspiration. Nor did most intellectual reflection on social relations argue for the legitimacy of the claim that all people possessed equal worth no matter their nation, race, gender, or religion. Indeed, even following these revolutions inequalities continued to be affirmed even by many among those who saw themselves as enlightened. Many of those who supported egalitarian politics in Europe and the United States did not seek similar standards of equality for African, Asian, or indigenous peoples of the Americas. Racial and cultural inequality provided continuing justification for European colonial control of non-European peoples until well into the twentieth century. Although non-Europeans, blacks, and women might possess a certain dignity, it was not understood to be equal to the dignity possessed by white European males. The emergence of the conviction that all persons deserve equal respect is at the heart of the development of the humanitarian and human rights movements.

Before the eighteenth century, people were generally understood to be located on a stratified scale, with those on upper rungs of the social ladder possessing higher status while those on lower rungs had less. Although all persons were seen as having dignity and worth, their dignity and worth were not seen as equal. Where one was located on this ladder of status depended on whether one was a prince, a noble, a cleric, or a commoner. Both prince and commoner possessed dignity, but the prince had more of it than did the commoner. One's status was also shaped by whether one was male or female, by one's culture or ethnicity, and by the color of one's skin. Those in the upper ranks of these hierarchies deserved greater honor. To deny them their due honor was to insult them. This premodern concept of honor was an expression of a normative understanding of how society should be structured. The rungs on the social ladder determined who should be honored and how much honor they were due. To change the metaphor, the differences among people also led to in-group/out-group divisions among them. Those in the in-group were due more respect and care than those in the out-group. Thus, "our people" count for more than do "your people." "We" deserve more than "they" do. The in-group might be distinguished from the out-group by nationality, ethnicity, religion, race, gender, or some other particular characteristic. No matter what characteristic might be used to draw the line, however, inequality of respect and treatment was regularly the result.

With the coming of modernity, however, a commitment to equal dignity and rights for all replaced the normative legitimacy of this system of unequal in-group/out-group organization.[24] As Jeremy Waldron has put it, modernity brought a shift from different grades of dignity ordered hierarchically to an egalitarian system in which all persons hold the same high level of dignity. In the premodern arrangement, the rungs on the social ladder were defined by different levels of dignity. In Waldron's formulation, the dramatic shift to an egalitarian understanding of dignity was, in effect, a promotion of all persons to the highest rank. This move to the modern notion of equal human dignity led to "an upward equalization of rank, so that we now try to accord every human being something of the dignity, rank, and expectation of respect that was formerly accorded to the nobility."[25] In class terms, every person has become the equivalent of a duke or duchess. The equal dignity of all means that an assault on an ordinary man or woman has now become what an assault on a prelate or a prince once was, a sort of sacrilege. Put in terms of caste, the equality of dignity means every person has become a Brahmin.

The move to the modern understanding of human dignity also involved expansion of the requirements of social responsibility from the duty to assist those belonging to one's own group to care for a notably wider, even universal community. Back in the thirteenth century, the theologian Thomas Aquinas noted the importance of commitment to one's closer group when he argued that the proper ordering of love (the "*ordo amoris*") for different persons could require giving priority to one's family members over strangers or to one's fellow citizens over those of distant communities.[26] Aquinas based his argument on the restricted reach of human agency. Since our finite and thus limited capacities mean we cannot assist everyone, responsibility can reach only as far as the scope of effective action. Because one's capacity to aid wider communities is limited, it can be legitimate to show special care for one's own children, for fellow citizens, or for those with whom one has special religious relationships. Sometimes this is the only way they will receive any assistance at all. On the other hand, if the capacity to assist those in need is broader, so is the responsibility to do so. Thus, Aquinas's stress on responsibility to those who are nearer can be contrasted with Pope John XXIII's 1962 statement that the scope of responsibility should be measured by the "needs of others" rather than by their physical or psychological proximity.[27] Responsibility can be broadened by greater interdependence and interconnection of people across national and cultural borders. Increased interdependence means that the well-being of people in one region is increasingly shaped by actions taking place in the larger human community. It arises from increasing contemporary capacity to assist people at much greater distances when they face crises than would have been possible in the past.[28] The range of one's responsibility can thus reach across national, ethnic, and religious borders when one's capacities have greater reach and when one's more distant neighbors are in need.

Waldron notes the relevance of this universal equalization of dignity for humanitarian crises. Common Article 3 of the Geneva Conventions forbids subjecting war prisoners to "outrages on personal dignity, in particular humiliating and degrading treatment" such as torture. This prohibition extends the chivalrous expectation that noble warriors like knights should be treated with dignity when taken captive to a demand that common soldiers be treated with a similar high respect for their dignity. Waldron calls this development a "transvaluation" of the idea of dignity, through which we have come to see dignity as belonging equally and universally to all persons, not just those at the top of society.[29]

Steven Pinker uses the more dramatic language of revolution to describe this change. Pinker has assembled an extraordinary range of evidence to show that there has been a rising commitment to universal and equal humanity in modern history. This commitment to equality has led to a notable reduction in the level of violence humans have been inflicting upon one another. Pinker's provocative study sheds light on the historical decline in crisis-level violence and the major increase in efforts to prevent and respond to this violence in the modern era. He calls these changes "the humanitarian revolution."[30] This revolution arose from the growing commitment to the equal dignity of all persons that began in the eighteenth century in the thinking of those whose work inspired American and French revolutions. The call for the equal respect for humanity contributed to the abolition of slavery, the restriction of legitimate grounds for war, growing concern for the protection of civilians in war, and new efforts to treat prisoners humanely. A further expansion of the commitment to equal dignity, which Pinker calls the "rights revolution," occurred in the second half of the twentieth century, with the drafting of the Universal Declaration of Human Rights, later rights covenants and conventions, and the human rights movement that seeks to implement these documents.[31] The data and historical narratives presented in Pinker's study make a strong case that the humanitarian and rights revolutions have led to a substantial decline in the death and suffering visited by human beings on each other over the past several centuries.

Pinker is not arguing that these revolutions have led to the end of humanitarian crises. Clearly, the suffering that conflict, oppression, and natural disaster continue to cause remains at a tragically high, unacceptable level.[32] Fulfilling the aspirations of the humanitarian and rights revolutions will require much more work—perhaps another, even deeper moral revolution. But rising concern for the humanity of those who suffer and for the equal human dignity of all across divisions of race, religion, nationality, ethnicity, and gender has had genuinely beneficial effects over the past several centuries. Keeping these positive developments in view will be an important source of hope. It can help sustain continuing efforts to respond to the needs of those whose humanity is violated by the effects of war and other emergency situations.

Pinker sees the emergence of the humanitarian movement as the triumph of a strongly secularist worldview. Despite the importance of Pinker's historical work, he is mistaken when he argues that the rise of the humanitarian movement required that the role played by religion be diminished or eliminated from public affairs. The next chapter highlights ways religious traditions have made important contributions to response to crisis in the past and contain valuable resources for continuing this response today.

CHAPTER 3

RELIGIOUS TRADITIONS AND HUMANITARIAN RESPONSE

Religious communities play important roles in alleviating the suffering caused by war and displacement. Faith-based agencies are highly visible on the scene of these upheavals, providing shelter for refugees, internally displaced persons, and others suffering due to conflict. They advocate public policies that will help prevent these crises or reduce their impact on those affected by them. Faith communities contribute significantly to the overall response to humanitarian crises. On the opposite side of the ledger, however, religion sometimes contributes to the suffering brought about by emergencies and disasters. Religious antagonism can be a direct cause of conflicts that lead to humanitarian crises and can sometimes exacerbate divisions that have political or economic roots. The relation of religious communities and their traditions to humanitarian response is therefore a complex affair. This chapter considers two ways of understanding the impact of religious traditions on the rise of humanitarianism and makes a normative argument about ways the traditions ought to influence the engagement of believers in humanitarian action, focusing particularly on Christianity, Judaism Islam, and, very briefly, Asian traditions.

RELIGIOUS TRADITIONS AND HUMANITARIANISM IN HISTORY

In his historical account of the rise of the humanitarian movement, Steven Pinker gives virtually exclusive emphasis to the negative role sometimes played by religion. He argues that religious traditions have frequently been sources of conflict and intercommunal division. In his view, the humanitarian revolution was a rebellion not only against the legitimacy of conflict but against the influence of religion as well. According to Pinker, the emergence of the inclusive, egalitarian understanding of human dignity at the heart of the humanitarian movement was the triumph of a secularist worldview. Pinker reads modern Western history as the victory of science, technology, and reason over religion, the supernatural, and superstition. The humanitarian revolution was the victory of secular enlightenment over religious irrationality. Pinker sometimes states that there is nothing really bad about religion, and that the humanitarian revolution is not necessarily atheistic.[1] Nevertheless, he repeatedly portrays religion as a source of conflict, violence, inequality, and even abuse and terror. For example, he asserts, "The scriptures present a God who delights in genocide, rape, slavery, and the execution of nonconformists." Religion elevates the parochial to the level of the absolute, making compromise impossible. Belief led to the slaughter of religious adversaries during the European Wars of Religion in the sixteenth and seventeenth centuries, and it continues to do so today in the Middle East and some Islamic countries.[2]

It is certainly true that religious believers have been and sometimes still are among those who commit grave abuses against human dignity. But Pinker's antireligious animus must be challenged. He simply rejects the idea that religion played any positive role in the rise of humanitarianism because he believes such a role "does not fit the facts of history." To make this claim, he takes positions that themselves go contrary to the facts, such as that Quaker participation in the abolitionist movement drew on Enlightenment rather than Christian thought and that Martin Luther King Jr. "rejected mainstream Christian theology."[3] Such claims surely go too far.

Peter Stamatov provides a very different reading of the origins of modern humanitarianism, drawing on rich historical evidence to show that religious communities made key contributions to the development of both the direct humanitarian service and the "long-distance advocacy" that goes on in the humanitarian movement today. His argument begins in the sixteenth century, when Roman Catholic Dominican friars raised their voices against the exploitation, forced labor, and enslavement of indigenous people in the Caribbean by representatives of the Spanish crown.[4] He also provides account of how a nineteenth-century group of English Quakers energized a movement that led to the abolition of slavery. He recounts how some early twentieth-century evangelical missionaries in the so-called Congo Free State helped stop the abuse of Congolese people by Belgian colonialists under

King Leopold II. Stamatov argues that these three historical movements helped shape the moral expectations and the models of action of humanitarian organizations of today.[5]

We can draw on Stamatov and other sources to illuminate how the sixteenth-century moral and religious argument about Spanish imperial exploitation of the indigenous people of the Caribbean helps clarify what is at stake today. In 1511 a Spanish Catholic missionary, the Dominican friar Antonio Montesino, gave a sermon to an assembled group of Spanish conquistadors on the island of Hispaniola (today's Dominican Republic). He directly challenged the colonial exploitation of indigenous people as effectively a form of slavery, appealing to values internal to the Christian tradition he shared with the Spanish colonialists. One of the justifications the colonial powers offered for their treatment of those native to the island was that they were not Christian. Spanish colonial control was justified as necessary to bring the gospel to the islanders and to open a path to salvation for them. Montesino challenged this by appealing directly to his Christian faith. He affirmed that the teachings of Christ called the Spaniards to treat those indigenous to the island very differently from the way they were. He set forth a ringing denunciation of the conquistadores, putting himself in the place of Christ and speaking in Christ's name: "I am the voice of Christ in the wilderness of this island.... This voice says that you are all in mortal sin and that you will live and die in it for the cruelty and tyranny with which you use these innocent people.... Are you not obliged to love them as you love yourselves?"[6] Here Montesino appealed to the commandment to love one's neighbor that was central to the Christian tradition of the Spaniards, calling them to a major change in their behavior. Christian belief calls those with faith to love and respect not only their fellow Christians but also those whom the Spaniards regarded as pagan barbarians. Montesino hoped that by pointing out values that are central to Christian belief and Christian tradition he could lead the conquistadors to treat the indigenous people with respect, or at least less oppressively.

A few decades later, other Christian critics of the colonial conquest in Peru and Mexico appealed to Christian tradition in a similar way to challenge Spanish domination of the indigenous in those regions. For example, in 1537–1539, the great theologian Francisco Vitoria delivered a set of lectures at the University of Salamanca on "the affair of the Indies" (*De Indis*). In this work, he objected to colonial treatment of indigenous people on explicitly Christian grounds. He argued that the duty to love all one's neighbors and to respect all for whom Christ died demanded a change in colonial practice. A few years later, about 1548, Bartolomé de las Casas, the bishop of Chiapas in what is now Mexico, wrote the prophetic *Defense of the Indians*.[7] Las Casas also appealed directly to Christian faith and the commandment to love the Indians as Christ did.

Montesino, Vitoria, and las Casas, however, did not appeal solely to Bible-based beliefs or only to distinctively Christian traditions in mounting their critiques of the conquistadors. They also pointed directly to the humanity of the indigenous people. In appealing to the Indians' humanity, they wanted to move the colonial powers away from an excessively narrow interpretation of Christianity, an interpretation that led them to an exclusivist belief that they owed full respect only to other Christians. They saw the humanity of the indigenous people as challenging the conquistadors to adopt a more inclusive, universalist understanding of their duties. It called them to see that Christian faith, when properly interpreted, required them to respect not only their fellow Christians but all human beings, including the non-Christian Indians. Thus, Montesino invoked the humanity of the indigenous in these words: "Tell me, with what right, with what justice do you hold these Indians in such cruel and horrible slavery? . . . Are they not men?"[8] His cry—are they not men, are they not human?—is a direct appeal to the human dignity of the indigenous people. The humanity of the Native Americans was a moral reality that itself challenged the values leading to oppressive behavior by the Spanish colonialists. In appealing directly to the humanity of the indigenous people, Montesino presumed that the conquistadors were as capable as he was of seeing the human dignity of the indigenous islanders and that the suffering being inflicted upon them was a violation of that dignity. The call to respect humanity was thus a call to a universalist ethic, an ethic that shows respect to all humans no matter their religion, race, or nationality. Montesino's cry—"Are they not human?"—called the conquistadors to recognize that the humanity of the indigenous people was itself a challenge to their behavior. It also challenged their in-place interpretation of their own Christian traditions, invoking the humanity of the Indians as a standard that called for a fresh interpretation of what Christianity required.

Vitoria backed up such direct appeals to the humanity of the indigenous people by drawing upon an understanding of natural law. Vitoria was a learned theologian and philosopher whose thinking on the "Indian question" was strongly influenced by the ethics of Thomas Aquinas.[9] Following Aquinas, Vitoria held that the demands of the moral law could be discovered not only from the Bible but also through reasoned reflection on human experience. Vitoria drew on the vicarious experience he gained from communication with his fellow Dominicans in the Americas. This shared experience helped him see the full humanity of the Indians and to recognize that what Spanish behavior was doing to them was morally unacceptable. Following Aquinas, Vitoria held that Christian faith can help clarify the requirements of natural law and of respect for humanity but that Christian faith is neither necessary for knowledge of moral duties nor for the capacity to live in accord with these duties. This natural law ethic also calls for respect not only for fellow Christians but for all human beings. The obligation to respect human beings arises from the human reality as discovered by reasoned reflection on experience. The basic requirements of morality are universal: wherever human persons are present, the moral requirement to show respect is also present.

Because these objections to the Spanish domination of Native Americans were based on a universalist understanding of the moral respect due to humanity and human dignity, they were a sixteenth-century anticipation of the twentieth-century understanding of universal human rights.[10] Indeed, Vitoria's *De Indis*, along with his other works such as *On the Law of War*, is often seen as a major contribution to the beginnings of modern international law. The objections by Montesino, Vitoria, and Las Casas to colonial domination were also anticipations of the modern humanitarian movement and its commitment to aid humanity whenever it is threatened with abuse or suffering.

These sixteenth-century figures drew simultaneously on their distinctive Christian beliefs and on reason to reach a universalist understanding of the requirements of humanity. This implies it is possible in the multireligious, multicultural setting of today's world to address the needs of humanity in crisis. Montesino's cry to the Spaniards—are they not human!—arose *both* from norms set forth by Christian tradition *and* from a direct appeal to the humanity of the indigenous people. When he appealed to the Christian commandment that the Spaniards ought to love the Native Americans as they loved themselves, he was calling them to live up to the requirements of their own religious tradition. He demanded they act in a way that would give authentic *expression* to their identity, an identity shaped by Christian tradition. At the same time, his direct appeal to the humanity of the indigenous people called them to a moral *response* to the actual humanity and dignity of the indigenous people they were exploiting and abusing. This dignity called the conquistadors to revise their understanding of what Christian tradition required of them.

The indigenous people were human beings just as the Spaniards were, and they should be treated as humans rather than as some kind of lesser being.

Montesino and Vitoria's challenges to the conquistadors, therefore, were based both on standards internal to the Christian tradition he shared with them and on a reality that could raise an external challenge to any tradition—namely, the humanity of the indigenous people. Of course, they appealed to the humanity of the indigenous people because their Christian faith helped them to see the indigenous as fully human. They also saw the humanity of the Indians as a reality that would require everyone, no matter what their tradition, to treat them with respect. Montesino and Vitoria appealed to the humanity of the Native Americans to challenge the misguided belief of at least some Spaniards that the indigenous were not in fact human at all and the belief of other Spaniards that the indigenous would become fully human only if they converted to Christianity. The critique of Spanish colonial practice rejected both of these beliefs and asserted that the indigenous were already fully human and should be treated as such. Indeed, Vitoria insisted that the capacity of the indigenous to become Christian showed their full humanity, for he held that only a human being is capable of embracing the Christian faith.

The thinking and actions of the reformist Dominican friars of the sixteenth century anticipated much of what the humanitarian movement of today seeks to accomplish. They also showed that an ethical approach can be simultaneously rooted in Christian tradition and committed to the defense of the dignity of all persons. They knew they did not have to make a choice between fidelity to a narrowly defined Christian in-group and abandonment of Christian tradition in favor of a secular universalism. They showed that one can be both a faithful Christian and a cosmopolitan humanist at the same time. Faith and reason can be complementary, not opposed in the way Pinker sees them. Christians today, and believers in other traditions as well, can learn much from these friars. We should keep their approach clearly in mind as we further explore how religious traditions can shape our response to humanity in crisis today.

The great world religions have diverse values and differing visions of ultimate meaning. These values and visions shape their normative understandings of how humans should act. They influence how believers will likely react to humanitarian crises and respond to the suffering of refugees. Therefore, some knowledge of normative religious traditions on these questions is important in shaping how religious communities can help those in crisis. A proposal about how a religious community should respond to an emergency is not likely to be effective if it conflicts with the faith commitments of the community's members. Attending to the normative stances of the great religious traditions on these matters is important to determining how these traditions should respond.

Therefore, I examine in the following some of the ways that specific religious communities draw on their normative traditions to respond to humanitarian crisis and to the needs of displaced people, first considering the great monotheistic traditions of Judaism, Christianity, and Islam, and then, much more briefly, the Asian religious traditions of Hinduism and Buddhism. The approach of Christian communities is of special concern since Christianity played a formative role in shaping the emergence of the humanitarian movement. Christian groups also receive particular attention because Christian agencies continue to be among the major responders to humanitarian crises today. Interreligious cooperation and the collaboration of faith-based agencies with secular ones are also important for effective response to the displacement caused by war. Such collaboration across traditions are considered briefly here and more fully in the next chapter.

CHRISTIAN RESOURCES FOR RESPONSE TO CRISIS

The Christian tradition plays a significant role in shaping responses to major crises today. Christianity was an important motivation for the rise of the humanitarian movement, and it guides the work of many humanitarian organizations of today. Nevertheless, although Pinker overgeneralizes, it is surely true that the "wars of religion" between Catholics, Lutherans, Calvinists, and Anglicans in sixteenth- and seventeenth-century Europe caused much bloodshed. Similarly, the links between Catholicism and the ancien régime that prevailed before the French Revolution often led to the conviction that modern human rights and religion are opposed. Given the history of religious conflict and the opposition by some religious communities to the emerging human rights movement, how did a positive role of faith communities in contemporary humanitarian efforts develop?

Roman Catholicism illustrates one way that this development occurred among Christians. The Catholic Church had strong alliances with the monarchies of Western Europe in the premodern era. Despite the American and French revolutions in the eighteenth century, the papacy continued to resist the modern democratic and human rights movements that arose with these revolutions. In the nineteenth and early twentieth centuries, the papacy saw movements for democracy and freedom of conscience as secularist forces that wanted to see Christian faith decline or at least to keep it privatized in the sacristy.

The Second Vatican Council (1962–65), however, moved official Catholicism from its alignment with authoritarian modes of political organization to support for democracy and human rights as conditions for peace. This shift was dramatic, even revolutionary. The destruction wrought by the two world wars led the Christian community to a growing awareness that the protection of human rights is a precondition for the preservation of peace. The persecution and death inflicted upon many millions of people by Nazi, Fascist, and Stalinist authoritarian regimes showed Catholic leaders the importance of placing limits on governmental power in order to protect the human dignity of all people. The grave abuses of religious freedom by these authoritarian regimes also gave the Church an experience-based knowledge of the threats posed to freedom by unrestrained state power. The long-standing Catholic tradition of commitment to the freedom of the Church enabled Pope John XXIII and the Second Vatican Council to see the right to religious freedom as in continuity with important dimensions of the larger Catholic tradition. At the same time, the broad range of the violations of human dignity by Adolf Hitler and Joseph Stalin showed that more than the Church's own well-being and freedom were at stake. The experience of multiple kinds of abuse by authoritarian rule led John XXIII to give strong support to the full range of human rights in his 1963 encyclical *Pacem in terris*. The Second Vatican Council went even further when it declared that the Church proclaims human rights "by virtue of the Gospel committed to her."[11] The Church thus gave its full official support to the agenda laid out in the United Nations' Universal Declaration of Human Rights.

Pope John XXIII and the Second Vatican Council thus moved the Catholic community to the forefront of the struggle for human rights and the protection of peace. Samuel Huntington concludes that, since Vatican II, the Catholic Church has become one of the strongest forces for human dignity, human rights, and democracy on the world stage. He sees the modern rise of democracy occurring in three waves. The first wave was the US and French revolutions in the eighteenth centuries; the second wave was the democratization of the former Axis powers of Germany, Italy, and Japan following World War II; and the third wave has been under way since the early 1970s. This third wave includes the coming of democracy to Spain and Portugal; the decline of military and authoritarian rule in Latin America, South Korea, and the Philippines;

and the end of communism in the Warsaw Pact nations. From his analysis of the data, Huntington concludes that "in its first fifteen years, the third wave was overwhelmingly Catholic. . . . Roughly three-quarters of the countries that transited to democracy between 1974 and 1989 were Catholic."[12] Monica Toft, Daniel Philpott, and Timothy Shah's studies have reinforced Huntington's conclusion about this dramatic contribution. They conclude that between 1972 and 2009 the Catholic community played a role in promoting democracy in thirty-six of the seventy-eight countries that experienced substantial advances for democracy, and that the Catholic community had a leadership position in the democratization of twenty-two of these countries.[13]

These commitments to human rights and democracy have had important consequences for the engagement of the Catholic community with the humanitarian movement. Both the preamble of the Universal Declaration and the overall argument of Pope John XXIII's encyclical *Pacem in terris* see the protection of human rights as closely linked with preventing humanitarian crises and responding to them when they occur. Work for human rights includes efforts to protect people from grave political crises that threaten their lives or drive them from home as refugees. It also includes efforts to protect peace, to recreate peace if conflict has already broken out, and to heal the wounds of conflict that can cause conflict to return if the cessation of hostility is superficial. The emerging commitment of the Church to human rights has gone hand in hand with its engagement with the humanitarian movement. It should not be surprising, therefore, that Catholic Relief Services is one of the major nongovernmental humanitarian agencies based in the United States. Caritas Internationalis, the international Catholic network whose 165 organizational members include CRS, describes its mission as "to respond to humanitarian disasters, to promote integral human development and to advocate on the causes of poverty and violence."[14] Caritas has extraordinary scope. It has one million staff members and volunteers. This broad reach enables Caritas and CRS to play significant roles in responding to most major humanitarian emergencies today.[15]

One might ask, however, how permanent the Catholic commitment to human rights and humanitarian response actually is. This commitment arose from inductive reflection on social experience, including the Church's experience of itself being persecuted. This experience can certainly change. Is the commitment simply a fortuitous development occasioned by circumstances that have been particularly propitious? Could it evanesce if the circumstances that occasioned it were to change or if the Church were to be in a position once again to exercise wide-reaching social control as it did in the ancien régime? In fact, however, the Catholic community did not move from opposition to human rights to support for these rights simply due to a change in context or in the Church's own self-interest. New social and political experiences led the Church to new discoveries of what Christian faith itself calls for when people's dignity is under threat. The experiences of twentieth-century war and totalitarianism have led the Christian community to the discovery that Christian faith itself requires participation in the struggle for human rights and in efforts to provide relief from humanitarian crises. The Second Vatican Council acknowledged that it was proposing a new interpretation of Christian faith and ethics when it said it "intends to develop the doctrine of recent popes on the inviolable rights of the human person and the constitutional order of society."[16] Further, it claimed that the development it was proposing was not merely a fortuitous expression of changed social conditions. Rather, the Council claimed that its development of the Church's commitment to human rights is "greatly in accord with truth and justice."[17] It therefore represents genuine progress in the Catholic community's insight into the demands of the Christian faith, not simply a reversible shift.

It will be useful to note several forms of this development in the Catholic community's understanding of its own beliefs that are relevant to humanitarian issues. The Christian tradition, along with the Jewish tradition as well, has long affirmed the creation of human beings in the image and likeness of God (Gen. 1:26). Persons possess a worth that should be treated with reverence. Made in God's likeness, human beings possess a sacredness analogous to the holiness of God. Thus, mistreating a human person is not only morally objectionable. It is a religious violation as well—a kind of sacrilege. By sharing in the experiences that led to the development of the Geneva Conventions and to the promulgation of the Universal Declaration of Human Rights, Catholic Christianity came to see that these aspects of its biblically based faith called it to engage actively in the humanitarian and human rights struggles. Further, because human beings are redeemed and recreated in Christ, believers are called to esteem human dignity even more highly.[18] The church's mission to defend human dignity and rights flows from the heart of Christian faith. In a similar way, the destructiveness of twentieth-century war and repression by authoritarian regimes led Catholic thinkers to recall that in the thirteenth century Thomas Aquinas had affirmed that human beings are "governed by divine providence *for their own sakes*."[19] This theological affirmation comes close to Kant's secular philosophical principle that persons are ends in themselves and never to be treated as means only, which Jean Pictet saw embodied in the ICRC's principle of humanity. The negative experiences of twentieth-century politics led the Catholic community to draw upon its traditional natural law–based conviction that ethical responsibilities can be grasped by human reason as well as in the light of faith. Such philosophical reflection on what it is to be human provided the Catholic community not only with a Christian imperative for humanitarian engagement but also with strong warrant for collaboration with non-Christians in assisting those facing humanitarian crisis. The possibility of new forms of collaboration with non-Christians was also strongly advanced by the Second Vatican Council's declaration that "the right to religious freedom has its foundation in the very dignity of the human person as this dignity is known through the revealed word of God and by reason itself."[20] Both the deep religious traditions of Christian faith and the requirements of reason reflecting on experience opened the way for the Church to see that its mission is an inclusive one, calling it to work for the dignity of all and to do so in collaboration with all who are committed to serving this dignity.

Vatican Council II also affirmed the need for strong bonds of cooperation and solidarity in social life. The Council cites Thomas Aquinas's appropriation of Aristotle's philosophical defense of the "social nature" of the human person, which implies that the development of the person and the advance of society "hinge on each other" and that each person "stands completely in need of social life."[21] From a more theological standpoint, the Council also taught that the God in whose image human persons are created is not a kind of monarch isolated in sublime solitude but a Trinitarian union of three persons, related to one another in mutual love. Because the God in whom Christians believe is radically relational, so too are human persons. As the Council put it, "God did not create the human being as a solitary.... For by his innermost nature the human being is a social being, and unless he relates himself to others he can neither live nor develop his potential"[22] Human dignity, therefore, cannot be achieved alone or in isolation but requires the possibility of active participation in social life.

This communal or solidaristic understanding of the person has important implications for the activity of the Christian community in the humanitarian and human rights movements. It supports a form of inclusiveness linked with a universalist understanding of the commandment to love one's neighbor as oneself. Such universalism has biblical roots. In Luke's gospel, for example, Jesus uses the parable of the good Samaritan to illustrate the meaning of love of neighbor. In the parable, love of neighbor is interpreted in a clearly inclusivist or universalist way. When a man on the road from Jerusalem to Jericho falls among thieves and is left half dead by the roadside, it is not the Jewish priest or Levite who comes to his aid but rather a Samaritan—someone whom the Jews of Jesus's time regarded as a religious outsider. Jesus holds up the action of this outsider as an example of the love of neighbor that is one of the two great commandments. When the parable ends with the words "go and do likewise," it challenges Christians to see in-group/out-group boundaries of religion, ethnicity, or nationality as irrelevant to their response to human need and thus to people facing humanitarian crises.[23]

The gospel of Matthew also highlights the importance of concern for those driven from their homes by political crisis. Matthew's narrative of the birth of Jesus includes an account of Jesus's "flight into Egypt." Just after his birth, Jesus, Mary, and Joseph were driven from their home by King Herod in his effort to destroy the infant Jesus as a threat to his regime. This can be seen as a form of persecution and, since it involved flight across a border, we could say anachronistically that Jesus met the contemporary international convention's definition of a refugee. As followers of Jesus, Christians should therefore have special sensitivity to the needs of those turned into refugees by humanitarian crisis.

Also in Matthew's gospel, Jesus teaches that, on the Day of Judgment, one of the criteria that will determine an individual's salvation or damnation at the last judgment will be whether one has welcomed the hungry, the thirsty, the stranger. As Jesus puts it, "Just as you did it to one of the least of these . . . you did it to me" (Matt. 25:40). When they follow this teaching, Christians see aiding the poor and hungry strangers as aiding Jesus himself. Thus, Christians should understand their relation with Jesus and with God as closely linked with the way they respond to suffering people who are not members of their own communities.

Jesus's radically inclusive understanding of neighbor-love reflects the book of Genesis's affirmation that all persons have been created in the image of God and are brothers and sisters in a single human family no matter what their nationality or ethnicity. This common creation gives every person a shared worth that reaches across national borders. As St. Paul put it, "From one single stock [God] . . . created the whole human race so that they could occupy the entire earth" (Acts 17:26). This challenges any understanding of the moral significance of borders that restricts the respect and care required by the love commandment to members of one's own religious, national, or ethnic community. *Sub specie aeternitatis*, there are no foreigners; all humans are equally brothers and sisters to one another. Extending care only to those who are "like us" is religiously unacceptable in a Christian normative perspective.

This does not mean, of course, that Christian communities and Christian-influenced societies always live up to the normative standards stressed in their traditions. There are clear examples of where Christians do not do so. For example, in the conflicts that led to the breakup of the former Yugoslavia in the 1990s, Christians fought each other as well as Muslims. In the violence that created massive internal displacement in Colombia, Catholics were in conflict with each other. Nonetheless, the developments that have taken place in a Christian understanding of one's responsibilities toward fellow humans does help explain emergent Catholic commitment to human rights and the strong responses by Catholic organizations to political emergencies and natural disasters today. The next chapter explores some of the ways Christian motives energize these responses and help to sustain those directly affected by crisis. First, the normative stances toward such crises in several other important religious traditions will be briefly considered.

SOME OTHER FAITH TRADITIONS

Most of the great religions of the world are significantly involved in responding to humanitarian crises. The themes of migration and exile play key roles in the founding narratives of many world religions, particularly Judaism, Christianity, and Islam. Thus, it should not be surprising that there are normative values that lead Jews and Muslims to respond to these crises along with Christians. Here the normative perspectives that shape the response of Judaism and Islam to these crises are sketched, followed by a very brief discussion of the normative stance of two Asian religious traditions, Hinduism and Buddhism. A central issue for these faith traditions, as for Christianity, is how the tradition's normative values promote respect toward outsiders, enabling the community to offer aid to victims of war and refuge to displaced people.

Judaism

The followers of the three great monotheistic faiths—Judaism, Christianity, and Islam—all see themselves as descendants of the patriarch Abraham, whose experience of God's call led him to migrate from the home of his kinsfolk in present-day Iraq to the land of Canaan, in present-day Israel. Jews, as well as Christians and Muslims, regard themselves as children of Abraham.

Thus, they see being migrants as a central aspect of who they are. They also see themselves as religiously called to respond to the needs of other migrants and exiles.

The story of the Exodus—a migration from slavery in Egypt to freedom in the land of God's promise—forms the core identity of Judaism. In this narrative, the Israelites had been forced to migrate to Egypt by a crisis of famine in their homeland. After a period in which they had been welcomed in Egypt, the Egyptians came to fear the Israelites as they increased in number and laid on them "the whole cruel fate of slaves" (Ex. 1:11–14). God saw their misery and heard their cries, freeing them and forming them into a people through bonds of a covenant. Moses led them to migrate across the desert into a land "flowing with milk and honey" that became their home (Ex. 3:7–8). Because God freed Israel from oppression and exile as strangers in Egypt, a special duty to respect strangers and migrants became a central tenet of Judaism. "Love your neighbor [your fellow Israelite] as yourself" (Lev. 19:18) was a central moral norm for the community of Israel. Repeatedly, however, the Hebrew Scriptures also declare that compassion and justice (*tzedakah*) are due not only to fellow Jews but also to strangers outside the Jewish community. While the command to "love your neighbor as yourself" appears once in the Hebrew Bible, the command to "love the stranger" appears no fewer than thirty-six times (e.g., in Ex. 23:9, Lev. 19:33–34, and many other places).[24]

The normative identity of Israel, as presented in the law and prophets of the Hebrew Bible, therefore calls the Jewish people to exercise special responsibilities to people fleeing slavery, abuse, and other crises. The story of the Exodus and its role in forming the identity of the Jewish people call Jews to support a humanitarian response to strangers in need. In particular, it calls for providing positive assistance to those fleeing oppression or persecution as forced migrants.[25]

The Bible also sees God's covenant with the Jewish people as the basis of a special relation between Jews and the land of Israel. This special relation to the land of Zion is a source of the unresolved problems today in the relation between Israel and Palestinians. Both Israelis and Palestinians claim the same land as their own, leading to ongoing conflict. This conflict has also made the Palestinians the single largest national group compelled to live as refugees. In much Jewish self-understanding, however, God's special covenant with Israel should have quite the opposite effect. The former chief rabbi of the United Hebrew Congregations of the Commonwealth, Jonathan Sacks, has argued that Jewish particularism should give Jews a special sensitivity to the duty to protect the distinctive identities of peoples different from themselves.[26] God's special covenant with the Jewish people calls them to protect not only the Jewish people themselves but also all who are different from them. It should make Jews especially sensitive to the need to "make space for difference" and to protect the right of others to be different.[27] God's covenant with Israel does not justify the denial of the fundamental rights of non-Jews but rather calls for commitment to the humanity, dignity, and rights of each people in its own integral identity.

Further, the narrative of the particularistic covenant with Israel is accompanied by the book of Genesis's story of the universal creation of every human being in the image and likeness of God (Gen. 1:27). Jews, like Christians after them, draw on this text to affirm the sacred dignity of all human beings. The creation of all men and women in God's image means all possess the same fundamental human rights. Although these rights do not set forth the full way of life that faithful Jews are called to, they do establish a minimum code that all persons, whether Jew or gentile, are required to follow. This minimal but universal orientation of the Creation story is reinforced by the covenant with Noah (Gen. 9:1–17). In the story of the covenant with Noah, God's care is extended to all persons and to "every living creature" (Gen. 9:10, 12, and 15), giving the Jewish people strict duties to respect the common humanity of all people.

Judaism is a complex blend of particularist values that require the support of members of the Jewish community and universalist values that call for respect for all people. These core values, in different ways, point toward strong obligations toward both Jews and non-Jews who are threatened or suffering due to political emergency or natural disaster. These values can energize vigorous efforts by members of the Jewish community to work on behalf of those in the middle of crisis.

Islam

Belief in the oneness of God and the unity of the entire human race are central to Islam, and these beliefs can have considerable significance for Islamic responses to humanitarian crises. The Qur'an affirms that the human race was created by Allah as *umma wahida*, "one community" (Sura 2:213). Despite the divisions that have arisen through history due to diverse beliefs and cultures, humanity remains one because it has a single origin and a shared destiny. The borders between nation-states, therefore, have only relative weight in Islamic political thought and close to no weight in Islamic ethics.[28] The Muslim community has a responsibility to work to retain human unity. Muslim duties reach across national, cultural, and religious borders, and this universalism has important implications for how Muslims should respond to people suffering from the effects of political conflict or natural disasters.

The normative tradition of Islam teaches that Muslims have a particular duty to assist those displaced from their homes by conflict. The event of Muhammad's *hijra* or migration from Mecca to Medina (622 CE) is considered the founding event of the Muslim religious community. In the *hijra*, Muhammad was fleeing from persecution by the Quraysh, the dominant clan in Mecca. So, again anachronistically, we could say that Muhammad met the contemporary definition of a refugee. He fled from Mecca to Medina so he could preserve the integrity of the message of monotheism that he had begun setting forth in the early suras of the Qur'an. The Quraysh's continuing adherence to their culture's many gods was in conflict with Muhammad's central message of the oneness of God. The conflict was also rooted in the Quraysh's desire to retain their economic power and their control over the *ka'bah* as the pre-Islamic tradition's central pilgrimage site in Mecca. Thus, Muhammad's flight was motivated both by his commitment to sustaining belief in the oneness of God in the face of religious persecution and by the threats he and his followers faced from those holding political and commercial power.[29] The origins of Islam are closely intertwined with a religious and political crisis leading to forced migration.

In continuity with this founding experience, the tenets of Islam include a core commitment to offer assistance and protection to "needy travelers." Being a traveler has been part of the Muslim experience from the very beginning. One of the five pillars of Islam is that it is each Muslim's duty, if possible, to make the hajj (pilgrimage) to Mecca in his or her lifetime. Both the founding *hijra* and the requirement of hajj call Muslims to appreciate the needs of people on the move. The Qur'an sees emigrants (*muhajirin*) such as Abraham, the people of Israel, and, above all, Muhammad and his companions in the *hijra* as falling under the special care of Allah (Q. 9:100). Those who welcomed Muhammad and his fellow migrants to Medina are known as the Ansar (the helpers), and they are especially blessed. The Qur'an notes that those fleeing from oppression face special vulnerabilities, and it teaches that Muslims have special responsibilities toward them (Q. 28:4). These responsibilities include the duty to provide asylum, including asylum to non-Muslims. In the words of the Qur'an, "If anyone of the disbelievers seeks your protection, then grant him protection so he may hear the word of Allah and then escort him to where he will be secure" (9:6). These and other Islamic teachings have led the Organisation of the Islamic Conference (today the Organisation of Islamic Cooperation), working with UN High Commissioner for Refugees, to conclude that "respect for migrants and those seeking refuge has been a permanent feature of the Islamic faith."[30]

Another of the five pillars of Islam, *zakat* or almsgiving, is relevant to Muslim responses to those facing humanitarian crisis. *Zakat* requires Muslims to donate a percentage of their income (generally understood to be 2.5 percent) to specified groups of recipients, including the poor, the destitute, and travelers in need. Above this obligatory practice of *zakat*, Muslims are also encouraged to donate more through the practice of *sadaqa*, or voluntary giving. Both *zakat* and *sadaqa* have led to the creation of permanent endowments known as *waqf*. A *waqf* provides resources to assist those in need over the longer term. All three of these practices provide means for a Muslim response to people suffering the effects of political conflict or natural disaster. They are obligatory religious requirements for all Muslims.[31]

A full picture of the Islamic tradition's interaction with the reality of humanitarian crisis, of course, requires noting some less admirable components. Just as some aspects of Jewish Zionism and Christian missionary activity have had negative consequences, so too complex links between the Muslim concepts of *hijra* and jihad have sometimes had negative consequences. Muhammad's flight from Mecca to Medina is seen as a struggle (jihad) against the adversaries of his monotheistic faith in the oneness of Allah. Most Muslims hold that the need for *hijra* as a way of expanding the reach of Islam ended with the establishment of Islam in Mecca. However, in the face of forces that would undermine Islam, the duty to defend Islam against attacks by non-Muslims continues. A hadith (a prophetic saying of the Prophet) indicates that there was no need for *hijra* once Mecca had become Muslim, but in the face of threats from unbelievers, "Jihad (struggle) and good intention remain."[32] Jihad, of course, does not necessarily mean armed struggle. Muslims understand the "greater jihad" to mean the struggle against unbelief within oneself, and jihad on behalf of Islam can be undertaken through persuasive words and the witness of an exemplary life. In some circumstances, however, it can refer to armed struggle. Thus, there are strands of Islamic tradition that have led some Muslim extremist groups to endorse armed jihad as an appropriate strategy in the struggle against Western colonialism and continuing Western influence in the

Muslim world. Nevertheless, there is serious argument under way within Islam today about the meaning of jihad and about the legitimacy of the use of force to either protect or advance the Muslim community. This discussion leads many Muslim thinkers to place the same kind of ethical limits on the use of force that the Catholic tradition developed to help it distinguish just from unjust war and that modern humanitarian law drew from the just war tradition in the West.[33] Extremist Muslims advocating violent struggle on behalf of Islam today have only partial or ephemeral continuity with the broad Islamic tradition.[34] In fact, in the larger Muslim tradition, struggle through word and example remains central, including through care for refugees and "needy travelers." This is the basis of Muslim efforts to respond to those suffering due to humanitarian crises throughout the history of Islam. It has also led to the recent foundation of Muslim faith-based agencies such as Islamic Relief. These new agencies are responding to crises with notable effectiveness today.

Religions of Asia

In contrast with the sizable number of analyses of the approaches of the monotheistic traditions to humanitarian and human rights issues, there are fewer studies of the approaches of Asian religions to these matters. Nonetheless, it is useful to note very briefly some of the core concepts underpinning Hindu and Buddhist responses, especially in the emerging tradition that has been called "engaged Buddhism."[35]

Hinduism is an internally pluralistic tradition—perhaps better called a family of traditions. Hindu responses to humanitarian crises are therefore quite diverse. Virtually all Hindus, however, have a strong conviction that human behavior should be guided by "dharma," a term whose rich meanings include "the moral order," "duty," and "justice." A central normative text for Hindus, the *Mahabharata*, summarizes dharma as requiring that "one should never do that to another which one regards as injurious to oneself."[36] Understood this way, dharma implies that all human beings have moral duties toward all other humans. This universality leads some contemporary Hindu thinkers to see dharma as a Hindu basis for human rights. Since the response of particular communities to humanitarian crises depends heavily on whether the sphere of rights and duties is understood inclusively, this universalistic meaning of dharma can be seen as a Hindu basis for duties to respond positively to the needs of people facing the suffering brought about by political conflict and natural disasters.

Dharma, however, also has other less universalist meanings. It can refer to duties based on caste or stage of life. Rulers have special obligations based on dharma, some of them toward the citizens of their own realm. Thus, a sense of religious duty leads some contemporary Indian nationalists to affirm the Indian state's obligation to advance Hindu traditions as the basis of Indian religious and cultural unity. This Hindu nationalism has been a cause of conflict both within India and across India's borders.[37] These religious sources of nationalism are woven in complex ways into historical and political events, such as India's struggle against British colonial rule and its strained relations with the regions that have become Pakistan and Bangladesh.

There are strands within Hindu traditions, therefore, that can lead to very positive responses to the needs of people affected by conflict and disaster. Such responses include India's welcome of millions of Hindus and Sikhs from Pakistan during the violent crisis accompanying the India-Pakistan partition at the end of the British Raj. India has also welcomed many thousand Tibetan Buddhist followers of the Dalai Lama fleeing Chinese repression since 1959. It hosted millions of Bengalis driven from their homes by the war between East and West Pakistan that led to the birth of the new nation of Bangladesh in 1971. At the same time, nationalist sentiments partly rooted in Hinduism continue to lead to conflicts with some non-Hindu people both within India and across its borders. Hinduism thus exemplifies both the positive and negative possibilities of religious response to humanitarian crisis.

What is today called "engaged Buddhism" has led to a number of significant new forms of Buddhist effort to relieve suffering caused by conflict, oppression, or persecution. Buddhism is often regarded as a spirituality of meditative focus on the interior life and of withdrawal from engagement with the struggles of social and political life. While it is true that Buddhists have often followed this path, there are significant resources within the Buddhist faith that have begun to be tapped in ways that energize engaged efforts to alleviate the suffering of the victims of humanitarian crises.[38] The Buddha was deeply aware of the suffering that afflicts the human condition. The first of the "four noble truths" taught by the Buddha after his enlightenment was the pervasiveness of suffering. Followers of the Buddha who are on the path to enlightenment are required to respond to this suffering with compassion, even delaying their own enlightenment in order to aid others who are suffering. Those on such a path of active compassion are called *bodhisattvas*. "Engaged Buddhism" seeks to follow this *bodhisattva* path.[39]

Among such engaged Buddhists were Maha Ghosananda, the Buddhist patriarch of Cambodia who died in 2007. Ghosananda began his leadership of a series of "pilgrimages for truth" in the refugee camps at the Thai border to which many Cambodians had fled from the Khmer Rouge's atrocities. These atrocities led to well over a million deaths, making what happened on the Cambodian killing fields surely one of the gravest humanitarian crises of recent history. Ghosananda's pilgrimages were efforts to stimulate support for peace and to heal the wounds inflicted by the Cambodian tragedy. Other Buddhists, such as Sulak Sivaraksa of Thailand, Thích Nhất Hạnh of Vietnam, and the Dalai Lama of Tibet, have also led nonviolent campaigns that seek to address some of the deep crises that have tragically unfolded in recent decades.[40] The Taiwanese Buddhist nun Cheng Yen founded Tzu Chi, a Buddhist nongovernmental organization that now has several million members in many countries, some of whom are engaged in international relief work. Cheng Yen teaches that offering assistance to those who are suffering from humanitarian crisis is a way of "following and applying the teachings of Buddha in our daily lives and transforming ourselves into living Bodhisattvas."[41] The work of the Tzu Chi organization included a significant response to Typhoon Haiyan that devastated parts of the Philippines in November 2013. Tzu Chi describes its relief work in an explicitly Buddhist way: "When people bring out the wisdom and compassion of a bodhisattva—to feel others' suffering as their own and work hard to relieve it—such sincere love will set off endless cycles of kindness. As everyone brings out their love and unites in collective effort, recovery is possible even after the worst of disasters, and in fact, the community can be rebuilt even better with survivors receiving and reciprocating abundant love."[42]

Buddhism, of course, like the other religions explored here, does not have an entirely positive record in relation to humanitarian crises. For example, Buddhism has been intertwined with the violent Sinhalese nationalism that contributed to the Sri Lankan civil war. This war displaced hundreds of thousands, with the number of the internally displaced reaching a peak of approximately eight hundred thousand in 2001.[43] Nonetheless, within Sri Lanka the Buddhist movement Sarvodaya Shramadana has sought a nonviolent resolution of the conflict.[44] Buddhism has also played a regrettable role in legitimating the grave abuse of the Rohingya people in Myanmar and the forced migration of many of them to Bangladesh.[45] The key factor affecting the role of Buddhism in the crises in Sri Lanka and Myanmar, as with other religious traditions in other parts of the world, is how the adherents of a religion understand the normative principles of their tradition and how they enact these principles in society.

Religious communities have significant capacities to assist those who are facing the suffering brought about by humanitarian crises and to help prevent such crises over the long term. The major world faiths and the organizations linked to them make many important contributions to alleviating and preventing the suffering caused by conflict and natural disaster. They are important contributors to humanitarian endeavor today. The way a faith community understands both its own identity and its relation to other faith communities will shape its response to crises. There are clearly important resources within all the major faith traditions that can lead to very positive responses. Religious traditions, regrettably, can also be drawn on in ways that lead to conflict. The key will be how the community draws on its tradition in light of its experience of the human needs and possibilities it faces. The trends sketched here indicate that positive responses by faith communities to humanitarian crisis are on the rise—in some communities, dramatically so. Before turning to those ethical considerations, the next chapter highlights some concrete ways that religious communities and their agencies can contribute to the humanitarian effort to help those threatened in humanitarian emergencies or who have been forcibly displaced today.

CHAPTER 4

RELIGIOUS ACTION TODAY

The central traditions of religious communities have long been important sources of the charity and compassion that lead people to come to the aid of those affected by wars and other crises. The Torah in the Hebrew Bible and the teachings of Jesus in the New Testament call Jews and Christians to love their neighbor as they love themselves. The scriptures of all the world religions teach versions of the "golden rule" that calls each person to "Do to others whatever you would have them do to you."[1] Islam names Allah the all-compassionate, all-merciful one, thus proclaiming that God calls Muslims to compassionate care for those displaced by war. Compassion is also a central duty in Buddhism, indicating that those on the road to Enlightenment should show care for the victims of humanitarian crises. Religious motivations such as these have long been sources of the efforts to assist those who are suffering because of conflict, as discussed in the previous chapter. A consideration of some of the more concrete ways religious belief can shape response to crisis today is the focus here.

THE IMPORTANCE OF FAITH-BASED ACTION

Several of the initiatives that generated the humanitarian movement in its present form rose from explicitly Christian roots, even when they were not formally linked to a specific Christian church. As the previous chapter showed, the humanitarian movement has deep historical roots in religious belief that all men and women are God's children. In a similar way, the founders of the Red Cross (ICRC) drew on their Christian faith and the ethics this faith supported when they launched the organization that serves as a model of contemporary humanitarian action. The ICRC, of course, is independent of any religious community and provides assistance independent of the religion of those being served. Its founders, however, had religious motivations of a nondenominational sort. Henri Dunant saw himself as "an instrument in the hands of God."[2] Jean Pictet understood the ICRC's principle of humanity as closely associated with the Christian duty to love one's neighbor. Pictet saw the ICRC's efforts to end the sufferings of war victims as reflecting the love that is the central norm and virtue in Christian morality.[3]

Despite these religious roots, in the twentieth century a notable secularization of humanitarian action seemed to occur as a number of new relief agencies with no explicit religious connection were created. In part, this was due to the growing institutionalization of the humanitarian effort. Until quite recently, responses to the needs of people facing grave threats to their well-being were rarely as institutionally organized as they have become today. Charity and benevolence were part of the everyday response to those who were suffering, but, as Michael Barnett has put it, there was "no regime of sympathy." Barnett characterizes the emergence of such an organized regime as "a revolution in moral sentiments" leading to a culture of compassion in which compassionate response to human suffering became "a central part of organized society."[4] This regime has been increasingly shaped by governments and by intergovernmental agencies like the UN High Commissioner for Refugees (UNHCR) and nongovernmental institutions of considerable scope. Because of the non-religious character of these organizations and their institutional reach, the overall scene appeared to become more secular. The conclusion that emergencies were increasingly being addressed by secular agencies was reinforced by the way that faith-based groups found it necessary to collaborate in their work with large, secular organizations. This often led them to stress the humanistic grounds of their activity, placing less explicit emphasis on faith commitment as the framework of their activities. As Alastair Ager and Joey Ager have put it, by the mid-twentieth century, "with non-governmental actors increasingly enmeshed within intergovernmental structures and governmental agendas, the principles and policies of humanitarianism were increasingly articulated in secular terms."[5]

Nevertheless, it is evident that faith-based organizations continue to play an important role in the overall humanitarian effort today. During the past several decades, the number of faith-based organizations dedicated to responding to humanitarian crises has grown. Particularly notable has been the creation of new Christian nongovernmental organizations (NGOs) with an evangelical orientation, such as Samaritan's Purse and the International Justice Mission, as well as Islamic humanitarian agencies, including Islamic Relief. It is also clear that many of the older religiously inspired agencies continue to play important roles in the overall humanitarian effort.

Estimates of the revenues expended by religious organizations on humanitarian assistance cannot be very precise. In part, this is because numerous parish churches, mosques, and other local and smaller religious communities provide direct assistance to those in need without their work being seen as humanitarian and without their expenditures being recorded as formally devoted to relief or development. Similarly, members of religious communities in one part of the world often assist members of their community in other parts of the world who are facing crisis without recording this as properly humanitarian aid.[6]

Despite these limits, it is clear from available financial data that agencies linked to churches, mosques, and other religious communities play major roles in the overall response to political emergencies and natural disasters. Expenditures for assistance work by the major religiously affiliated organizations in the United States are similar to the amount spent by secular agencies.[7] The overall operating expenditures of some of the largest secular and religious NGOs responding to humanitarian crises, drawn from their annual reports for 2016, are gathered in tables 4.1 and 4.2.

Thus, the evangelically inspired World Vision International's annual expenditures of about $2,000 million are somewhat larger than Oxfam International's budget of about $1,200 million, while the US-based Catholic Relief Service's expenses of $970 million are just slightly less than the $1,173 million spent by Médecins sans Frontières (Doctors without Borders). These data support Michael Barnett's observation that "it is impossible to study humanitarianism without being impressed by the importance of religion."[8]

TABLE 4.1 Annual Expenditures of Secular Humanitarian Organizations (2016)

Organization	*Annual Expenditures (millions)*
Oxfam International	€1,007 (approx. $1,195)
Médecins sans Frontières	€989 (approx. $1,173)
International Rescue Committee	$772
Save the Children	$698
Care USA	$610
Mercy Corps	$432

TABLE 4.2 Annual Expenditures of Religious Humanitarian Organizations (2016)

Organization	Annual Expenditures (millions)
World Vision International	$2,153
Catholic Relief Services	$970
Samaritan's Purse	$583
Islamic Relief USA	£115 (approx. $136)
Islamic Relief Worldwide	$99
Hebrew Immigrant Aid Society (2011)	$50

The continuing importance of the role played by faith-based organizations runs counter to the secularization hypothesis that many social theorists have held until quite recently. Through much of the twentieth century, social scientists presumed that history was on a one-way path toward increasing secularization. They concluded that religion was declining, with fewer believers than in earlier days, or that religion was being privatized, with less influence in public domains such as politics or the economy. Due to this decline or privatization, they expected religion to become increasingly "invisible," with less influence on public life than in earlier epochs.[9] The evidence of the past several decades, however, points in a markedly different direction. It suggests that the secularization hypothesis is not an accurate description of what is happening, at least when applied outside Western Europe.

The role of religion in public life has thus been undergoing significant reassessment over the past several decades. This rethinking is evident in the appearance of serious academic books with provocative titles such as *The Revenge of God: The Resurgence of Islam, Christianity, and Judaism in the Modern World*; *The Desecularization of the World: Resurgent Religion and World Politics*; and *God's Century: Resurgent Religion and Global Politics*.[10] In most parts of the world, religion is neither declining nor becoming purely a private affair. Indeed, José Casanova argues that "religious traditions throughout the world are refusing to accept the marginal and privatized role which theories of modernity as well as theories of secularization had reserved for them."[11]

The continuing public influence of religion seems particularly notable in international politics. The support of some faith communities for the human rights movement has been increasingly evident. For example, Catholicism has played a particularly important role in the advancement of human rights and democracy since the Second Vatican Council concluded in 1965.[12] The positive role of religious action is also evident in the assistance that religious communities and their agencies continue to provide to displaced people and to others affected by humanitarian crisis. Faith-based organizations remain important players in the humanitarian movement today.

POSITIVE AND NEGATIVE EFFECTS

The activity of faith communities, of course, has both positive and negative effects in international affairs. Religious communities are major responders to humanitarian crises. Sometimes, however, they are among the causes of the conflicts that lead to these crises. The negative face of religion is evident in the politicized assertions of religious identity and self-defensive fundamentalisms that contribute to several of the world's conflicts today. The record in the first years of the twenty-first century is distressing. Brian Grim and Roger Finke draw upon data gathered by the US State Department, the Pew Forum on Religion and Public Life, and several other sources. They conclude that between 2000 and 2007, 86 percent of the 143 countries with populations of more than 2 million have experienced at least some cases of people being abused or displaced from their homes because of their religion.[13] As noted earlier, the religious beliefs of some Jews and some Muslims have been among the factors driving the Israeli-Palestinian conflict over multiple generations. Intra-Muslim conflict is one of the causes of the Syrian civil war, which has displaced huge numbers of people both as refugees and within Syria itself. In India, Muslim reaction to the Hindu nationalist convictions of the Bharatiya Janata Party contributed to the rise of Lashkar-e-Taiba, a Muslim group with ties to Pakistan that in 2008 carried out terror attacks in Mumbai, killing many. These Hindu-Muslim tensions also contribute to the dangerous instability between the nuclear-armed powers of India and Pakistan. Buddhist control of the government in Sri Lanka led to resistance by the minority Hindu community that generated a bloody civil war, and Buddhist efforts to exclude Muslim Rohingya people from Myanmar have displaced many thousands of Rohingya to Bangladesh. There are severe cases of religious persecution and conflict in Africa as well. In Sudan, for example, the long civil war between south and north before South Sudan became an independent country in 2011 had religion as one among its several driving forces. Christians and adherents of traditional African religion in the south resisted efforts by the north to Islamize the whole of Sudan. The conflict took over 2 million lives and created over 5 million displaced persons.[14] In central Europe, communal hostilities between Orthodox, Muslim, and Catholic believers contributed to the fragmentation of the former Yugoslavia into separate countries, including Serbia, Bosnia-Herzegovina, and Croatia.

On the other hand, the previous chapter has shown that the normative values of the major world religions call believers to work for peace and to respond to the needs of persons adversely affected by war and displacement. In their vigorous pursuit of these values, religious leaders like Mohandas Gandhi, Martin Luther King Jr., the Dalai Lama, Pope John Paul II, and Archbishop Desmond Tutu have played vigorous roles in the pursuit of human rights and democracy, peace and reconciliation. Gandhi's nonviolent campaign for the independence of India from British rule was grounded in his Hindu beliefs, interpreted with the help of his reading of the Christian Leo Tolstoy. Gandhi's nonviolence inspired movements for justice and peace among Christians. These included King and his campaign for racial justice in the United States as well as Tutu, whose participation in the antiapartheid movement enabled South Africa to elect Nelson Mandela president in 1994. John Paul II was deeply involved in Poland's struggle for freedom from control and domination by the Soviet Union. The pope's support for the Solidarity movement in Poland contributed in significant ways to movements that led to the tearing down of the Berlin Wall in 1989 and to the collapse of the Soviet Union and its empire in 1991. The Dalai Lama has been a powerful Buddhist voice raised on behalf of the people of Tibet in the face of their oppression by the People's Republic of China. His voice, like that of many other religious people engaged in campaigns for justice, has appealed for significant change through nonviolent means.

One of the most notable developments of recent international affairs has been the significant rise of nonviolent movements for justice and political change, and many of these movements have been religiously inspired. Many of these movements have been notably successful, particularly when they have been pursuing justice internally within states, despite the conviction of political realists that nonviolence is unlikely to be an effective political strategy.[15] The commitment to respect those who are different, including those who are religiously different, has enabled these movements to seek greater justice in public life in vigorous ways while remaining committed to the use of peaceful means. Many of these movements have been faith-based.

In a similar way, humanitarian agencies linked to religious communities have played significant roles in responding to the suffering caused by major crises. These communities and their leaders have contributed to ending some of the major humanitarian crises and to promoting the reconciliation needed to prevent the return of conflict. Their role in responding to natural disasters has also been significant.

Scott Appleby is surely correct, therefore, when he says that religion plays an "ambivalent" role in relation to the conflicts that so threaten peace and human well-being.[16] Faith communities sometimes contribute to these conflicts and sometimes play important roles in overcoming them. A key question, therefore, is what *kind* of faith and faith-based tenets motivate religious communities to engage in the activities that have significant consequences for humanitarian crises. If a community's beliefs lead it to respect the dignity and rights of all persons, including those of other faiths, and to call on governments to guarantee the rights of all, the believing community will make positive contributions to peace and to the protection of people from the effects of war and disaster. As the previous chapter has argued, most of the religious traditions of the world hold normative commitments that call for such positive contributions. Many of those who adhere to these traditions live out these norms in action. In doing so, they make positive contributions to alleviating the suffering caused by conflict, displacement, and other harmful effects of humanitarian crisis.

In recent years, therefore, there has been a notable rise in the recognition of the importance of religious communities and their agencies in the humanitarian response to the crises that cause displacement and threaten human dignity. For example, António Guterres, who in 2012 was serving as UNHCR, convened a meeting of leaders of religiously based humanitarian agencies on faith and protection. This meeting gathered more than four hundred representatives of faith-based organizations, academics, and government officials in Geneva to explore forms of partnership in efforts to improve protection of the displaced. The report on the consultation states that the discussion was a "journey of mutual discovery," leading to a "deeper appreciation for and understanding of the role religion and spirituality play in the lives of those UNHCR serves." The conference affirmed the importance of partnerships between the High Commissioner's office and faith-based agencies for the protection of displaced people. It called for the enhancement of what the report called "faith literacy" among UNHCR staff, implying that appreciation of the role of faith-based efforts could be improved.[17] The consultation led to the writing of a further document titled *Welcoming the Stranger: Affirmations for Faith Leaders* that drew upon the sacred scriptures of Hindu, Buddhist, Jewish, Christian, and Muslim traditions. This statement declared, "The call to 'welcome the stranger,' through protection and hospitality, and to honor the stranger or those of other faiths with respect and equality, is deeply rooted in all major religions."[18] These "affirmations" were formally launched at a signing ceremony at the Religions for Peace 9th World Assembly on November 21, 2013, in Vienna. They were signed by more than 1,700 religious leaders.

It is increasingly clear, therefore, that religious belief remains important in the humanitarian sector. Although secular humanitarian organizations are surely important responders to crises, so are faith-based agencies. Indeed, a recent historical review of response to the needs of displaced people over the past twenty-five years concludes that the contribution of faith might well be "the big new theme in refugee studies."[19] Because of this growing recognition of the influence of faith in humanitarian efforts, it will be helpful to explore some of the specific ways religious belief and religious communities support efforts to assist displaced people and others facing humanitarian crisis today.

SOME CONTRIBUTIONS OF FAITH

Religious belief can help sustain those who are suffering the effects of crisis. It energizes the work of those who seek to assist the displaced. The normative values of religious traditions also give faith-based agencies distinctive approaches to their work. Faith traditions and communities contribute by sustaining meaning in the face of the suffering that is a common effect of war and displacement. Faith communities provide communal support that victims of crisis often need in the face of the isolation from their homes brought by displacement. Faith can also provide the hope needed to sustain long-term response to the deeper causes of humanitarian crisis.

Meaning in the Face of Suffering

Wars, earthquakes, and other disasters not only wound, kill, and displace many people; they shatter the personal relationships that provide people with support and help sustain meaning in the ordinary routines of life. Such crises fracture the taken-for-granted worlds in which affected people had been living, causing a kind of intellectual and emotional earthquake. This upheaval calls into question the patterns of meaning that hold life together. Since "secular" means "of or pertaining to the world" (*Oxford English Dictionary*), when the suffering brought by humanitarian crisis shatters the meaning of one's world, this splits open the surface of the secular domain itself. As an earthquake cleaves the crust of the earth, a humanitarian crisis fractures secular explanations of life's purpose. A humanitarian crisis can thus bring about a kind of seismic upheaval on the spiritual level for those it affects. Both the victims of humanitarian crises and those desiring to help them stand before a rift in the structure of meaning that sustains the relationships and routines of their ordinary activity. These emergencies destroy expectations about how life will normally be lived. They raise the question of whether evil and destruction have gained the upper hand in human existence.

Humanitarian crises, therefore, point to two possibilities. First, those who face these crises can conclude that the rift they open up in this-worldly routine descends into depths where all hope of meaningful life should be abandoned. For example, theologian Jon Sobrino has described several types of religious response to the earthquakes that devastated El Salvador in 2001 that moved in this direction. Some Salvadorans saw the destruction as punishment by God for the sins of the people of the country. This religious interpretation led some to believe that the appropriate response was for people to repent from their sinful ways or even simply to accept the destruction they faced. Others saw the earthquakes as God's will, in some mysterious way. This interpretation led them to believe they should simply accept God's inscrutable will and give thanks for the continuing life of those who survived. A third approach was to doubt the goodness of God, asking, "What's wrong with God" if God allows this sort of harm to come to so many innocent people?[20] A further response is less explicitly religious. It sees a disaster such as the Salvadoran earthquake as having destroyed all meaning and hope, whether religious or secular, by throwing its victims into an abyss of absurdity. When a crisis is experienced this way, the outcome can be despair. In all of these interpretations, even when the outcome is not total despair, efforts to respond can seem largely pointless. The result will be passive acceptance. Crises like the earthquake are just the way things are. Little can be done to protect people from their harmful effects.

Yet, in an alternative approach to crisis, people may come to perceive, however dimly, a source of hope that goes deeper than the fractured world. Sobrino proposes an understanding of Christian faith that sees God as radically engaged in the suffering of humanity and in crises such as the Salvadoran earthquake. There is a way of understanding Christianity—a theology—that sees the death of Jesus on the cross as an invitation to trust that the ultimate mystery surrounding our lives—God—lovingly embraces those who struggle right in the midst of their suffering. Should death come,

God will be in solidarity with them even in death. For the believer, the cross of Jesus reveals that the mystery at the heart of the world is not meaningless absurdity but a loving God who has utter compassion for all who suffer and die. The cross is a revelation of divine solidarity with every human who undergoes the distress and loss caused by war, displacement, earthquake, or injustice.

Such a Christian vision invites the victims of crisis to trust that the redeeming love of God is present in their struggles and to hope that God's love is stronger than the threats they face, enabling them to carry on and actively work to rebuild their lives for a better future. It also invites other believers to undertake compassionate efforts to alleviate the suffering caused by crises and to act to prevent this suffering.[21] This is a form of Christian faith that leads to both hope and action in the face of wars or other disasters. When the routines of ordinary life have been fractured, secular patterns of meaning can themselves be shattered. If this happens, secular meaning may no longer be able to provide the hope needed to sustain active engagement. Thus, when one faces the great losses that wars or displacement can bring, transcendent meaning may become a precondition of hope and of the action that hope sustains. Both the victims of such crises and those who seek to aid them may eventually need a source of meaning and hope that is deeper than that provided by their daily routines. Religious experience and faith can provide this kind of meaning and hope. For Christians, such meaning and hope can rise from their belief that the cross of Jesus points to how God's love is present even amid human suffering. For Buddhists, it could rise from a conviction that the compassion exemplified by the Buddha offers meaning that goes deeper than the routine expectations fractured by crisis. Such faith can help sustain people who are facing disaster. Faith can also motivate and energize humanitarian workers when they face diminished hopes as they confront the sufferings of the victims of war, displacement, or other crises. The power of faith to provide such meaning and hope is surely at the heart of religion's continuing engagement in the humanitarian effort.

This theological argument is reinforced by some recent empirical literature on the importance of faith and spirituality in the humanitarian effort. Several studies have shown that faith helps people cope with humanitarian crises by sustaining their hope and by providing them with meaning in the midst of loss. These studies also point out that faith can be a source of support for humanitarian workers themselves, who sometimes face questions about whether their work makes sense when setbacks seem to have the upper hand.[22] The staying power needed for the long-term effort required to grapple with a crisis may be strengthened by the hope religious faith can support.

Communal Support through Accompaniment

Faith communities also provide communal support that helps strengthen the resilience of people facing emergencies.[23] Data on the way communal support sustains hope and action suggests that the commitment by some faith-based agencies to "accompany" the victims of crisis is on the right path. For example, Jesuit Refugee Service (JRS) sees being on the ground with those who suffer from crisis as central to its mission. JRS mission has three dimensions: accompaniment, service, and advocacy. For JRS, accompaniment means JRS staff should stay in close and respectful contact with the refugees they seek to assist, listening to their stories and showing them through the personal presence of JRS staffers that they are not forgotten. Many refugees say this has been the most important help they have received from JRS. This response is a key reason why JRS sees accompaniment as a central focus of its work. Being in personal relationship with those driven from their homes affirms the displaced as persons. It helps keep their hope alive and enables them to continue the struggle to overcome their plight.

Accompaniment also has a significant impact for those who are assisting the displaced. Listening to the stories told by refugees both stimulates commitment to action by the JRS staff and shapes their understanding of what kind of action is needed. In this way accompaniment guides service. It also helps form JRS's advocacy agenda. Without strong roots in the communal interaction that takes place through accompaniment, service and advocacy could easily come to be shaped more by bureaucratic requirements or external agendas than by the real needs of those facing conflict or disaster. Keeping the focus on the actual needs of those who are suffering requires at least some personal relationships with them. This relational presence is itself a form of help, for it lets those being served know that they still count as persons. It helps keep meaning and hope alive. JRS therefore sees accompaniment as truly central to its mission.[24]

For Christians, the provision of such communal support for those suffering the effects of war or disaster will be significantly motivated by the call of Christian love. Action based on love will often lead to personal presence and deepened respect. Christian efforts to assist other Christians in crisis situations will also sometimes include responding to their explicitly religious needs, perhaps by making available worship services or some form of explicitly religious counseling. Thus, JRS does not hesitate to say that its work includes explicitly pastoral care for those being accompanied.[25] At the same time, JRS accompanies and serves people in need regardless of their race, ethnic origin, or religious beliefs.

In a similar way, Catholic Relief Services states that all of its work is "motivated by the Gospel of Jesus Christ to cherish, preserve and uphold the sacredness and dignity of all human life, foster charity and justice, and embody Catholic social and moral teaching." At the same time, CRS will "assist people on the basis of need, not creed, race or nationality."[26] Islamic Relief has greater access to people suffering from emergencies in Muslim countries, so it is particularly able to build bonds of communal trust and support when assisting Muslims. The growth of trust arises at least in part from the shared bond of Muslim faith between Islamic Relief's staff and those being aided. This bond is evident when the organization assists those it serves in organizing such Muslim practices as prayer and the observation of Ramadan.[27] Islamic Relief International also works to provide humanitarian assistance to those who are not Muslim. Its commitment to interreligious cooperation is clear in its partnership with the Lutheran World Federation in developing a "faith-sensitive" approach to humanitarian response.[28]

This points to the question of whether agencies acting based on Christian or Islamic belief can at the same time serve all persons in need and can do so with full respect for the beliefs of those from other traditions. On one level, Christian and Islamic organizations have much in common with secular humanitarian organizations, chiefly because their understandings of their Christian or Muslim beliefs enable them to affirm the dignity of every person independent of the person's religion. Respect for this dignity requires not discriminating among people because of their religion when support and services are being provided. In faith-based organizations like CRS and Islamic Relief, however, many staff members have personal knowledge of how faith can be an important source of strength during crisis. They are thus able to talk with those they are serving about the role of faith in sustaining hope. They can also provide some support for religious practices, provided they do not do so in a way that makes assistance dependent on religion or that uses aid as a vehicle for proselytizing. Combining support for faith with nondiscrimination is, of course, a very delicate undertaking. The wrong kind of support would exclude some people from the aid they need because of their faith or lack of it. On the other hand, if nondiscrimination leads to a strictly secular stance, it could lead to an approach that prevents faith from sustaining the meaning and hope people need in the midst of emergencies.

A possible way to deal with this tension between recognizing the importance of faith and serving in a nondiscriminatory way is for faith-based agencies to adopt a strong commitment to interreligious understanding and collaboration. The criteria for genuine interreligious exchange presented by Catherine Cornille can indicate what this would mean. Interreligious understanding requires *humility*. One needs to be convinced that one can actually learn something by listening to someone with a faith different from one's own faith. Thus, when a Christian seeks to accompany Muslims driven from their homes by war, listening to a Muslim talk about what her faith means to her can create a form of support that would not be possible if such a conversation were regarded as inappropriate. Second, interreligious understanding requires *commitment*. A person on the staff of a Christian or Muslim agency should not be afraid to speak with those being served about how her faith supports her efforts to assist. Expressing this commitment in a humble way can create bonds between agency staff and those they aid, bonds that will help sustain both in their efforts. Third, interreligious understanding depends on seeing that the different faiths of those struggling together share an *interconnection* in their diverse ways of trying to alleviate and prevent the suffering caused by conflict or disaster. Finally, cooperation across faith traditions requires a concrete, experiential *empathy* for the role of specific beliefs in the life of a person who is a member of another community.[29]

For example, staff of Christian agencies assisting those displaced from and within Syria are working largely with Muslims, many of whom have been displaced because of intra-Muslim conflict. Christian staff will thus benefit from having at least a rudimentary appreciation of the Muslim beliefs of those they are helping and of some of the tensions among diverse Islamic traditions that are party to the Syrian conflict. When the staff of Christian agencies are able to talk in a humble way with the Muslims they are serving about what the conflict means to Muslims, and about why they as Christians are seeking to help, this will help strengthen the communal support that sustains hope. It will be a component of what JRS calls accompaniment. In addition, some staff members working in Christian agencies aiding those displaced from Syria are themselves Muslim. Interreligious understanding will therefore strengthen staff collaboration. Interreligious understanding will be similarly valuable for the Christians and Buddhists collaborating on the staffs of Christian agencies that are aiding Buddhists displaced from Myanmar into Thailand. Intra-staff dialogue about how the Christian, Buddhist, and Muslim faiths address displacement will help staff members respond more effectively and more humanly to those they are seeking to aid. Humble interreligious exchanges among staff and those they serve, and among the staff of agencies seeking to help, will make it possible to accompany those facing emergencies in a deeper and fuller way than would remaining silent about religion because of a desire to treat all faiths equally. Equal treatment and nondiscrimination call for humility in the face of difference and for respectful listening to those who are different, not efforts to overlook differences and to keep quiet about them.

Long-Term Response—Compassion Becomes Justice

Compassion is a key motivation that leads humanitarian agencies to respond to the needs of people facing emergencies and disasters. This is particularly true for faith-based organizations. Christian love or Buddhist compassion are often referred to in the mission statements of Christian and Buddhist humanitarian NGOs. This love and compassion goes into action when a humanitarian worker helps a person in need with direct assistance. But as admirable as action based on love or compassion surely is, it is nevertheless sometimes regarded as a form of voluntary philanthropy rather than a strict obligation. This can lead to assistance being seen as optional rather than as a requirement to treat displaced persons according to their human dignity. If humanitarian action is seen as beyond the call of duty in this way, there is also a risk that it will slide into a form of paternalism, in which the strong and capable provide aid to the weak and vulnerable. The commitment to accompany those facing crisis seeks to avoid this kind of condescending paternalism by providing assistance in a way that respects the equal dignity and capacity for agency of those being aided. Accompaniment seeks reciprocity and mutuality in the relationship between aid workers and those they assist, rather than condescension and paternalism.

Although compassion can lead to appropriately personalized ways of aiding displaced persons, there is also a danger that compassion might overlook the institutional dimensions of crisis. If this happens, assistance will address only the symptoms rather than the deeper causes of conflict and other emergencies. Thus, a stress on justice and rights is important because of the way that such an emphasis calls for long-term commitment to the dignity of those being assisted and for efforts to overcome the structural causes of crisis.[30] This raises the question of the relation of religiously motivated love and compassion to the norms of justice and rights. Must one choose between love and justice, between compassion and rights? If so, does one have to choose between a faith-based response rooted in love and a secular response based on justice and rights?

Recent reflection in religious ethics indicates that this is a false choice. In Christian ethics, for example, love can be seen as requiring action for justice, not as an alternative to it. Christian love, of course, has several meanings.[31] It can be seen as a kind of *self-sacrifice* in which one surrenders oneself in order to support the well-being of another. Action based on love or compassion, understood this way, could be seen as a voluntary act that goes beyond the requirements of strict duty since self-sacrifice is often seen as a supererogatory rather than a strict duty. If love is seen as a standard that motivates actions that go beyond duty, there is a danger that it may lead to forms of paternalism. The desire to base humanitarian response on justice rather than love seeks to avoid this kind of condescension. Love, however, need not lead to a form of condescension. It can take the form of *mutuality* that exists between good friends or close companions. Accompaniment seeks this kind of reciprocal relationship among equals. Nevertheless, because this kind of mutuality requires a certain degree of immediate presence of one person to another, its institutional implications are indirect.

A third meaning of Christian love has been called love as equal regard. The biblical commandment to love one's neighbor as oneself affirms that self and neighbor should be cared for equally. This commandment also makes no distinction between one neighbor and another. The love commandment, understood this way, calls for recognition of the equality of all one's neighbors and for equal treatment of each neighbor. Equal treatment, of course, does not require treating every person in an identical way. Equal love of one's neighbors is not the same as identical treatment of each neighbor.[32] Special responsibilities toward one's spouse or children surely exist. However, the equality among persons presumed by the call to love all one's neighbors as oneself requires an effort to provide all persons with the minimal resources that are essential to their lives and their welfare simply as persons and to alleviate the unnecessary suffering they face. Thus, the normative principle that one should love one's neighbor as oneself (love as equal regard) has a significant overlap with the idea of egalitarian justice.[33] Understood this way, love requires working to secure the treatment of all persons in ways that respect their equal human dignity. It leads to a commitment to the basic human rights of all persons. In addition, it implies that there are particularly stringent obligations toward persons who have been deprived of the basic requirements of their human well-being by conflicts they have not initiated or by disasters they have surely not caused. The commandment to love one's neighbor, therefore, should lead faith-based humanitarian agencies whose identity and mission are based on this commandment to a vigorous pursuit of justice and rights for those suffering the effects of conflict or disaster.

The several dimensions of love and compassion should be related to each other in a dynamic and developing way.[34] An encounter with a person who is suffering, whether that encounter happens directly or through knowledge passed on by others, can awaken compassion that leads to a desire to help. It may lead to a desire to accompany those affected by emergency conditions and to share their struggle for a better situation. Such a compassionate response can in turn reveal that the causes of the suffering are deeply rooted. One can discover that alleviating the suffering is beyond one's own power as an individual and even beyond the efforts of modestly sized relief groups. This discovery can lead to the recognition that most conflicts have deep institutional or political causes. It can show how the sufferings brought about by many natural disasters are compounded by economic and political institutions that make some people much more vulnerable than others. This awakening to the institutional dimensions of a crisis can in turn lead to a recognition that care or love for those suffering calls for organized response that seeks to change the social institutions that cause suffering for some but not others, or that make some particularly vulnerable in ways that others are not. Equal care for one's neighbors who are suffering, therefore, can and should lead to efforts to change the institutions that distribute suffering in unjustifiably unequal ways. Love can lead directly to working of justice. In particular, it leads to the pursuit of social justice—that form of justice that governs social institutions so that they protect the equal human dignity of all people, particularly those who are suffering because of the way these institutions are presently functioning.

An appropriate understanding of the relation between love, justice, and social institutions implies that humanitarian action based on justice and human rights is not an alternative or supplement to action-based love but is an expression of love. This has been much stressed by Christian agencies that provide humanitarian protection and assistance, such as Catholic Relief Services. The development of "engaged Buddhism," with its move from compassion to the pursuit of institutional change, suggests that justice can be an expression of Buddhist compassion as well. When love is understood as equal regard for all one's neighbors, as the commandment to love one's neighbor as oneself suggests it should be, love will be seen as requiring both justice and institutional change. Faith-based action shaped by such an understanding of love or compassion should be at least as committed as is secular action to shaping institutions in ways that secure justice and human rights. Indeed, it is possible that the depth of commitment arising from faith-inspired love for the displaced may lead some faith-based agencies to become more engaged in efforts for institutional change than are some secular agencies that fear they may violate humanitarian neutrality by coming too close to politics.

Our discussions so far have sketched an overall stance toward humanitarian crises. The following chapters cover more specific ways we ought to address the humanitarian and several ethical issues that can arise for humanitarian actors, governmental and nongovernmental, both secular and faith-based. These chapters will address the challenges we face in a more concrete way.

CHAPTER 5

BORDERS AND SHARED HUMANITY

Both humanitarian values and religious norms imply that all people share a common humanity. This shared humanity means that every person is a member of a single human community that extends across the borders separating countries and cultures from each other. The bonds that link persons to one another across these borders, of course, are not as strong as those that link them in closer groups such as families, ethnic groups, or even nations. Nevertheless, the humanitarian ethic holds that the moral ties that reach across these borders are real. The duties to aid those who suffer because of war or disaster extend not only to the members of one's own country, culture, or creed but to all men and women. Similarly, there are ethical obligations to grant asylum to people from a culture different from one's own when they need refuge from persecution or war. Humanitarian principles, human rights, and religious norms relativize borders. They call for a moral solidarity that links people together despite their cultural, national, or religious differences. In the framework of the humanitarian ethic, people from distinct cultural, national, or faith communities become neighbors to those they would otherwise see as strangers.

Such is the humanitarian moral vision. But we need to ask about its relevance in today's political context and whether it can be pursued effectively. These questions have quite practical implications. Do individuals have a duty to use their money, talents, or votes to assist those from other communities who face crisis? Do countries have a duty to admit asylum seekers when many of these countries face economic and political challenges of their own? Do states have a responsibility to take diplomatic, economic, or even military action to come to the assistance of people in another community who are severely threatened by being driven from their homes? Such questions call for careful consideration of the moral significance of borders. Here I address the issues in a more general way. Later chapters consider the ethical questions that arise in more specific kinds of crisis situations.

DUTIES ACROSS NATIONAL BORDERS

The growing global interdependence among peoples is leading some analysts to call for a serious rethinking of the relevance of national borders for our ethical responsibilities. The displacement of refugees is an important human manifestation of this interdependence. Because of rising displacement, political philosophers such as Joseph Carens and refugee scholars such as Philip Marfleet have argued that the time is ripe to make borders fully open to all who are fleeing persecution, conflict, or disaster.[1] In a similar spirit, philosopher Martha Nussbaum has argued that a cosmopolitan community that ties all human beings together morally has primacy over narrower communities defined in terms of nationality, ethnicity, or religion. Some years ago Nussbaum called nationality a "morally irrelevant" characteristic of personhood, a position that amounted to an ethical call for open borders.[2]

The principle of "humanity" that guides the actions of the International Committee of the Red Cross and the broader humanitarian movement has been shaped by such a universalist, cosmopolitan ethic. Humanity includes the whole of humankind and all its members. Concern for humanity therefore means that responsibilities reach across borders. There are real duties to *all* members of the human race. To act in accord with humanity is to act with inclusive concern toward all men and women, with special concern for those who face persecution, oppression, or suffering. The borders separating people according to their ethnic, religious, cultural, or national differences do not set boundaries on the moral duty to respect human dignity.

As we have seen, this universalist, cosmopolitan vision can be supported on secular philosophical grounds, such as Kant's insistence that all human persons are ends in themselves, independent of the cultural, religious, or national differences among them. Every person has an intrinsic dignity and worth rather than a negotiable price or a value that depends of some distinctive characteristic such as gender, ethnicity, race, or nationality. This universalist vision also has religious warrants. In both Judaism and Christianity, all persons are brothers and sisters in a single human family no matter what their nationality or ethnicity. Every person has been created in the image and likeness of God (Gen. 1:27). This common creation gives every person a shared dignity and worth that reaches across all boundaries. The borders between peoples are subordinate to the respect due to the dignity of every person, including people displaced by war or other severe crises. Citing the New Testament, the Second Vatican Council affirmed that all human beings "should constitute one family and treat one another in a spirit of brotherhood," since God "from one man has created the whole human race and made them live all over the face of the earth (Acts 17:26)."[3] Pope Francis drew on this biblical vision when he visited the Greek island of Lesbos and assured Syrian refugees seeking entrance to Europe that "God created mankind to be one family." Drawing on such a biblical and cosmopolitan vision, the pope called Europe to "build bridges" to enable the Syrian refugees to enter rather than "putting up walls" to exclude them.[4]

Pope John XXIII appealed to this normative universalism in 1963 when he drew on both religious and secular warrants to affirm that national boundaries do not limit the reach of moral duty. John XXIII maintained that citizenship has a global meaning not limited by national boundaries. In his words, "The fact that one is a citizen of a particular State does not detract in any way from his membership in the human family as a whole, nor from his citizenship in the world community."[5] This affirmation of world community relativizes the moral significance of national borders and state sovereignty. It means that the duty to protect human rights reaches across borders. Such transborder duties have particular relevance to the plight of refugees, who by definition lack the protection normally provided by their home state. Since refugees have lost the protection of their home state, they will effectively end up with no rights at all unless the duty to protect their rights is genuinely transnational. As Pope John XXIII stressed, "Refugees cannot lose these rights simply because they are deprived of citizenship of their own States."[6] The duty to protect the displaced must therefore reach across borders if they are to receive the protection they need.

SHIFTING MODELS OF SOVEREIGNTY

The relation between humanitarian responsibilities and national borders is closely related to the way state sovereignty is understood. The significance of sovereignty has undergone notable historical changes over the past several centuries. Daniel Philpott's study of shifting models of state sovereignty sheds considerable light on the humanitarian responsibilities of states and of other actors as well. He argues that there have been two "revolutions in sovereignty" over the past three and a half centuries and that a third revolution may be under way today.[7] The first revolution was the transition from the political arrangements that prevailed in medieval Europe, where the nation-state did not yet exist, to the modern European state system whose beginning is conventionally marked by the Peace of Westphalia in 1648. The second revolution was the expansion of the modern European nation-state system to the entire globe, accomplished through the anticolonial movements that followed World War II.[8] These two revolutions created the global system of nation-states supported by the UN Charter, in which each country holds the prerogatives of sovereignty, self-determination, and territorial integrity.

Philpott seeks to show that each of these revolutions was driven primarily by the power of new ideas. In the case of the Westphalian revolution, the central ideas were theological and ethical convictions that emerged in the Protestant Reformation. These ideas led German Protestants, and subsequently other European peoples as well, to demand that they be able to determine their religious beliefs for themselves within their own territories. This required freedom from religious control by the formerly dominant Holy Roman Empire, and eventually from all external powers. As the identities of the key political groups became less religious, these initially religious demands gradually evolved into the secular norms of self-determination, territorial integrity, and nonintervention that became the central norms of the modern nation-state system. In this framework, each country's principal international duty was to respect the self-determination of other countries. Nonintervention across state borders became the European norm.

An analogous, second revolution occurred following World War II. Rising anticolonial and antiracist ideas meant that all peoples, not only Europeans, had the right to religious, cultural, and political self-determination. With the gradual abolition of colonial domination, the system of self-determining, sovereign nation-states spread to the entire globe. Each state has the responsibility to respect the sovereignty of all the other states and to allow each country to determine for itself what goes on inside its own borders.

This history is relevant to the contemporary task of specifying responsibilities toward people displaced by war and other crises. It shows that the system of sovereign nation-states is not the only way to organize the world. The global political system can change and develop. Indeed, a third revolution in sovereignty may have begun today that is analogous to the two revolutions that created the state system in Europe and led to its spread throughout the world. This contemporary revolution is also idea driven. It appeals to the ideas of human dignity and human rights as limits to state sovereignty.

The humanitarian and human rights movements are contributing to the revolution in sovereignty that appears to be under way. In recent decades, the ethical ideas embedded within these movements imply that states not only have the responsibility to protect the dignity of their own citizens but also have transborder duties to respect the human rights of the citizens of other countries. Both the humanitarian movement and humanitarian law affirm the existence of transnational responsibilities to protect people from sufferings caused by conflict or natural disaster. Just as the idea that people should be liberated from imperial control led to the historical rise and global spread of the nation-state system, so too the idea today that people should be free from persecution, tyranny, and poverty has generated the normative standards of human rights and humanitarian law that make claims on states themselves. States have a responsibility, both morally and legally, not to abuse either their own citizens or the citizens of other countries. If states fail to uphold the values of human rights, peace, and order, the legitimacy of their action can be questioned.[9] When a state violates the rights of its own citizens in extreme ways, people in other countries may have "duties beyond borders" to come to the aid of those in distress.[10] The nature of such aid and the kind of intervention it may require is explored in the chapters to follow.

To be sure, humanitarian ideas and human rights norms are not the only forces helping to reduce the importance of national boundaries today. The role of borders is also being reshaped by the growth of global trade, by the movement of money in international financial markets, by ecological forces that threaten the atmosphere and the seas, and by other forms of growing interdependence. These global pressures surely do not mean that states are unimportant or disappearing. They do indicate, however, that the interests of individual countries have increasingly transnational dimensions.

Both recent normative discussions as well as actual events on the ground suggest that state sovereignty can no longer be regarded as absolute. The interests of states as well as their normative responsibilities reach across borders. Pope John XXIII observed in his 1963 encyclical, *Pacem in terris*, that the emergence of responsibilities across borders is one of the principal developments in contemporary international affairs. He argued, however, that existing international structures are inadequate tools for the governance of our increasingly interdependent world. He wrote that these institutions "are unequal to the task of promoting the common good of all peoples." In response, John XXIII called for a "public authority, having worldwide power and endowed with the proper means for the efficacious pursuit of its objective," namely, the worldwide common good.[11] He gave particular endorsement to the United Nations. Pope Benedict XVI went even farther in his 2009 encyclical, *Caritas in veritate*. He wrote, "In the face of the unrelenting growth of global interdependence, there is a strongly felt need, even in the midst of a global recession, for a reform of the United Nations Organization, and likewise of economic institutions and international finance, so that the concept of the family of nations can acquire real teeth."[12]

Both John XXIII and Benedict XVI thus called for both institutional and moral change in the international sphere. Institutionally, they called for innovations in governance that support more effective efforts to secure the human rights of persons whose dignity is jeopardized by the dynamics of interdependence, including the victims of war and displacement. Morally, the increased interdependence of our globalizing world requires a new form of solidarity. Pope John Paul II saw this as a deeper sense of the humanity we share across the borders. This solidarity will "take up interdependence and transfer it to the moral plane."[13] Without this moral solidarity, the de facto interaction of peoples with those from other nations and cultures frequently leads to conflict. Such conflicts are among the chief sources of humanitarian crises and the displacement they cause.

Former UN secretary-general Kofi Annan echoed this moral appeal for solidarity across borders when he insisted on the limits to sovereignty. In Annan's words, "State sovereignty, in its most basic sense, is being redefined. . . . States are now widely understood to be instruments at the service of their peoples, and not vice versa. . . . When we read the [United Nations] charter today, we are more than ever conscious that its aim is to protect individual human beings, not to protect those who abuse them."[14] Full adoption of the revision of sovereignty that Annan saw occurring would be a change in the international system parallel in scope with the creation of the nation-state and the abolition of colonialism. It would be a genuinely revolutionary development.

For Christians, however, the call to develop institutions that reflect the worldwide scope of the human community is not really a revolutionary idea at all. Such a revision of the Westphalian system reflects key elements in the Christian tradition. Pope John Paul II suggested that such a shift would have traditional roots, for the Bible "continually speaks to us of an active commitment to our neighbour and demands of us a shared responsibility for all of humanity."[15] In a similar vein, Pope John XXIII appealed to Christian tradition to support his insistence that citizenship in a particular country does not deprive a person of "membership in the human family, nor of citizenship in that universal society, the common, world-wide fellowship of human beings."[16] These religious beliefs are among the reasons that the Catholic Church has held, from Westphalia to the present, that state sovereignty should be limited. For example, Pope Innocent X (d. 1655) condemned the treaties signed at Westphalia that helped create the modern nation-state system as "null, void, invalid, wicked, unjust."[17] This was largely due to the way Westphalian sovereignty restricted the role of the Church in the public life of European society. Before the Reformation, Catholicism had played a central unifying role in the *res publica Christiana* of European Christendom. Following the Westphalian peace arrangements, Europe became religiously divided and politics more secular, with Catholicism in a less central position. Nevertheless, Catholic resistance to sovereignty also arose from reasons going beyond the self-interest of the Church and a nostalgia for the medieval order. Both Catholic theology and an understanding of the requirements of a reason-based philosophy of human personhood gave the Church a strong commitment to the unity of humanity. This commitment played a role in the Church's rejection of the absolute sovereignty of nation-states at the time of Westphalia, and it continues to do so today.

The religious and moral stress on the limits to sovereignty has continued to be visible in Catholic engagement in international affairs in the post–World War II period. After the war, the Christian democratic parties of Germany and France that were inspired by Catholic social thought became important advocates of the limitation and pooling of sovereignty that led to the European Union. During the pontificate of John XXIII in the 1960s and following conclusion of the Second Vatican Council in 1965, the Catholic community became increasingly engaged in advocacy on behalf of human rights. The Council transformed Catholicism into a significant player in the struggle for human rights worldwide. It made the Church a strong advocate for limits on state sovereignty and for the creation of the transnational institutions needed to secure human rights.[18] Although the strengthening of such global institutions would be in considerable continuity with Catholic tradition, it would also call for dramatic—even revolutionary—change in the international system. Since revolutionary change can be risky business, it is important to consider how local communities, nation-states, and nongovernmental agencies also continue to have important roles in the response to humanitarian crises and needs of displaced people.

THE LOCAL AND THE GLOBAL

From a normative point of view, an authentically cosmopolitan ethos calls for recognition that all persons share a common humanity. At the same time, philosopher Kwame Anthony Appiah has persuasively argued that a cosmopolitanism that shows genuine respect for all persons requires not only recognition of the common humanity of all but also for each person's distinct and differing characteristics. Cosmopolitanism that overlooks local differences can degenerate into a form of imperial tyranny. An ethically adequate politics, therefore, should both support the common humanity of all people and recognize the ways people differ from each other.[19] People differ from one another in their languages, cultural values, and religious traditions. Respect for all persons requires respect for these differences among them. People also differ in their nationality and citizenship. Recognition of this fact has recently led Nussbaum to reverse her earlier position that national borders are morally irrelevant. She now affirms that one of the ways that people exercise their freedom and express their dignity is by shaping the institutions of their own nation-state.[20] Nussbaum now argues that the protection of human dignity requires respect for the self-determination of states. At the same time, her continuing support for the common humanity of all persons means that states that are worthy of respect are those accountable both to the rights of their citizens and to the rights of others whom their actions affect. The sovereignty of accountable states arises as an expression of the rights and freedoms of their citizens and limited by the rights and freedom of others. There is a local duty to protect the rights of those in one's own nearby community; there is also a cosmopolitan duty to protect the fundamental human rights of all, including migrants and refugees. The local and the global both make real demands from an ethical standpoint.

How these duties are related is one of the central questions on the political scene today. There can be tension, even conflict, between a universalist commitment to people's common humanity and a more particularist desire to show positive regard for their differences. Indeed, the tensions between cosmopolitan universalism and nationalist particularism has become a point of sharp, even violent conflict in the politics of several countries and regions today. An adequate response to the needs of refugees and other forced migrants calls for discovering ways to combine a normative commitment to the common humanity of all members of the human family with respect for the local, national, and regional differences that also support human dignity. Adequately responding to the needs of people whose humanity is threatened requires finding new ways to support human dignity on the local, national, and global levels simultaneously. Nation-states alone are not enough. Nor would the creation of some sort of "world-state" be either politically effective or ethically desirable. The task of finding new ways to relate the local and the global is both a pragmatic and moral challenge.

The Jewish and the Catholic traditions each provide some helpful insight into how to combine universalist respect for all and particularist recognition of differences in the effort to protect people facing crisis. As seen above, the Jewish and Catholic traditions both affirm the duty to respect the common humanity of all people. These traditions also maintain, in somewhat different ways, that there are duties to respect the distinctions that form people into differing religions, cultures, nations, and states.

As noted in chapter 3, Judaism stresses the common humanity and sacredness of all persons as created in the image of God, which is proclaimed in the first chapters of the book of Genesis. The story of God's covenant with Noah supports a similar universalism, for this covenant extends beyond Israel to all human beings. Indeed, through the covenant with Noah, God promised to protect and to sustain the entirety of creation (Gen. 9:1–17). On the other hand, the belief that God's covenant with Israel gives the Jewish people a distinctive religious and national identity is also central to the Jewish tradition. The special covenant with the Jewish people calls Jews to special concern for the well-being of other Jews and for the distinctiveness of the Jewish people. In Jonathan Sacks's felicitous phrase, it calls for special sensitivity to the "dignity of difference." The particularist identity of Jews has transcendent significance that should make Jews sensitive to the differences of others as well. It should lead them to affirm the importance of the "right to be different."[21] Generalizing from the desire to secure their own particular identity, Jews are also called to support the distinctive identities of other people as well. Indeed, Sacks argues that the Jewish awareness of the dignity of difference can help other traditions come to a similar recognition of the need to respect differences. Thus, Judaism has resources within its own tradition that lead Jews to affirm both cosmopolitan and particularist values. Judaism calls for respect for all persons as part of the human family created by God. It also requires respect for the differences among people, differences exemplified first in Jewish difference through the covenant but analogously present in other peoples as well.

In addition, because God's special covenant with Israel set the Jewish people free from bondage as strangers in Egypt, Jews also have duties to others in bondage and to strangers in their midst. The Hebrew Bible repeatedly stresses that the Jewish people have duties not only to fellow Jews but also to the strangers they encounter in the land of Israel. "You shall not oppress an alien; you well know how it feels to be an alien, since you were once aliens yourselves in the land of Egypt" (Ex. 23:9; see Lev. 19:33–34 and many other places). Judaism combines universalism and particularism in a way that recognizes both the right of the Jewish people to their own distinctive identity and their onerous duty to others, especially to migrants and refugees. For Jews, duties to those in need reach across the borders of Israel and the Jewish people.[22] This Jewish stress on the rights of those who are different illustrates one way that particularist stress on one's own identity can be combined with universalist concern for those who are different. It suggests that, for Jews, the local and particular need not be seen as alternatives to the universal and cosmopolitan. Normatively, both kinds of commitment are supported by the Jewish tradition.

The Catholic tradition also brings helpful insight into ways to combine cosmopolitan universalism with respect for the distinctive identities of peoples, and it adds useful reflection on the institutional dimensions of the issue. The Catholic conviction that persons are brothers and sisters in a single human family that reaches across borders supports this kind of universalism. All are called to treat one another with mutual respect and concern, even when they come from differing countries or cultures. This call arises from the commandment that sums up all other duties: "Love your neighbor as you love yourself."

At the same time, Catholic tradition combines this universalism with recognition of the importance of national and cultural differences. For example, St. Augustine and St. Thomas Aquinas both affirm a Christian duty to love all humans as our neighbors, while they also recognize the importance of special relationships, such as those with family members or co-citizens of one's own country. Love of neighbor requires respect for those with whom we have special relationship in family, culture, or country as well as for each fellow human. An important aspect of Christian ethical reflection, therefore, is to determine the order of priorities that should exist among these diverse loves (an *ordo amoris*, as Augustine called such priorities). In some circumstances, love for those who are nearer should take precedence over concern for those at greater distances. In an analogous way, those in one's own cultural or national communities may take priority over those less closely related in more distant lands. On the other hand, when those farther away have greater needs, they can take precedence. The commandment to love one's neighbor can require special concern for those whose dignity is in danger, including those facing displacement or some other humanitarian threat. The proper order among our loves must be determined in light of specific circumstances.

Catholic social thought also appeals to what has come to be called "the principle of subsidiarity" to determine whether the more local or more global should take priority. This principle affirms that there are special duties within smaller, proximate communities. However, it also insists that when there is serious need at a greater distance or when a local community is not responding to the needs of its members, larger regional communities or the international community as a whole can have a duty to respond. Pope Pius XI first developed the idea of subsidiarity in his 1931 encyclical *Quadragesimo anno*. He argued that it is an injustice "to assign to a greater and higher association what lesser and subordinate organizations can do."[23] Thus, national governments should let local agencies take action to protect the rights and well-being of their people and should act only when smaller or local groups are unable to act effectively. Similarly, regional and more broadly international agencies should let more local or national groups take the initiative unless these smaller groups are incapable of addressing urgent issues or need transnational help to do so. Further, when larger or more distant agencies do act, they should provide help (*subsidium*) to local agencies rather than undermine local activity and initiative. This presumes that social vitality comes from the grass roots up, from free people shaping society through their agency rather than from a top-down imposition of authority.[24] Nevertheless, there are frequent occasions today when action by the larger and more distant agencies of government, including international governance, is needed to address the challenges of growing interdependence.

Thus, in the face of grave need or when serious human rights violations are occurring, national borders and cultural differences carry considerable moral weight, but they are not morally determinative. The good of more local national and cultural communities must be seen within the framework of the larger solidarity of the global human family, and this larger solidarity requires protecting the rights of all persons even if, in the extreme case, this calls for intervention across a national border. Support for the global common good and respect for human rights of all persons are complementary commitments.[25] Regional and global institutions should respect the self-determination of nation-states and the distinctiveness of particular cultural communities. Indeed, the regional or global institutions should seek to aid those that are more local in supporting the agency of their members.[26] The requirements of the wider solidarity override the requirements of respect for the distinctiveness of smaller, more local communities only if the local communities are incapable or unwilling to provide the respect due to their members. Subsidiarity therefore calls for respect for the local unless the demands of a more inclusive human solidarity require otherwise. The local should be sustained, supported, and assisted by the cosmopolitan, not replaced by it.

Although the subsidiarity principle was developed within Catholic social thought, it also has considerable support in secular political thinking. The European Union uses subsidiarity to describe its understanding of the proper relation between the responsibilities of the larger structures of the EU and the role of each of the EU's member states. The treaty governing the structures of the EU invokes subsidiarity to affirm that the union itself should act only when member states cannot achieve required goals or when the union itself is better able to achieve what is needed.[27] In other words, the larger transnational community of the EU does not replace the communal bonds that exist in the member states. EU governance should supplement the action of its member states when they are unable to take needed action or when the union itself can act more effectively.

From these Jewish, Catholic, and secular European insights into the relation between the more local and the more cosmopolitan, we can conclude that the responsibility toward people being harmed or displaced by war or other crisis conditions falls on multiple communities. In most cases, the primary duty to assist persons facing severe threats to their dignity and well-being falls upon those in their local community and their own country. If, however, their nearby neighbors or their country of citizenship fails to protect them or actively threatens them and compels them to flee, the duty can move to neighboring countries, to nongovernmental organizations, and to the larger global community. Duties to fellow citizens do not always trump duties to refugees, nor do duties to refugees always override duties to co-citizens. Both local and cosmopolitan duties are real and important.

POLYCENTRIC RESPONSIBILITY

Multiple agents carry diverse responsibilities to alleviate a concrete humanitarian crisis. Specific duties to one's own people are the routine expression of shared citizenship. Duties to people from other lands can arise when these people face severe threats to their dignity from war or displacement. These multiple duties will have to be weighed in relation to each other to determine what ought to be done under the prevailing circumstances. We might call this polycentric responsibility rooted in polycentric solidarity, borrowing the term "polycentric" from economist Elinor Ostrom. In 2009 Ostrom became the first and only woman to receive the Nobel Prize in Economic Sciences "for her analysis of economic governance," especially governance of goods shared in common such as natural resources and the earth's atmosphere.[28] She argues that the governance of these shared goods needs to occur on multiple levels, with active support by different communities of people.[29] The communities that benefit from the protection of shared goods such as the seas or the atmosphere are often in several states or nations, so the responsibility to govern these resources effectively reaches across borders. International collaboration is often needed to protect these goods. However, Ostrom also stresses that responsible local engagement is often simultaneously needed, for it stimulates interest and empowers grassroots action. Without local engagement, people are less likely to contribute actively to the pursuit of the needed response.

For example, Ostrom notes that the protection of the endangered stock of lobsters and threatened codfish in the Gulf of Maine required action by multiple groups, including fishing co-ops based locally in particular harbors and larger associations of those involved in the fishing of these stocks. Effective protection also required government action, ranging from coordination of local groups by the state of Maine to the hammering out of international regulations by the United States, Canada, and the United Nations. This kind of action exemplifies what Ostrom means by polycentric governance carried out by multiple agents, including nongovernmental actors in civil society, faith communities, businesses, markets, states, and intergovernmental organizations.[30]

Ostrom's approach suggests that the responsibility to respond to the harms caused by humanitarian crises and displacement should also be polycentric. Humanitarian threats often reach across borders, so the agents capable of making effective response will rarely be located within one country alone. Multiple agencies from different countries and traditions will very often have to share in the effort to assist people facing crisis. Protecting the basic humanity of the tens of millions of displaced people today is surely too large and complex a task for any single agent to deal with alone. Assisting these millions of displaced people is simultaneously a local, regional, and global challenge. Action by international organizations like the UN High Commissioner for Refugees and the Office for the Coordination of Humanitarian Affairs is needed. Effective action also requires the engagement by the nation-states who have caused the crisis or the displacement in the first place. Responsible action is also required by the countries where the displaced seek asylum. When the number of refugees being hosted in a country exceeds its ability to provide relief or protection, the responsibility must be shared internationally with other countries who have greater resources or who are presently less burdened. Multiple nongovernmental organizations should be routinely involved in virtually all efforts to provide humanitarian assistance to displaced people. No single community or agency has the capacity to assist the displaced acting alone. Helpful action will have to rely on multiple actors.[31] Because the effectiveness of the assistance will require engagement of multiple communities and agencies, the responsibility to act will fall on multiple actors as well. The responsibility is polycentric. It will require both local and cosmopolitan solidarity at the same time.

It is increasingly evident that the world today is neither divided into self-contained nation-states nor is it a single global community composed of all human beings in an undifferentiated unity. In addition to states, many transnational actors have major influence, including multinational corporations and financial institutions; nongovernmental advocacy networks that focus on issues such as human rights, peace, and environmental protection; and religious communities with their significant presence on many levels of global interaction.[32] Anne-Marie Slaughter points out that the "new world order" she sees emerging is actually a network of multiple agencies. These networked groups include governments and parts of governments. The governmental agencies are frequently networked with their counterparts in other countries, vertically networked with agencies "above" them in global and regional intergovernmental organizations, and linked with many different types of nongovernmental organizations.[33] This leads Slaughter to argue that competition among nation-states ruled by sovereign governments is increasingly complemented by networks that link persons and nations across borders in a thickening web of mutual dependence.[34]

Each community's linkage with other bodies gives it the capacity to act in an increasingly interconnected world. In Slaughter's words, "However paradoxical it sounds, the measure of a state's capacity to act as an independent unit within an international system—the condition that 'sovereignty' purports both to grant and describe—depends on the breadth and depth of its links to other states."[35] Sovereignty should be seen as "a place at the table," interacting with other states, with intergovernmental bodies on both regional and global levels, and with many nongovernmental agencies, including religious communities and their many agencies. If this is correct, attempting to defend the interest of one's nation by disengagement from the struggles of other nations and peoples could produce exactly the opposite effect from what is desired. For example, failure by the West to make adequate efforts to address the civil war in Syria has led to massive movement of Syrian refugees through Turkey and across the Mediterranean, producing a populist resistance that is threatening the long-term stability of the European Union itself. Engagement with crises that may initially seem removed from the self-interest of one's community is increasingly necessary to secure national well-being in the long or even medium term. National interest and duties across borders are increasingly intertwined.

This polycentric, networked picture of the world of today has important implications for the way we understand the responsibility to respond to the humanitarian crises and to the millions of refugees these crises have created. The responsibilities fall on multiple agents, ranging from the very local to the fully global. Whether the response should be primarily local or heavily international depends on the nature of the crisis and on the distinctive capacities of the local in international agencies at issue. In some situations, it is best for the local community or particular country to respond to the needs of its own members who are facing crisis. Thus the responsibility to assist the people internally displaced by Hurricane Katrina when it slammed into the Louisiana coast in August 2005 fell on US governmental agencies such as the Federal Emergency Management Agency, branches of the Louisiana and New Orleans governments, and numerous local private groups, including churches, that had the capacity to assist. In other cases, such as the displacement caused by the civil wars in South Sudan or Syria, local, national, and international responses are all clearly needed. Some of these will be by governments, others will be nongovernmental. Thus, response to both the Syrian and South Sudanese crises rightly rely partly on the work of nongovernmental agencies, both secular and faith-based, such as Oxfam, Médecins Sans Frontières, Catholic Relief Services, World Vision, and Islamic Relief. But in crises that have significant political causes and political effects, and where effective response requires political action, as is true in both Syria and South Sudan, action by governments and larger international bodies is required. In all of these cases, action is most effective when the responding agencies cooperate through humanitarian networks that reach across the division between the governmental and the nongovernmental and across national borders.

The responsibilities to address the needs of humanity in crisis fall on multiple institutions that act on different scales and with diverse competencies. A polycentric understanding of responsibility means that no one community, country, or agency bears the responsibility to act all on its own. As polycentric and network-based, the responsibility is shared among local, regional, and global actors. When responsibility is seen as shared, the needed action becomes more likely.

The chapters that follow spell out in more detail several responsibilities toward those in crisis today and how these responsibilities can be carried out collaboratively.

CHAPTER 6

RIGHTS AND NEGATIVE DUTIES

This chapter explores some of our moral and legal duties to refrain from behavior that imperils people's humanity, especially by violating their fundamental human rights. It highlights several important duties *not* to act in ways that contribute to humanitarian crises by threatening human rights in serious ways. The call to protect people from threats to their humanity and to prevent crises that violate human dignity is in fact a moral call. It is important in the requirements spelled out in humanitarian law as well. Both the moral and legal dimensions of protection are often expressed today in terms of human rights. I begin, therefore, with a sketch of an understanding of human rights that shapes how protection should be understood. The issue of who deserves protection is then considered, followed by some examples of the kind of human rights violation that is often at the center of humanitarian crises today. Avoiding serious violations of basic human rights will go a long way toward reducing the number and intensity of humanitarian crises, so I conclude with an overview of several negative duties that are important to avoiding crisis events, including ethical and legal duties that limit what can legitimately be done in conflict. Duties to take positive action in response to emergencies, such as granting asylum to refugees and addressing the deeper causes of emergencies, are considered in subsequent chapters.

RIGHTS AND PROTECTION

The ethical dimensions of the effort to protect people from the harms brought by war and other humanitarian crises overlap considerably with the challenges raised by the broader effort to protect human rights. Since the proclamation of the Universal Declaration of Human Rights in 1948 and the subsequent growth of the human rights movement in recent decades, human rights have become a central reference point in ethical discussion of public affairs on a wide range of practical issues. The expansion of human rights discourse has been particularly evident within the humanitarian movement. Chapter 2 notes the advance of a "rights-based" approach to humanitarian action over the past several decades. More recently this rights-based approach has been accompanied by a growing stress on "protection." These two emphases, taken together, suggest that a key ethical aim in the humanitarian field is to encourage people to live up to their duties to protect the rights of others.

The stress on protection has been the result of the experience of the crises that have occurred over the past several decades. I noted earlier the massive human suffering that took place in Rwanda and Bosnia. The need to find ways to protect people from the tragic effects of war and civil conflict has intensified in more recent years by several similarly grave crises. For example, the civil war in Sri Lanka came to a very bloody end in May 2009. In this conflict, up to seventy thousand civilians perished, and several hundred thousand Tamils and other minorities were held captive under brutal conditions. A 2015 report by the UN High Commissioner for Human Rights, Zeid Ra'ad Al Hussein, indicated that massive human rights violations were committed by both sides of the Sri Lanka conflict. Al Hussein did not hesitate to say that these rights violations were war crimes and that they may well have reached the level of crimes against humanity. Al Hussein was compelled to ask how the UN and the broader international community could have allowed this to take place. He concluded that a much higher standard of human rights protection would be required in the future.[1] People should be shielded from such brutalizing suffering by effective protection of their human rights.

Similarly, the crisis in Syria, which has caused the largest human displacement since World War II, can also be seen as a major breakdown of the human rights regime. A nearly total failure to protect the human rights of the Syrian people has been unfolding in that heartbreaking conflict.[2] For example, in 2017 the UN Commission of Inquiry on Syria reported that "the parties to the conflict continue to perpetrate unthinkable crimes against civilians" through the violation of their fundamental human rights. The violations included deliberate attacks against civilians by parties to the conflict, including the Islamic State in Syria (ISIS), the government of Syria, and the coalition led by the United States. Siege warfare denied many civilians their rights to free movement, food, access to education and health care, and even the right to life. Attacks on civilians have been deliberately carried out, targeting religious minorities. The delivery of humanitarian aid to civilians suffering because of the warfare has been forcefully restricted in order to compel adversary forces to surrender. The Syrian government repeatedly used chemical weapons against civilians as well as combatants in ways that are both severe and illegal.[3] These events led Al Hussein to make a passionate denunciation of the failure to protect the people of Syria. In his words, "the Syrian conflict has been characterized by its absolute disregard for even the most minimal standards of principle and law," particularly the principles and the law of human rights.[4]

A more recent crisis has been the forced flight of more than 720,000 Rohingya refugees from Myanmar to Bangladesh that began in August 2017 due to the outbreak of conflict in Myanmar's Rakhine State.[5] The Rohingya are a Muslim minority in the primarily Buddhist Myanmar, and the conflict has been caused by a complex combination of religious, ethnic, and political factors. The Rohingya refugees reaching Bangladesh are mostly vulnerable women and children. They also include many elderly people who need additional aid and protection. Most of the displaced Rohingya have lost everything in their flight from Myanmar and are in great need. Al Hussein, the High Commissioner for Human Rights, has characterized the treatment of the Rohingya as a "textbook case of ethnic cleansing." The UN Special Adviser on the Prevention of Genocide, Adama Dieng, has suggested that the forces attacking the Rohingya may even be seeking their total elimination as a people.[6] If proven, this would constitute the crime of genocide. Whether the Rohingya crisis is genocidal or not, it certainly involves massive violations of human rights.

Severe violations of human rights like these are the source of the rising emphasis on protection as a central objective of humanitarian action. According to the Interagency Standing Committee, which coordinates the humanitarian work of key UN agencies and their non-UN partners, the "central" goal of humanitarian action should be protecting people in the face of crisis. For this committee, protecting people means saving their lives, ensuring their safety, alleviating their suffering, and restoring their dignity.[7] This requires, of course, not only safeguarding individuals one at a time but also shaping social contexts so that people remain safe. To do this, political, military, or environmental conditions must be addressed so that threats to human safety and dignity are reduced.

The Interagency Standing Committee explicitly formulates the meaning of protection in human rights terms. It defines protection as "all activities aimed at obtaining full respect for the rights of the individual in accordance with the letter and the spirit of the relevant bodies of law (i.e., human rights law, humanitarian law and refugee law)."[8] This definition of protection includes a commitment to secure the full range of human rights proclaimed in the Universal Declaration, including both civil/political rights to religious and political freedom and the social/economic rights to the fulfillment of one's most basic needs. The requirements of humanitarian law include the right of wounded soldiers and prisoners of war to humane treatment and the right of civilians to freedom from attack (noncombatant immunity). By including the requirements of refugee law, the definition implies that protection should be provided to people who have had to flee their own country because of persecution. People who have been driven from their home have the right to seek and secure asylum. Protection also includes defending their right to live in a human way in their country of refuge, with access to the level of employment, housing, education, and freedom of movement that is available to other noncitizens in the country of their asylum. It means that they are not to be involuntarily returned to the country they were compelled to flee (non-refoulement).[9] Since the number of refugees is so high today, providing protection in accord with these standards of the Refugee Convention presents a huge challenge.

WHO NEEDS PROTECTION? REFUGEES AND BEYOND

By including the standards of refugee law as well as of human rights and humanitarian law, the Standing Committee sets forth a very demanding agenda for humanitarian action today. Securing the human rights of all displaced people requires responding not only to record-high numbers of refugees but to internally displaced persons (IDPs) and many others as well. The extensive nature of human displacements today calls for a broad understanding of who needs to be protected. The 1951 Convention on the Status of Refugees requires protection for those who have been compelled to flee across the border of their home country because of "well-founded fear of being persecuted for reasons of race, religion, nationality, membership of a particular social group or political opinion."[10] Persecution, strictly understood, is a relatively narrow kind of threat when it is compared to the many kinds of abuse people face in situations of war and oppression today. The understanding of who should receive protection has been gradually broadened over the years since the promulgation of the 1951 convention. The General Assembly's approval of the 1967 Protocol Relating to the Status of Refugees dropped the convention's limitation of its applicability to people displaced within Europe before January 1, 1951—that is, chiefly those forced to flee by World War II.[11] This shift effectively enabled the High Commissioner for Refugees to expand relief efforts to people driven from their homes by Stalinist oppression in the USSR and to people fleeing the threats brought about by anticolonial and Cold War struggles. In addition, in the decades since the 1967 protocol was approved, the scope of international efforts to assist the displaced has been further broadened.

Today not only those persecuted but also many who are fleeing war or civil conflict, human rights violations, and other severe threats are often seen as "of concern" to the High Commissioner for Refugees. Refugee law specialists Guy Goodwin-Gill and Jane McAdam summarized these developments, concluding that the mandate to protect the displaced now reaches beyond those who are fleeing persecution and have crossed the border of their country. It should also protect those not effectively protected by their own government as well as people displaced by "conflicts, human rights violations, breaches of international humanitarian law, or other serious harm resulting from radical political, social, or economic changes in their own country."[12] This is a significant expansion of the way the responsibilities toward displaced people are understood. A key trigger that indicates the presence of a duty to provide protection is the presence of violence. Violence or the threat of violence is an important dimension of many of the threats causing today's massive displacements. Because conflict is a major cause of displacement, the UNHCR titled its 2014 report on the global refugee trends *World at War*.[13]

In addition, a significant number of those driven from home by crisis today are IDPs, that is, they remain within their home countries.[14] At the end of 2017, of the 68.5 million displaced people in the world, 40 million were IDPs.[15] These IDPs are not guaranteed protection under the Refugee Convention. Nor are people in flight because of negative consequences of failed or fragile governments or because of economic deprivation that is severe enough to threaten not only their well-being but even their lives. An increasing number of people are being forced to abandon their homes by the effects of climate change, such as long droughts, expanding deserts, and rising sea levels, as well as more frequent hurricanes and typhoons. Chapter 9 considers some of these issues. It has become clear that limiting those who should be assisted to refugees as officially defined in the 1951 convention means many people will continue to face extreme danger.

Both the legal and moral norms for response to the displaced will have to be rethought if people in crisis today are to be assisted in a way that protects their human rights.[16] One response to the changed historical circumstances has been a shift in the vocabulary used to name the people affected by crisis and entitled to protection. Those in need of protection are increasingly called "forced migrants" rather than "refugees." More recently it has been suggested that those on the move because of humanitarian threats to their safety should be called "crisis migrants" or "survival migrants."[17] Alexander Betts defines survival migrants as persons who are outside their home country "because of an existential threat for which they have no access to a domestic remedy or resolution."[18] Such an existential threat could be persecution, but it could equally well be the conflict of war, the failure or fragility of one's home government, grave economic need, or danger arising due to climate change.

Refugees, of course, are one type of survival migrant, but there are many others as well, including IDPs. Both refugees and IDPs have a status that is officially recognized in international law and policy. This status is determined by being forced to move by a particular cause (by persecution, in the case of refugees) or in a particular way (across the border of one's country, for refugees, or within one's homeland, for IDPs). The proposal that protection should be provided to "crisis" or "survival migrants," on the other hand, means that there are people in need of protection whose movement has not been forced by persecution or led to transborder flight. Protection can be required simply when a grave crisis or the need for survival has compelled people to migrate. "Crisis" or "survival migrants" are people driven to move because of severe threats to their lives or their human dignity.

This discussion has been carried a step further in a recent study that suggests people need protection above all because of their "vulnerability" to grave threats to their dignity.[19] Such vulnerability arises when one's access to food and water is insecure and may fail. Similarly, when the destruction of social networks blocks participation in the workplace and in markets, large groups can become vulnerable to severe economic deprivation. Such vulnerabilities can be present when migration is happening, before it happens, or after it has occurred. Whenever severe vulnerability occurs, however, it can threaten people's dignity. Since such vulnerabilities often force people to migrate, Roger Zetter calls them "displacement vulnerabilities."[20]

The expectation that people will be protected when their human dignity is violated or vulnerable to violation sets a more demanding norm for protection than the requirement to aid refugees as they are officially defined in the convention. These "official" refugees certainly continue to deserve protection. The normative basis of the convention's insistence that those it defines as "refugees" have a right to seek and obtain asylum is the recognition that people in flight from persecution face severe threats to their human dignity. This suggests, however, that people may need protection whenever their human dignity is in grave danger, whether they are fleeing persecution or some other threat and whether they have crossed a border or not. People should be protected not only from persecution but also from the other threats to their dignity, including the dangers arising from war and disaster. Reducing the harmful effects and vulnerabilities brought by war and other grave crises should be a central normative requirement of humanitarian response.[21]

HUMAN RIGHTS AT THE CENTER

Whether people who are facing severe crises should be called refugees, forced migrants, survival migrants, or simply vulnerable is more than a terminological question. How the question is answered is a substantive matter that may determine who survives in a crisis. For example, proposing that protection should be provided to forced migrants or survival migrants and not just refugees would add an additional 40 million internally displaced people to the 24.4 million refugees legally entitled to protection at the end of 2017. It could also add to those who deserve assistance many millions displaced by state failure, by environmental change, and by grave economic need. Such changes would mean a significant shift in the norms of humanitarian action. Calling for the protection of people who are vulnerable to severe threats to their human dignity makes further demands, for it adds many who have not fled from their homes to the list of those in need of some form of assistance.

Despite these significant practical consequences, these redefinitions of who has a claim on protection are surely needed because of the new threats to the well-being and dignity of many people today. The new terminology has arisen because of the need to overcome the gap between the protection actually being provided and what is required to protect the dignity of people facing conflict and disaster today. This gap is in fact an ethical one—the painfully evident distance between the *is* of the conditions confronting people caught in crises and the *ought* of what human dignity requires. Responding to this gap will require pursuing more inclusive normative goals than those often sought today. It will call for new action by governments, intergovernmental agencies, and nongovernmental organizations. Determining what changes are required involves answering two basic questions, both ethical in nature. First, who has a justified moral claim or right to be protected when they face threats from humanitarian crises? Second, who has a duty to provide the assistance required?

The development of the humanitarian movement sketched in chapter 2 suggests that the concepts of humanity and human dignity, and especially of human rights, are the roots of the ethical norms that can help answer these questions. The phrase "human dignity" points to the inherent worth of each person, a worth that can be violated or made vulnerable by the threats people face in war, natural disaster, state failure, or other forms of crisis. Chapter 3 argues that the obligation to respect human dignity is affirmed by the major religious traditions of the world and by secular humanistic traditions. This dignity makes a claim on others when it is vulnerable or violated. It requires that those causing the violation or vulnerability cease doing so and calls on those in a position to alleviate the violation or vulnerability to take action. Thus, we can say that one human being *is* a kind of *ought* in the face of another. Each person's dignity should be respected by all others. The obligation to show such respect leads to negative duties to refrain from action that would violate another person's worth. It also implies positive duties actively to protect people from denials of their worth or to help them regain their dignity when it has been violated.[22]

The idea of dignity therefore plays a central role in forming the ethical norms that should guide humanitarian action. But human dignity is a rather general notion that lacks the specificity needed to address complex crisis situations through concrete action. To develop an ethical approach that addresses contemporary humanitarian challenges in an effective way, we need more specific guidance. Proposing more concrete norms requires identifying what Margaret Farley has called "obligating features of personhood."[23] One might also call these the "obligating features of human dignity"—features that indicate the specific human traits or abilities we are obligated to respect in order to protect human dignity. Such features indicate not only *that* persons should show respect toward one another but *what* such respect requires. Farley identifies two such obligating features: autonomy and relationality. Autonomy requires respect for persons' capacity to be self-determining and not to have their lives shaped or manipulated by other persons or external powers. Relationality requires respect for the interpersonal and social relationships that all humans must depend on if they are to thrive or even survive as persons.[24] Because autonomy can be interpreted in an excessively individualistic way, I would prefer to call the first of these features of personhood "freedom." Freedom is not simply the result of being left to act independently on one's own, as might be implied by the term "autonomy." Human freedom comes into being only in interaction with others, as Farley's stress on relationality implies. In addition, I think we should add "basic needs" to these obligating features of personhood. Without meeting one's needs for nutrition, clean water, shelter, necessary conditions of health, and a basic level of education, no one can live with human dignity. Respect for human dignity requires meeting the basic needs, protecting the key freedoms, and sustaining the key relationships for all people. At a minimum, it requires *not* inflicting the harms that will befall people when their basic needs are unmet, their most important freedoms are denied, or their sustaining relationships are shattered.

The importance of respect for these needs, freedoms, and relationships in the context of humanitarian crises is evident from their relation to both human capacities and human vulnerabilities. Long ago Aristotle observed that human beings possess some of the capacities of the Greek gods, such as freedom, the ability to think, and the capacity for communication with others. In addition to these god-like characteristics, however, humans also have bodily needs like those of the other animals, whom Aristotle called beasts. Aristotle went on, however, to stress that humans are neither beasts nor gods and should be treated differently from both beasts and gods.[25] Human personhood therefore generates both negative and positive obligations for others. Not being treated as a beast means not having one's basic freedom denied or threatened by persecution or oppression. It means not being denied the relational interaction with others needed to shape one's social and material environment. Such relational interaction requires that one have a political voice and be able to participate in the economic life of one's community. Not being treated as if one were a god, on the other hand, means having one's bodily and material needs met to at least a basic level. Human dignity can be realized only if these material conditions are present, and it cannot be realized if they are lacking. Severe material deprivation assaults a person's dignity just as surely as does persecution or the denial of political or religious freedom. If people are denied access to the work that will enable them to meet their needs, they cannot simply fly off to heaven as might a mythical god or angel. Unlike the gods, humans are necessarily embedded in the social and material worlds. If they are denied basic social relationships, their dignity is assaulted, their freedom is undermined, and their needs are unmet.

Human dignity requires that one's freedoms and capacities for political participation be protected and that one's need for social relationship and participation be secured. It also requires that one's most essential needs be met through food, shelter, bodily integrity, basic medical care, and a number of other material supports. Since the dignity of a human person confronts others with a kind of *ought*, so do these more concrete obligating features of human dignity. Respecting key freedoms, protecting essential relationships, and meeting basic needs are all required if we are to respect human dignity. Basic needs, core freedoms, and essential relationships, therefore, can help specify and concretize the more general concept of human dignity.

Amid humanitarian crises, all three of these dimensions of dignity are threatened for many people, who are rendered vulnerable to the deprivation of the most basic requirements of their dignity when they face persecution because of their religion, ethnicity, or other group membership. This deprivation can be equally threatening when the fog of war rolls in or when society falls into chaos due to the collapse or weakness of government. The conditions required for life with dignity can also be undermined by major shifts in the physical environment on which people depend—abruptly in the case of a typhoon or earthquake, more slowly but nonetheless surely in the case of rising seas or expanding deserts. It thus makes sense to conclude that human dignity requires that people be protected from these threats. It also follows that others have duties not to inflict such threats on the dignity of their fellow humans and to assist them in dealing with these threats when this is possible.

Seeing such basic needs, core freedoms, and essential relationships as key dimensions of human dignity can help identify more specific ethical norms that should govern humanitarian action and shape humanitarian policy and institutions. This effort can be further advanced by showing how these needs, freedoms, and relationships can be further spelled out in terms of the fundamental human rights that must be respected in order to protect human dignity. Human rights can thus be seen as specifications of the obligating features of personhood. They express in greater detail what is required by human dignity. Human rights, therefore, are central norms that indicate what must not be done to people by undermining their dignity through persecution, violence, deprivation, or isolation. They also indicate when there are duties to alleviate severe threats to dignity in crisis situations.

Human rights are used in this way by Alexander Betts in his recent proposal on the normative humanitarian standards. Betts argues that the protection of truly basic rights is the ethical requirement that should govern response to humanitarian crises. He draws on Henry Shue's earlier proposal about which human rights are in fact most basic.[26] Basic rights are those that specify the threshold below which people should not be allowed to fall, even in desperate circumstances. For Shue, human rights are basic when they are required for the enjoyment of all other rights and thus for living with dignity. In his words, "Basic rights are the morality of the depths. They specify the line beneath which no one is to be allowed to sink."[27] These basic rights fall into three categories: the right to *physical security*, the right to *subsistence*, and the right to *basic liberties*. The categories overlap with the three dimensions of human dignity, noted above.

The basic right to physical security requires that one be safe from murder, rape, and other physical threats that arise in warfare or in the chaos that can result when states are weak or have collapsed. Such abuses may also be tools of the persecution stressed by the Refugee Convention. The right to physical security thus protects one from murder and rape and from many other threats to human dignity. Physical security requires a form of governance effective enough to prevent crimes or the social anarchy that endanger human life and basic freedom. Failure to protect the right to physical security is widespread in situations of humanitarian crisis. The right to security therefore has much relevance to crisis situations.

The right to subsistence should also be central in the development of normative ethical standards for response to crises. This right ensures access to clean water, adequate food, protective shelter, and other essentials for a reasonably healthy life of more or less normal length. It is evident that people are often deprived of these essentials when they are affected by conflict between or within states, by lack of adequate governance, or by droughts, hurricanes, or other natural disasters. When such causes prevent people from meeting their most basic needs, human dignity is threatened and human rights are denied. Ethical response to humanitarian crises requires addressing these subsistence needs.

Finally, basic rights include the guarantee of basic liberties, such as holding and expressing one's own religious, intellectual, and political convictions; exercising some influence on the social institutions and policies that shape one's milieu; and having access to security and subsistence.[28] Persecution based on race, religion, ethnicity, or political opinion often attacks such liberties. In denying these liberties, persecution threatens other basic rights by leaving those in power free to mistreat all those under their sway. The Refugee Convention recognizes how persecution threatens basic rights and, thus, human dignity in this way. It sees the threat as so serious that those who flee across a border to escape the threat have a normative claim to be granted asylum. This is discussed further in the following chapter. Basic liberties, however, can also be threatened in many ways besides persecution. For example, if a society's economic elite denies large parts of the population freedom of access to land, thus preventing them from obtaining a basic livelihood, it is a grave assault on dignity. If efforts at change are obstructed by force, the result can be a long-standing, crisis-level denial of basic rights both to liberty and to subsistence.

There is little doubt that people affected by humanitarian crises in recent years are experiencing severe denial of their basic human rights. The rights of people in crisis are not being protected, and their basic needs are not being met. When António Guterres was High Commissioner for Refugees in 2015, he observed that "the human rights agenda is losing ground to the national sovereignty agenda, and that is making humanitarian work more and more difficult in several parts of the world." He added that inadequate financial support is preventing the multilateral humanitarian system from "responding to the most basic needs of populations in distress around the world."[29] The populist and nationalist currents in international politics that led Guterres to make these statements have only intensified since he made them. Changes in current, business-as-usual approaches to humanitarian crisis are thus clearly called for. A new way forward is needed.

DUTIES NOT TO HARM

More effective responses to these urgent humanitarian challenges first require that both state and nonstate actors live up to their duties not to harm others by depriving them of their basic rights. The remainder of this chapter spells out more concretely several specific negative duties not to harm, drawing on the requirements of both ethical and legal tradition. The following chapters focus on more positive duties to make active efforts to protect people's rights and to aid those who have been deprived of their rights.[30] The aim is to address particularly urgent moral aspects of the need for protection.

The long tradition of reflection contained in the just war ethic—the ethical standards for the legitimate use of force—points to some of the most important negative duties relevant to crises brought about by armed conflict. Since this tradition distinguishes morally legitimate from morally illegitimate uses of force, it could more accurately be called the just/unjust war ethic.[31] It has deep roots in Christian thought, especially (but not exclusively) in Catholicism, and it overlaps in important ways with the secular tradition of the international law of armed conflict. In recent years there have also been several explorations of analogies in non-Christian and non-Western traditions.[32]

In its modern form the just/unjust war tradition stresses that morally legitimate use of force must respect the fundamental rights of those affected by the conflict.[33] The line between just and unjust conflict is the boundary between force used in the defense of human rights and force that violates rights. The primary negative duties in conflict, therefore, are to avoid the direct violation of the human rights of those affected. These duties can be further distinguished in light of the just war tradition's two sets of moral criteria: the *jus ad bellum* norms that determine whether going *into* war is legitimate, and the *jus in bello* criteria that govern the legitimacy of means used *within* combat. Both sets of moral criteria require respect for human rights.

The *jus ad bellum* norm of just cause requires that force be strictly limited to defending the rights of innocent persons to life, security, and freedom or the rights of nation-states to self-determination and territorial integrity. Conversely, there is a negative duty *not* to use force against other persons or communities to deny them their political freedom, to exploit them economically, or to eliminate them because they are culturally or religiously different. If force is used to deny other persons or communities their rights in one of these ways, it becomes aggression, not self-defense. Aggressive use of force in this way is both immoral and criminal, for it violates both the moral demands of justice and the legal requirements of international law. When this happens, self-defensive resistance to the aggression becomes justified, provided the other standards noted below are also met.[34] Use of force that attacks the basic rights of innocent persons or communities is thus excluded; it falls under a moral and legal prohibition that declares "thou shalt not."

A tragic example of such a violation of the moral and legal duty not to use force in ways that violate others' rights was the Rwanda genocide of 1994. The just war tradition's just cause requirement that force be used only in defense of basic rights was clearly and massively violated in Rwanda. There had regrettably been considerable mutual violation by the Hutu and Tutsi peoples of each other's rights in modern Rwandan history. None of this history, however, justified the Hutu attacks that slaughtered eight hundred thousand Tutsi people in three months. What took place was not simply an effort to vindicate Hutu rights. The goal was genocide of the Tutsi, defined in international law as action intending "to destroy, in whole or in part, a national, ethnical, racial or religious group, as such."[35] Such a goal unequivocally violates the moral and legal criteria for the legitimate use of armed force. There was an unambiguous negative duty not to do what was done in Rwanda. Genocide falls under a clear "thou shalt not" in both the moral and legal traditions.

This prohibition also applied to the slaughter at Srebrenica. Thousands of Bosnian Muslims were intentionally killed at Srebrenica because of their identity. Serbs pursued ethnic cleansing, seeking either to kill all Muslims or to drive them from territory that the Serbs sought for themselves. This was in clear violation of the norm that using force is legitimate only in defense of human rights. There was a duty *not* to do to people what was done to the Bosnian Muslims. What happened at Srebrenica was a clear violation of the duty not to harm people by denying their most basic human rights.

The *jus in bello* norms of the just/unjust war ethic also specify criteria for distinguishing means that are legitimate in conflict from those that are illegitimate. The central *jus in bello* conditions are noncombatant immunity, which requires civilians not be the targets of attack, and proportionality, which requires that the harm caused by the means employed in conflict be minimized and not outweigh the good those means are seeking. In this way, the *jus in bello* norms highlight several additional "thou shalt nots" that are relevant to the contemporary humanitarian situation. They specify some further kinds of action that must be avoided if human dignity and basic rights are to be protected. Indeed, the *jus in bello* norms suggest that much of the violence taking place in the humanitarian crises of today is in fact unjust.

The *jus in bello* criterion of noncombatant immunity has direct relevance to humanitarian crises. This norm forbids direct, intentional attacks on those not participating in combat. In addition, proportionality requires the protection of civilians from disproportionate harm even if such harm is a collateral side effect of the attacker's intended goal. International law sets forth similar prohibitions. The Geneva Conventions 1977 Additional Protocol on the Protection of Victims of Armed Conflict insists that civilians be distinguished from soldiers and protected both from direct attack and from disproportionate collateral harm.[36] Violation of these standards can be war crimes. If such attacks on civilians are carried out by a state or organized nonstate group in a way that is "widespread and systematic," they can become crimes against humanity.[37] Regrettably, such violations of moral and legal norms through indiscriminate and even systematic attacks on civilians have been all too frequent in recent conflicts. Some recent conflicts have become humanitarian crises precisely because of the extent of their violations of the *jus in bello* norms.

For example, tactics used in the civil war that began in South Sudan in December 2013 have regularly violated the right of civilians to basic security.

Early in the conflict, a respected human rights organization concluded that both the government of South Sudan and the forces in opposition had "committed extraordinary acts of cruelty that amount to war crimes and in some cases potential crimes against humanity."[38] A panel of experts appointed by the UN Security Council later reinforced the judgment that civilians were being directly targeted by both sides to the conflict.[39] The killing of civilians was widespread and appears to have been systematically organized in some cases. Thus, both sides in the South Sudan conflict have committed flagrant moral violations of the basic rights of civilians and appear to have violated legal prohibitions of war crimes and crimes against humanity. In South Sudan both sides have also used rape as a weapon. Rape is obviously a serious moral offense; legally, it can be a war crime and, if it is systematic and widespread, a crime against humanity.[40] Adding to the chaos, the conflict in South Sudan has threatened the right to subsistence of millions of people, leading to widespread hunger and the malnourishment of hundreds of thousands of children. In the face of this mayhem, it is not surprising that many South Sudanese have been driven from their homes. In March 2018 almost 2.5 million South Sudanese had become refugees, and an additional 1.85 million were internally displaced.[41] The strategies and tactics used by both sides in the South Sudan conflict have themselves turned the South Sudan situation into a grave humanitarian emergency. Alleviating the crisis will thus require significant initiatives to reestablish at least rudimentary respect for both basic rights and the rules of conflict.

The Syrian crisis reinforces the conclusion that armed conflict can lead to deep crisis when the adversaries violate their duty not to attack basic rights of civilians. The UN Human Rights Council's Independent International Commission of Inquiry on Syria concluded that over the course of the conflict there had been an "exponential rise in the perpetration of war crimes, crimes against humanity and human rights violations."[42] The actions of all sides, both the government and the multiple opposition groups such as ISIS and Al-Nusra, were in clear violation of the law of armed conflict and of moral norms as well. Civilians have felt the brunt of the violations, while those inflicting harm remain free of accountability. Once again the rights violations have led to massive displacement—the single-largest forced migration in recent history. The flight of refugees has also threatened the stability of the neighboring countries, including Turkey, which in 2018 was hosting the largest number of refugees of any country in the world; Lebanon, which is hosting the highest per capita number of refugees in the world; and Jordan. This has placed unprecedented strain on the economies and infrastructure of these countries. Syrian displacement has also severely strained the politics of the European Union due to disagreements about how to respond to the extraordinary number of Syrian refugees seeking asylum on the continent.

These emergency situations indicate why the duty not to violate basic human rights is central to protecting people from the ravages of humanitarian crises. They show why strengthening adherence to the requirements of the just war ethic and of the international law of armed conflict is so important to reducing humanitarian abuse. These norms forbid grave offenses against human dignity and human rights, such as genocide, ethnic cleansing, war crimes, and crimes against humanity. Reducing these serious rights violations would be an important step toward diminishing the most severe humanitarian effects of conflict. It would both save many lives and reduce the flight of refugees and IDPs. When lives are in danger and threats to their human rights are widespread, people often have little alternative but to flee from their homes. This is especially true when the violations rise to the level of atrocities like genocide or crimes against humanity. Protecting people from atrocity-level threats to their basic rights is thus essential to overcoming the harms brought by humanitarian crises and massive forced migration.

Increasing the respect for human rights in this way requires significant reinforcement of conscientious commitment by leaders of both states and nonstate bodies to the duty not to attack civilians indiscriminately or with disproportionate consequences. Pressure from public opinion in the countries where conflicts are occurring and on the regional and global levels can help strengthen such commitment by political leaders. The prospect of legal enforcement also has an effect by letting potential violators know that they are likely to be held accountable. The International Criminal Court (ICC) was established in 1998 to hold people accountable for egregious violations of international law. The Rome Statute that created the ICC gave it jurisdiction over the atrocities of genocide, crimes against humanity, war crimes, and the crime of aggression.[43] The ICC has so far not been able to bring to trial some of those it has charged with such atrocities due to its lack of effective ways to enforce its decisions. For example, Omar al-Bashir of Sudan faces charges of genocide and crimes against humanity for his actions in the Darfur region of Sudan, but obtaining his arrest has so far been impossible. ICC's charges against Uhuru Kenyatta of Kenya had to be dropped because the prosecutor had difficulty getting witnesses to testify. Nevertheless, although the ICC's record has so far been mixed, it has had success in several other cases. The

ICC has launched a process that promises to strengthen the accountability faced by leaders responsible for the atrocities that help create humanitarian emergencies.[44] Duties not to violate basic rights are more likely to be enforced today than in the past, and those who do violate them are less likely to get away with it than used to be the case.

The reduction or elimination of the atrocities over which the ICC has jurisdiction may seem like a very limited goal in the face of extensive human suffering taking place in the humanitarian emergencies of today. Indeed, preventing atrocity is a limited goal. But it is an essential step. Preventing atrocities that massively violate human rights by ignoring the moral and legal norms of war would surely help reduce the harm that is so evident in humanitarian emergencies today. It would reduce the large number of casualties and the massive displacements today's conflicts often bring.[45] Further, serious consideration of these issues in public debate could waken public opinion to the scope of the harm armed conflict does to civilians today, including the harm to many millions of displaced people. This could increase the public's awareness of the harmful consequences that very often flow from the use of force, even in a good cause. Reinforcing the moral and political barriers to the use of force in this way would thus help reduce the frequency of humanitarian crises and the number of refugees in the world today. It could also increase pressures to curtail the arms trade that feeds the fires of many unjust conflicts today. Not selling arms to those who are likely to use them to conduct ethnic war or create refugees would go a considerable way toward helping reduce such evils.

Greater adherence to the duties not to commit atrocities that massively violate human rights would thus be an important first step toward alleviating the crises faced by humanity today. Taking this step will call for action by political and military leaders. It will also be an important goal in the advocacy efforts of both secular and faith-based agencies that seek to influence both public opinion and public policy. This first step will not eliminate all the suffering that mars the human scene today. Far from it. But it would make an indispensable, concrete contribution. The following chapter considers some further positive steps in this effort.

CHAPTER 7

POSITIVE DUTIES AND SHARED RESPONSIBILITY

History teaches the sad lesson that political communities and their leaders do not always live up to their duties to protect people's basic rights. Violation of the negative duty not to harm others is too often a regrettable occurrence in international politics. This raises the question of what states, nongovernmental organizations, and individuals should do when immoral or illegal action threatens human rights and brings about humanitarian emergencies. When a state or rebel group violates the *negative* duties we have sketched, what *positive* obligations do others have to assist those who are suffering from the harmful effects of the violation?

To specify some of these positive duties, we need to know who has a responsibility to provide help when somebody else has caused the problem and what that responsibility is. Can a country have a duty to aid people facing ethnic cleansing when that country has not been involved in forcing them to flee? Can private citizens have a responsibility to assist a group of refugees when they had nothing to do with the refugees' displacement? There is certainly a duty *not* to commit ethnic cleansing and *not* to act in ways that turn others into refugees. This leaves the question open, however, of whether one has a duty to take positive action to alleviate suffering one has not caused.

In this chapter, I first sketch a set of criteria that have proven useful in determining when there is a duty to take positive action to help people whose basic rights are threatened in an emergency. Second, I consider the responsibility to grant asylum to those threatened by war or other emergency conditions. Third, I discuss the growing evidence that effective response to emergencies often requires that multiple countries and agencies share responsibility to provide help. I examine how the capability to assist helps determine one's share in the duty to provide assistance. The concern in this chapter is with the duty to provide immediate, short-term assistance to people whose well-being and basic rights are already under direct threat. The following chapter considers some aspects of the ethical responsibility to prevent emergencies from arising. The final chapter discusses duties to seek change in larger social institutions so they protect people from emergency conditions over the longer term.

CRITERIA FOR RESPONSIBILITY

A mode of moral analysis originally developed in another context is helpful here in addressing the question of when positive duties arise to aid people facing humanitarian threats. This ethical approach emerged in the 1970s during debates about who had a duty to respond to the harm caused by apartheid in South Africa. As is well known, the apartheid regime separated South Africa's people by race and ethnicity, requiring them to live apart from one another. It denied human rights to black, Asian, and mixed-race persons, including basic rights such as political participation through the vote and freedom of movement within their own country. These forms of political oppression forced blacks into deep poverty and kept them there, while South African whites lived at nearly the same high level as whites in Europe and the United States. Under apartheid, South Africa was the economically most unequal country in the world. In the face of the injustice of the apartheid system, some decision-makers in the US and the UK maintained that the duty to abolish and change the apartheid system fell solely on the white South Africans who had created it and were enforcing it. In this view, the governments, corporations, and investors who were engaged in political interaction or business in South Africa had a duty not to act in ways that actively discriminated against black South Africans on racial grounds, but they had no duties to take positive action to get rid of apartheid as a system. White South Africans had created the system that was inflicting harm on black South Africans, so it was the duty of the white South Africans—according to some in the US and UK—to dismantle the system. They believed that countries, companies, and investors outside of South Africa did not have a duty to take positive action to help abolish the apartheid system as such.

Several scholars at Yale University, however, proposed a quite different ethical analysis. They argued that their university had a duty to take positive action to help eliminate apartheid through the way the university administered its endowment funds. Under certain circumstances, persons or institutions could have positive duties to help remedy harms they had not themselves caused. They called their approach the Kew Gardens Principle, for it arose from reflection on a tragic event that occurred in the Kew Gardens section of New York City in 1964.[1] According to press reports, a young woman named Kitty Genovese was viciously stabbed and died a slow, agonizing death while thirty-eight nearby people watched and did nothing, failing even to call the police. It has since been learned that the initial reports of what happened were not fully accurate.[2] However, the public outrage stimulated by the press reports points to the fact that most people have a moral conviction that there can be positive duties to aid others in emergency situations. It is not enough to avoid causing harm. In some situations, not acting to alleviate injury can be as much a moral failure as acting in a way that causes injury. Omission can become as immoral as commission. Those who observed Kitty Genovese's death should have at least made some minimal efforts to prevent it.

Analogously, one can have positive duties to protect those whose rights are being violated amid humanitarian crises even though one is not causing the violations. As most people were disturbed by learning that not even one of the thirty-eight witnesses to Kitty Genovese's murder phoned the police, we can question the idea that there is no obligation to respond to a humanitarian crisis when one has not caused it. There can be positive moral duties to aid people in grave danger that go beyond the obligation not to cause harm.[3] In the Rwanda genocide, for example, the governments of the US and the UK had a responsibility to do more than they did to protect the eight hundred thousand Tutsi who died there, even though they were not involved in organizing or carrying out the killing.[4] They had a positive duty to provide political and perhaps some financial support to sustain the UN peacekeeping efforts that were under way in Rwanda. In fact, however, the US and the UK not only failed to contribute to UN peacekeeping efforts but, along with France and Belgium, they took action to stop peacekeeping efforts from continuing. Bill Clinton, who was US president during the genocide, has since acknowledged that action by the United States could have saved three hundred thousand lives.[5] Clinton now recognizes that his decision not to take more vigorous action was a serious mistake. As he put it to a reporter in Kigali several years after the genocide, "I blew it. I just, I feel terrible about it, and all I can ever do is tell them the truth, and not try to sugarcoat it, and try to make it up to them."[6] Clinton now sees his inaction as a failure, perhaps a moral one. His recognition that he failed to do what was required of him implies that there are duties to take positive action to protect people from harm as well as duties not to harm them.

Drawing on such convictions, the Yale authors who developed the Kew Gardens Principle argued that there can be a positive duty to respond when four conditions are present: (1) there is a critical *need*; (2) one has *proximity* to the need; (3) one has the *capability* to respond with some effectiveness; and (4) one is likely the *last resort* from whom help can be expected.[7] Subsequent reflection has added a fifth condition: (5) help can be provided *without disproportionate harm* to the one providing the assistance. Discerning the implications of these criteria is often a delicate process. They can be quite useful, however, in the effort to specify the scope of positive responsibilities that may exist in the face of the suffering in places like Rwanda, South Sudan, and Syria.

For example, there is little doubt that many people in both Syria and South Sudan are in deep need due to the conflicts that have thrown their countries into chaos. Those still inside the borders of these deeply divided countries face dangers that are already violating their human rights and could lead to their deaths. Those who have been forced to flee as refugees have already lost one of their most basic rights—the right to live at peace in their own homeland.

The duty to respond to these needs falls first upon those whose proximity to the crisis makes them more likely to have knowledge of the need and better understanding of how to respond to it. This means, of course, that the government of a nation where crisis is occurring and local communities within that nation bear prime responsibility to address the need. In South Sudan and Syria, therefore, both the governments and the opposition forces in each country have the negative duty to stop the atrocities that are causing crisis, as indicated in the preceding chapter. Their proximity to the suffering also means they have a duty to take positive action to lift the burden of suffering. The duty to take positive action, however, does not extend only as far as the national borders of the countries where conflict and crisis are present. As I argue in chapter 5, national borders do not set limits to the reach of moral obligation. A strictly local specification of the scope of responsibility will leave many without the protection and help they need. In addition, proximity should not be understood as just physical or geographical nearness. When people become aware of a crisis in a neighboring country or even in a country a great distance from themselves, this awareness leads to what can be called intellectual or psychological proximity. It puts them in *moral* proximity to those who are suffering. To be sure, those in the geographical neighborhood often have the most immediate duties to respond to grave need. If they are unable or unwilling to respond, however, that duty can transfer to those farther away.[8] Seeing the scope of responsibility as limited to the home states of those suffering from widespread upheaval and displacement effectively denies the common humanity of all people on the globe.

There has in fact been some response by neighboring countries both to the civil war in the still-unified country of Sudan and to the later civil war in South Sudan after it had become an independent country. The effectiveness of these responses has varied. The Intergovernmental Authority on Development (IGAD) is a regional organization of the countries near Sudan and South Sudan. Its members are Djibouti, Eritrea, Ethiopia, Kenya, Somalia, Sudan, and Uganda. These countries played a helpful diplomatic role in mediating the internal conflict between northern and southern Sudan while they were still one country. IGAD mediation was one of the factors contributing to the 2005 Comprehensive Peace Agreement that ended fighting that had killed about 2 million people in the still-unified country of Sudan and displaced 4 million both internally and as refugees to other countries. The Comprehensive Peace Agreement included plans for the 2011 referendum in the southern regions of the still-unified Sudan that led to the creation of South Sudan as an independent country. IGAD has also been engaged in efforts to bring peace to the conflict that began in the newly independent South Sudan in 2013, although its role in that conflict has been somewhat less effective. Proximity to South Sudan has given the countries of IGAD both an awareness of the human suffering caused by the conflicts and a desire for peace because of the harmful effects of the conflicts in the entire region, especially through mass refugee movement. Proximity has led South Sudan's neighbors to recognize their responsibility to try to help. Regrettably, economic and political self-interest has sometimes distorted the mediation efforts of several of these countries, particularly Uganda and Ethiopia. Peace has not always been their sole goal.

The limited success of IGAD efforts in the conflict raging in South Sudan since 2013 has also led several countries from outside the region to become involved through an effort known as IGAD Plus. This larger group includes the African Union, the United Nations, the European Union, the United

States, the United Kingdom, China, and Norway.[9] A sense of moral responsibility arose in these more distant countries through intellectual proximity to the suffering, displacement, and death being caused by the conflict. This awareness led them to join the effort to overcome the crisis in South Sudan. This combined regional and global mediation effort has been far from perfect, and it has not yet brought peace. Both regional and international agencies could have paid more attention to local peace efforts within South Sudan and to how aspects of their mediation benefited some South Sudanese elites in unhelpful ways. In addition, the engagement of more distant powers has declined. The United States under presidents Barack Obama and especially Donald Trump has played a considerably less active role in seeking peace in the South Sudan civil conflict than it did under President George W. Bush in the earlier civil war in the still-unified Sudan. Nevertheless, regional and international engagement is probably the only source of hope that the South Sudan conflict can be ended in the near future. Despite the limits of the IGAD and IGAD Plus efforts, the Sudan crises show that both physical proximity and proximity through awareness can generate a sense of positive ethical responsibility to take action, both regionally and internationally.

The criterion of capability also helps answer the question of whether there are positive duties to respond to a specific crisis. We routinely link responsibility to help someone in need with the capacity to do so. If a person is unable to provide help, there is no obligation to do so. For example, someone who cannot swim does not have a duty to come to the aid of a child who is drowning if providing the aid will require swimming some distance. It makes no sense to risk two drownings rather than just one. A good swimmer, however, can have a duty to try to help if this can be done without undue risk. As Kant suggested, "ought" implies "can"; if one cannot provide help, there can be no duty to do so.[10] When one possesses the ability to take effective action, however, one has a responsibility to do so if the need is great.

Being the last resort in an effort to assist someone in great danger also increases the responsibility to take action. Whether one is in fact the last one who can be expected to help is rarely self-evident, however. So this standard can be understood to mean that if one is better positioned to help than are others, one's responsibility will be greater. Conversely, if others are better able to take helpful action, their responsibilities will be greater and one's own duties reduced.

Finally, the existence of a duty to take positive action to help alleviate harms that one has not caused depends on whether helpful action can be taken without disproportionate burdens. This means, of course, that in this context the duty to act should be understood in light of the expectations of day-to-day political morality, where the criterion of duty is justice rather than self-sacrificial love. In Christianity and in other religious traditions, self-sacrifice rooted in compassionate love for others can be a true duty. Nevertheless, when we are dealing with decisions about how governments should respond to a humanitarian emergency, justice rather than self-sacrifice is the appropriate ethical standard. Whether there is a positive duty to act in a political context should be determined by seeking a just and proportional distribution of the burdens. All should carry a fair share. Determining what justice demands requires paying attention to the burdens faced by all who are affected by an emergency, not just by those who are considering whether to respond. Whether assistance can be provided without disproportionate burden requires careful attention to the burdens already being carried by those in need of assistance, not only to the burdens that the responder might have to carry. This is essential if estimates of proportionality are to avoid self-serving magnification of the costs to those who are considering action and diminished estimates of the afflictions faced by those already affected by emergency conditions.

Using these criteria calls for both political insight and good moral judgment. It requires that the relevant decision-makers possess the virtue Aristotle called practical wisdom or prudence.[11] Decision-making guided by practical wisdom is not a mechanical process. It grows out of sensitivity to the deep needs of those who are confronted by urgent humanitarian threats. This kind of sensitivity calls for moral solidarity with those in danger, a solidarity that leads one to appreciate the challenges and needs they face. It draws upon an intellectually well-grounded understanding of the causes and possible resolutions to the conflict at hand. It also requires political know-how, the kind of savvy that enables one to grasp what responses are likely to produce helpful outcomes. Such practical wisdom enables the relevant international bodies to take actions and propose policies that actually help those in danger. It shapes responses that can move events in the right direction both ethically and politically. It also helps strengthen those institutions that can support a more stable and lasting peace.

The following sections draw on these criteria of need, proximity, capability, last resort, and proportionate burden to clarify some of the more concrete ethical responsibilities that arise in the context of humanitarian crises today.

REFUGE AND ASYLUM

The criteria of need and proximity converge when people in flight from severe threats seek refuge across the border of a neighboring country. A country near an emergency that drives people to flee can have a duty to admit people in need of refuge because of the danger they face. If the country of potential asylum has the economic resources and political stability to admit people facing grave threats without disproportionate harm to its own people, its duty to admit those in need of refuge will be strong. This duty may be proportionally diminished, of course, if the possible host country is very poor or politically fragile. When migrants have been driven across borders by existential threats to their lives or basic rights, countries with the capacity to admit them have a duty to do so. This is a consequence of the fact that our common humanity relativizes the moral significance of national borders. The borders of nation-states are important means for the protection of the human dignity and human rights of citizens of these states. They protect people against domination or colonial exploitation by powers with no interest in their well-being and freedom. Borders, however, are not moral absolutes. If the dignity of fellow humans can be protected only by granting them asylum in another country, the moral relevance of national borders will be diminished. When the criteria of need, proximity, and capability converge, a proximate country with the capability of doing so will have a moral obligation to grant asylum to those who need protection. In such circumstances, a country capable of providing protection to a needy person in flight will have a duty to grant asylum.

An example of such a convergence of need, proximity, and the capability to provide help is the plight of those who have been seeking asylum in the United States from El Salvador, Honduras, and Guatemala. Over the past several years, large numbers of families, women with their children, and unaccompanied children from these three countries have been seeking entry to the United States because of the dangers they were facing at home. In 2014 over a half a million migrants from this region, often called the Northern Triangle of Central America, were apprehended crossing the southwest border of the United States. Since 2014, and especially following the election of Donald Trump in 2016, the US has been taking an increasingly hard line in denying them asylum. Stronger efforts have been made to exclude all migrants from the Northern Triangle and to deport those arriving even when they claim to have a valid legal claim to asylum. The effort to close the border to people from the Northern Triangle led to a decline in the number seeking admission during the early days of Donald Trump's presidency. In 2018, however, the number increased again.[12] Many were fleeing from the armed conflict raging among gangs and other criminal groups in Central America. The homicide level brought about by gang and criminal fighting in the Northern Triangle is similar to that in many of the most destructive wars of today.[13] Flight from this violence is the principal driver of migration to the United States from these Central American countries.

A strong case can be made that many of those in flight from the Northern Triangle countries have valid claims to refugee status as defined by the 1951 Convention and under the standards set forth in international law. This would imply that many of those in flight have solid legal claims to asylum in the United States. The convergence of the need of these people for protection and the fact that the United States has the capability to provide this protection surely means that there is also a moral obligation to admit them. Despite these legal and moral duties, however, when the number of asylum seekers from the Northern Triangle began to again rise in 2018, the Trump government announced that it intended to arrest and detain anyone crossing the US border without legal approval in advance. In a dramatic threat, US Attorney General Jeff Sessions declared that families entering the US without the legal approval in advance would not only be detained but the children in these families would be separated from their parents and placed in separate detention centers. Sessions put it this way: "I have put in place a 'zero tolerance' policy for illegal entry on our Southwest border. If you cross this border unlawfully, then we will prosecute you. It's that simple. If you smuggle illegal aliens across our border, then we will prosecute you. If you are smuggling a child, then we will prosecute you and that child will be separated from you as required by law."[14] John Kelly, the chief of staff to President Trump, further stated that the separation of children from their parents aimed to deter additional Northern Triangle people from seeking asylum in the US, saying that the "name of the game is deterrence" and that family separation is an appropriately "tough deterrent." He expressed the hope that it would lead to "a much faster turnaround on asylum seekers"—that is, to quicker denial of asylum to those seeking it.[15]

Through this policy the United States was violating its moral duty to admit people fleeing from grave threats to their most basic human rights. Several US courts have seen the policy as a legal violation as well. The murder rate in the Northern Triangle countries is among the highest in the world. In

2016 the conflicts among gangs and other criminal groups made El Salvador the homicide capital of the world, with 91.2 murders per 100,000 people. In nearby Honduras, the annual rate that year was 59.1 homicides per 100,000 of population, and Guatemala had to endure 27.3 homicides per 100,000.[16] Although these rates have recently declined slightly, they remain among the highest murder rates in the world. Latin America has about 8 percent of the world's population but accounts for 38.5 percent of the world's criminal killing. In 2017 murders took 140,000 Latin American lives, more deaths than the annual loss of life in almost all the wars of the twenty-first century.[17] People in the crossfire of the conflict among criminal gangs in Central America are fleeing because their very lives are on the line. Those in flight are surely what Alexander Betts has called "survival migrants."[18] They seek refuge because of existential threats to their basic human rights. There is little doubt that they need protection. Thus, the ethical criteria of need and proximity, sketched above, converge and indicate that when persons fleeing Central American violence seek refuge in the United States, they deserve to receive it. Because those fleeing the Northern Triangle face grave threats to their basic rights and because the United States is both proximate and capable of responding without disproportionate burdens, the US has an ethical duty to grant asylum to many of these people.

Regrettably, the United States is not only failing to act in accord with this duty but is taking active steps to deny admission to these people and to discourage them from even applying for asylum. The US launched a policy of separating children from their parents to "deter" families from seeking safety in the US. This policy violates the basic human right to the integrity of the family. The right to family integrity continues to be present for those who are seeking asylum.[19] The use of strategies that deliberately fracture families in order to discourage people from seeking the protection they need is doubly immoral. It both fails to provide protection to people who need it and breaks apart families in order to achieve its goals.

These ethical objections are reinforced by contrasting this policy with the significant increase in the number of Venezuelans who have been granted asylum in the United States over the past several years.[20] Greater US openness to the Venezuelans is partly political, for many of the Venezuelans are in opposition to the leftist politics that the US government opposes. It is partly economic, for the greater wealth of many of the Venezuelan asylum seekers has enabled them to arrive in the US on tourist visas and to afford legal assistance when seeking refuge. The asylum seeker from the Northern Triangle needs protection at least as much as the Venezuelans do, but the pressure of politics and money is leading the US to exclude the Central Americans without even considering their asylum claim. The treatment of many of the Central Americans seeking refuge in the United States therefore lacks moral justification.

Denial of asylum by the United States to those fleeing violence and murder in the Northern Triangle is morally objectionable and may be illegal as well.[21] The Universal Declaration of Human Rights proclaims, "Everyone has the right to seek and to enjoy in other countries asylum from persecution."[22] This statement is deliberately ambiguous. It affirms the right of a person in danger to seek asylum, but it does not say there is a corresponding duty in law to grant asylum to such a person. Also, the right "to enjoy" asylum has been interpreted to mean that a refugee who has already been granted asylum by a country of refuge has a right to continue enjoying what has been granted.[23] From an ethical point of view, however, the Kew Gardens Principle implies that when a person is in grave need due to widespread homicide, persecution, the dangers of war, or other threats to basic human rights, a proximate country can have a moral duty to grant admission. Granting asylum is often essential to meeting the extreme need of many of those in flight. This moral duty is intensified when the country of possible asylum is proximate to the crisis that is causing displacement and has the capability of providing refuge without placing disproportionate burdens on the people of the admitting country.

In addition, the legal obligation to provide refuge to persons fleeing from severe threats to their basic rights becomes very clear in some circumstances. If someone has already entered a country of possible asylum, and if they can demonstrate that they are in flight from serious danger, there is a legal duty to grant refuge. Article 31 of the 1951 Refugee Convention recognizes this ethical duty and enshrines it in law. This article states that when refugees enter a host country without legal authorization due to threats to their life or freedom, they should face no penalties, provided they can show "good cause" for their presence.[24] The criterion of need is called on here to set forth a duty that goes beyond what is said elsewhere about the duty to grant asylum, particularly for those who have already crossed the border of the potential host country, whether legally or not.

The same is true of the so-called doctrine of non-refoulement set forth in Article 33 of the 1951 Refugee Convention. This article states, "No Contracting State shall expel or return ('*refouler*') a refugee in any manner whatsoever to the frontiers of territories where his life or freedom would be threatened on account of his race, religion, nationality, membership of a particular social group or political opinion."[25] The introductory note to the Refugee Convention sees the duty of non-refoulement as so basic that "no reservations or derogations" are legitimate. Therefore, there is a very strong responsibility toward displaced people facing grave threats who have already crossed the border of another country. Under no circumstances should they be sent back to their country of origin or onward to another country if this would put them in serious danger.[26]

Thus, despite some ambiguity surrounding the legal duty to grant asylum, there is little doubt that there are both ethical and legal responsibilities toward people fleeing from persecution, conflict, and many other severe threats to their life and rights. The ethical duties are clear when those seeking refuge face threats to their basic rights and when the needs of those seeking refuge can be met without placing disproportionate burdens on the people of the receiving country. Further, when such ethical duties are present, this suggests that the legal regime should be refined and further developed so the law more adequately reflects the commitment to protecting human dignity that has been at the heart of international humanitarian law from its beginnings.

CAPABILITY AND SHARED RESPONSIBILITY

The capability of nearby countries to assist people whose basic rights are in danger is increasingly salient because of the size of the forced migrations taking place today. The relevance of the capacity to assist is magnified because of the poverty of many countries that are hosting the large number of refugees today. The limited ability of poor, often politically fragile nations to deal with massive numbers of refugees suggests that the responsibility to provide protection should be shared by many countries, including by those with greater capacities to help. It is not a responsibility that should be carried by just a few poor- or moderate-income countries.

The seriousness of the problem is evident from the way that refugee populations are very unevenly distributed among host countries with very different capacities to assist them. The High Commissioner for Refugees reported that in 2017, 85 percent of the world's refugees were being hosted in developing countries, with almost one-third of the world's refugees being hosted in sub-Saharan Africa. Worldwide, five of the host nations (Pakistan,

Uganda, Bangladesh, Sudan, and Ethiopia) are among the world's poorest countries. Turkey is hosting a larger number of refugees than any other country (3.5 million), almost all from Syria, although Turkey is a middle-income country facing fragile political and economic conditions. Uganda has a rapidly growing refugee population. Nearly 1.4 million people have been forced to seek protection in Uganda, largely due to the conflict in South Sudan, even though Uganda is one of the world's poorest countries.[27] In a similar way, over 720,000 Rohingya Muslims fled from Myanmar to Bangladesh between August 2017 and May 2018, and the number continues to grow.[28] Bangladesh is also among the world's poorest countries, and the arrival of so many refugees has put great pressure on its resources. Small villages have taken many of the new arrivals, putting great strain on their already limited resources.

The resources available to assist refugees in the countries of the developed world is in stark contrast with the capacities of poor nations like Uganda and Bangladesh. The contrast between the capabilities of developed nations and those of the middle-income countries like Lebanon and Turkey is significant though less dramatic. These differences imply that countries' differing capabilities to assist are increasingly important from both an ethical standpoint and as a matter of national and global policy. The various levels of political stability among countries is also important in determining how they should share responsibilities for the displaced.

The 2016 UN General Assembly's Global Summit on Refugees and Migration made a global commitment to "shared responsibility" to assist displaced persons in its New York Declaration. The heads of state of most of the world's countries supported this declaration, which is the basis of the developing Comprehensive Refugee Response Framework. This framework seeks to create more effective global response to large-scale movements of refugees and protracted refugee situations. The New York Declaration makes a strong commitment to sharing the responsibility to assist refugees in an equitable way among nations. As the New York Declaration puts it, "We acknowledge a shared responsibility to manage large movements of refugees and migrants in a humane, sensitive, compassionate and people-centered manner. We will do so through international cooperation, while recognizing that there are varying capacities and resources to respond to these movements. International cooperation and, in particular, cooperation among countries of origin or nationality, transit and destination, has never been more important; 'win-win' cooperation in this area has profound benefits for humanity."[29] The Global Compact on Refugees that was approved in December 2018 also gives strong emphasis to sharing the responsibility to assist displaced people. It observes that countries that host refugees make very large contributions to the global collective good, often over extended periods. Many of these host countries are very poor. The Global Compact therefore declares that "it is imperative that these countries obtain tangible support of the international community as a whole" to enable them to carry out their essential work for refugees effectively.[30] This commitment to having all countries share in protecting and assisting refugees is a breakthrough development.

There is, however, a considerable way to go before countries share the responsibilities to aid displaced people in a fair way. For example, European and North American countries have the capability and resources to grant asylum and resettlement to a much larger number of refugees than is happening today. Despite the capacity to assist many more, some political leaders in Europe and the United States want to admit even fewer than they presently do. In 2015 Germany did admit an extraordinarily large number of Syrian refugees, perhaps over a million, following Chancellor Angela Merkel's reassurance to the German people that "we can do it [*wir schaffen das*]."[31] However, since Merkel took this strong stand on Germany's duty to share responsibility for displaced Syrians, antirefugee sentiment has increased sharply in Germany. The antirefugee fears have contributed to the rise of the nationalist Alternative für Deutschland party that has become a significant player in German politics. Antirefugee nationalist politics has been growing in other European countries and in the United States as well.

It is crucial, therefore, that public opinion recognize that the number of Syrians seeking resettlement outside the Middle East today is not proportionally even close to the number already within the borders of Syria's nearby neighbors. For example, in 2018 Lebanon had received so many Syrians that it had the largest number of refugees per capita of any country in the world—one out of every six persons within the country's borders. With a population of about 6 million, there were nearly a million displaced Syrians in Lebanon who were officially registered by UNHCR, with an estimated million and a half not officially registered.[32] This is in addition to the many Palestinian refugees who have been living in Lebanon for several generations. When David Cameron, then prime minister of the United Kingdom, announced in 2015 that his country would grant asylum to twenty thousand Syrians over the next five years, he was appropriately reminded that Lebanon had admitted that many Syrians over the past two weekends. The burden of these forced migrants on the Lebanese people has been very heavy. Three-quarters of Syrian refugee households in Lebanon were unable to meet their own needs for food, health, shelter and education, and 58 percent were living in extreme poverty, below the level needed for survival.[33] This puts extraordinary strain on Lebanon's economy. In addition, Lebanon has long been a politically fragile nation, and the presence of so many Syrians adds to its existing instability. Lebanon has evidently reached the limits of its capacity to receive more refugees. Turkey and Jordan are similarly overburdened. In 2018 the number of displaced Syrians in Turkey reached about 3.5 million; in Jordan, the number was over 600,000.[34] Under such circumstances, surely it would be reasonable to conclude that Lebanon, Turkey, and Jordan no longer have a duty to receive additional refugees because they lack the capability of doing so.

On the other hand, the wealthy nations of Europe, North America, and the oil-exporting Gulf states have a much greater capability to aid those in flight from Syria. These richer countries have a duty to respond to the Syrian crisis in a way proportionate to their substantially greater ability to do so. They possess economic resources that would enable them to provide asylum to considerable numbers of refugees. They could also share the responsibilities by providing more assistance to Syria's already overburdened nearby neighbors. They could do this by substantially increasing their contributions to UNHCR funds that assist refugees within those countries. They could also provide more support for development efforts in the region. Regrettably, financial assistance to the countries bordering Syria has been inadequate. The regional plan for response to the Syrian crisis remains significantly underfunded. The same is true of Uganda's need for help in assisting those who have fled from the conflict in South Sudan. Uganda, despite its poverty, has received over 1.3 million South Sudanese refugees.[35] Since Uganda is one of the world's poorest countries, a fair sharing of the responsibility for the many displaced South Sudanese who have settled in Uganda will require significantly greater assistance to Uganda.

A genuine sharing of responsibility for the massive movement of refugees today requires the rich nations of the Northern Hemisphere to admit sizably larger number of displaced people. Shared responsibility also calls for increased financial and political support for the poor and fragile states that already host most of the world's refugees today. The countries of the global north have the capability to admit more refugees and to aid those countries already hosting so many refugees. Because they have this capability to assist those in deep need, they have a responsibility to do so.

Each nation's fair share in the responsibility to assist cannot, of course, be mechanically determined, for this fair share depends on a variety of considerations. Some factors are relatively easy to measure, such as gross domestic product per capita. Other factors, however, such as political stability and the cultural readiness to interact with strangers, are less easy to measure. In addition, a factor such as cultural resistance to the increased presence of people from other lands can and should change. Loyalty to one's own country is a positive value, but it must not be allowed to obscure all other values. When fellow human beings from other countries or cultures are in great need, the duty to assist them should take priority over an exclusivist loyalty to one's one people, especially when one is capable of assisting. Increased recognition of the duty to help when one is capable of doing so will contribute to developing the fairer, more just sharing of the responsibility toward refugees that is urgently needed today. To achieve this, the rich nations of the Northern Hemisphere must overcome tendencies toward racially or religiously driven xenophobia and the mistaken fear that refugees are likely to be terrorists.

The fair distribution of responsibilities can also sometimes require taking account of historical facts such as a potential host country's colonial or military involvement with the region from which refugees are fleeing. France and the United Kingdom, for example, reaped significant economic benefits from their colonies in Africa and Asia, so France and the UK have special duties to be open to refugees from the regions they colonized. They have not only benefited from the resources of these colonies, but past colonial domination has often contributed to the injustices at the root of the conflicts that are causing displacement today. In addition, a country with a history of military involvement in a region can have a significant share of the responsibility to aid people displaced from that region. Thus, the United States recognized its duty to receive refugees from Vietnam after its war in that country. Similarly, although the US intervention in Iraq in 2003 was certainly not the sole cause of the displacement of many Iraqis, it contributed significantly to the political chaos that led to the huge forced migration of Iraqis that has occurred. The crisis in Iraq flowed over into Syria, so the US also has a proportionally larger share of the responsibility to aid Syrian refugees as well. Political scientist Stephen Walt observes that if the United States and its allies had not invaded Iraq in 2003, "there almost certainly would be no Islamic State today."[36] Thus, there would be fewer people seeking asylum from Iraq and Syria. This deepens the duties of the US and its allies to resettle more Syrian and Iraqi refugees. Regrettably, the US's willingness to receive Syrians and Iraqis in flight from the conflicts to which the US contributed has been decreasing rather than increasing. This is not a fair or just way to share responsibility toward those driven from home by the Syrian and Iraqi emergencies.

In addition to fair distribution of the number of refugees being resettled, shared responsibility also calls for a fair sharing among countries of the costs of hosting the displaced. This will require increased assistance to Lebanon, Turkey, and Jordan. These three countries are already massively overburdened by the number of forced migrants they are hosting. They do not possess either the economic resources or the political stability to provide asylum for many additional refugees. On the other hand, the resources of the wealthy nations of northern Europe, North America, and the oil-producing Gulf states give them the capability not only to receive many more asylum seekers but also to share the economic burdens being carried by Syria's already overtaxed neighbors. The assistance being provided to the countries bordering Syria is woefully inadequate. The nations of Europe, North America, and the Gulf have substantially greater economic resources than do Syria's and Iraq's neighbors, so they have a duty to provide more assistance to Syria's nearby neighbors than they are providing.[37]

How to achieve greater fairness in sharing the responsibility toward those affected by emergencies is perhaps the greatest ethical challenge facing the humanitarian movement today. Fairness, of course, does not mean that each country should be asked to make a numerically equal contribution. Justice can require different countries to contribute in ways that are proportional to their capability to assist effectively. Fairness in sharing responsibility will be proportional to a country's proximity to the emergency, to its historical contributions to causing it, to its capability of making a helpful contribution, and to its ability to help without placing disproportionate burdens on its own people. All of these criteria, taken together, suggest that the countries of North America, Europe, and the Gulf should make significantly greater contributions to the humanitarian effort than they are making. Their responsibilities can be carried out by granting asylum to more refugees, by providing larger opportunities for resettlement, and, perhaps most importantly, by providing economic and other forms of assistance to countries that are already carrying disproportionate burdens. Providing such assistance should be a political and economic priority for countries with the capacity to do so. The common humanity of those facing crisis requires this. It is an ethical demand of justice and fairness. The humanity that those in crisis share with those having greater resources demands nothing less.

CHAPTER 8

ACTING ACROSS BORDERS

The preceding chapter argues that there can be a positive duty to grant asylum to migrants whose dignity is severely threatened in their home country if this can be done without taking on disproportionate burdens. Our common humanity requires that we be ready to receive people from other nations if this is the only way to protect them. This chapter goes beyond the duty to grant asylum to consider possible responsibilities to take action within other countries. It considers possible duties to try to change the behavior of other nations if such change is the only way to protect people from serious violation of their rights. This, of course, can raise alarm in some political contexts, especially if the effort to influence another nation's behavior is identified with the use of armed force. Here, however, we are concerned with a much broader range of activities than military engagement. Action across borders to protect threatened people can include diplomatic activity for human rights, initiatives to restore or sustain peace, development work by NGOs, and other initiatives.

More specifically, I consider here three areas where duties to take positive action across borders arise. First, I discuss the responsibility toward internally displaced people within the borders of another nation. Second, I explore the scope and limits of the duty to protect people in other countries against violations of their rights that reach the level of atrocity. Finally, I briefly outline several longer-term ways to help other countries move from crisis to a just and sustainable peace and, thus, to assist the refugees and IDPs produced by those countries. Each of these matters, of course, could be explored at great length. Here the discussion is kept brief by drawing on the values and norms highlighted in earlier chapters.

DUTIES TO INTERNALLY DISPLACED PEOPLE

The United Nations' *Guiding Principles on Internal Displacement* define internally displaced people as "persons or groups of persons who have been forced or obliged to flee or leave their homes or places of habitual residence, in particular as a result of or in order to avoid the effects of armed conflict, situations of generalized violence, violations of human rights or natural or human-made disasters, and who have not crossed an internationally recognized State border."[1] Following this definition, IDPs are not refugees as described by the 1951 Refugee Convention since they have not crossed an international border. Nevertheless, Richard Holbrooke, former US ambassador to the UN, preferred to call IDPs "internal refugees."[2] He wanted to stress that there is often little concrete difference between the suffering of official refugees and the suffering of IDPs. Indeed, those displaced within their own country can sometimes be worse off than those who have actually escaped persecution or some other form of abuse by fleeing across the border.

The number of IDPs has been growing dramatically in recent years and is now very large. According to the Internal Displacement Monitoring Centre, as of the end of 2017 there were over 40 million people in the world displaced within their home countries by conflict and violence, along with an additional large but unknown number of people displaced by disasters. Of these, 30 million had been newly displaced during 2017. This surge in forced movement was due to the very high levels of conflict and violence in 2017 and due to a record-breaking number of hurricanes in the Caribbean and Atlantic as well as major typhoons in Asia and the Pacific (indeed, 2017 could be called the "year of cyclones").[3] The large number of IDPs in recent years means that today they are about two-thirds of all the world's forcibly displaced persons.

The plight of IDPs is exacerbated by the fact that most of them are in the developing world, where resources to assist them are small. According to the World Bank, at the end of 2015, developing countries were hosting 99 percent of all IDPs, and most of these were in states made fragile by conflict.[4] More than half of those who were internally displaced by conflict were in just three countries: Syria, the Democratic Republic of Congo, and Iraq. More recently, internal displacement due to civil conflict has risen sharply in South Sudan, Ethiopia, and the Central African Republic. Internal displacement by weather-related hazards like storms or floods was also on the rise in 2017.[5] The importance of local conditions is reinforced by the fact that the help IDPs receive also depends heavily on what their own society is able and willing to provide for them. This bodes ill for the quality of the relief that IDPs are likely to receive. Not only are most IDPs in poor countries but the source of their suffering is frequently their own government. It is surely ominous when one's own government becomes the chief threat to one's basic rights. IDPs thus often face a double threat: not only have they been driven from their homes but the ruling power of their country has become their enemy. The threat to IDPs will increase further if their own government prevents them from receiving aid from abroad. Relief assistance by governments of other countries and by international humanitarian organizations ordinarily requires the approval of the IDP's home state. Regrettably, such assistance from outside is sometimes denied when the IDPs are members of a political, ethnic, or religious group in conflict with the government.

Because IDPs remain within their own nation, the conflicts that drive them from home often receive less media attention than do those that drive refugees to seek asylum in Europe and the United States. The plight of IDPs is thus notably less visible than that of refugees. The UN's emergency relief coordinator, Stephen O'Brien, recently called IDPs "the invisible majority" among the world's displaced.[6] The needs of the IDPs within the Central African Republic, for example, are nearly invisible compared to the needs of displaced Syrians when they arrive en masse at the borders of European countries. Despite their invisibility, however, IDPs have the same dignity and the same human needs as do the asylum seekers knocking at the doors of the rich northern countries. Like asylum seekers, the lives of IDPs have been turned upside down by war and disaster. They undergo the same suffering when they lose their homes and their familiar communities, as do the refugees who have fled across international borders. They frequently receive less help than do refugees; for since they are technically not refugees, they are not officially entitled to international assistance through the UN High Commissioner for Refugees. In addition, IDPs often have fewer initial resources than do those who have traversed borders, so their displacement can lead to greater deprivation than that faced by refugees.

Principle 1 of the *Guiding Principles on Internal Displacement* insists that IDPs possess "the same rights and freedoms under international and domestic law as do other persons in their country." They should "not be discriminated against in the enjoyment of any rights and freedoms on the ground that they are internally displaced."[7] South Sudanese scholar and diplomat Francis Mading Deng led the project of drafting the *Guiding Principles*. Deng's team drew on existing norms of human rights, humanitarian, and refugee law to assemble a framework of principles that should shape international response to IDPs. The *Guiding Principles* are not a formal treaty or convention, so they do not have the force of "hard law" that is readily enforceable. They are called "guiding" principles because they rely on the readiness of those to whom they apply to follow their guidance. Nevertheless, the principles do set forth norms found elsewhere in binding international law. Quite a few countries have already incorporated the guidance of the principles into their own domestic laws and policies, and the number of countries that have done this is growing. The *Guiding Principles* therefore set forth both ethical and legal standards for the treatment of IDPs.

Nevertheless, the effective impact of these demands is weakened by the tension between their claim to set forth universally binding standards for the treatment of IDPs and the continued stress on national sovereignty as a basic requirement of the international system. On the one hand, the primary responsibility for the protection of internally displaced people lies with the state within which they located.[8] On the other hand, these principles strongly affirm the full gamut of human rights held by all persons. There can be a sharp conflict between these two affirmations when the state under whose power the IDPs fall is unwilling to defend their rights. The conflict is even sharper if, for political reasons, the government is itself the source of their displacement. In such a situation, it will not be much help to the displaced to suggest that they look to their own government for protection since their own government is threating their rights.[9]

Deng fully recognized the tension between sovereignty and human rights in his work on the *Guiding Principles*. He knew the tension between the rights of the displaced and state sovereignty from his personal experience as a citizen of the still-unified country of Sudan. Sudan's government in Khartoum was denying Deng and his fellow Dinka people many of their rights, including denying them access to the benefits produced by the oil under their land, treating them as second-class citizens for racial and ethnic reasons, threatening them with forced religious conversion, and even attacking them with indiscriminate military force. These violations turned many southern Sudanese into displaced persons, with more than 2 million of them internally displaced within their own country during the civil war between southern Sudanese and their government in Khartoum that did much harm from 1983 to 2005. Drawing on his experience in Sudan as well as on what was happening in Somalia, the former Yugoslavia, and elsewhere, Deng helped formulate an understanding of sovereignty that sought to make room for the duties to assist those facing serious harm in countries other than one's own. He called this understanding "sovereignty as responsibility."[10]

The concept of sovereignty as responsibility has important ethical content. Like more traditional understandings of sovereignty, it protects each state's right to govern and to carry out its responsibilities to its citizens. When the state governs this way, others should not disturb it from without by aggression or unjustified intervention. Thus, sovereignty as responsibility protects the state's ability to carry out the tasks expected of an effective government. This emphasis, however, reinterprets sovereignty in light of a democratic ethos. It sees sovereignty as an expression of the people's right to govern themselves rather than being ruled by some oppressive imperial or colonial power. Because of this democratic emphasis, sovereignty requires that a government preserve the rights of its own citizens. When it does this, it should remain undisturbed by external powers. If a state is unable to protect its own people's rights, it may voluntarily call on other nations to help it do so. If the state is unwilling to protect its people's rights, or worse, if the state itself attacks those rights, its sovereignty can be limited involuntarily. The responsibility to protect or help restore those rights can transfer to other nations or to international organizations.

This revised concept of sovereignty is directly relevant to the needs of internally displaced people. This is not surprising since Deng developed the concept of sovereignty as responsibility while he was helping to draft the *Guiding Principles on Internal Displacement*.[11] The idea of sovereignty as responsibility can help clarify some important ethical dimensions of response to IDPs.

The 2018 Plan of Action formulated by the UN special rapporteur on the human rights of IDPs proclaims a threefold set of duties toward IDPs: to *prevent* internal displacement from occurring; to *protect* the displaced; and to *resolve* the crises that lead to displacement.[12] Here I consider how better to protect those who are already IDPs. I use the case of IDPs in the still-unified Sudan before the south became independent in 2011 to illustrate what is possible. The last chapter of this book considers the prevention and resolution of crises over the longer term.

The *Guiding Principles* begin by affirming that states are the primary agents for the protection of their own people and thus for the protection of their citizens who have been internally displaced. In the Sudan civil war, the international community sought to aid Sudanese IDPs by putting pressure on the government in Khartoum and on its adversary in the war, the Sudan Peoples' Liberation Movement/Army (SPLM/A). International efforts to help the millions who were displaced within Sudan aimed to facilitate a peace treaty between Khartoum and the SPLM. To this end, international diplomatic pressure was applied in several interacting ways. As noted in the previous chapter, the Intergovernmental Authority on Development (IGAD), composed of Sudan's neighboring countries, pressured Khartoum and the SPLM to undertake negotiations. One of these neighboring countries, Kenya, played a particularly important role. Kenya hosted negotiations between Khartoum and the SPLM in the Kenyan town of Machakos in 2002 and again at Lake Naivasha in Kenya from 2002 to 2005. A Kenyan military leader, Gen. Lazaro Sumbeiywo, served as the moderator and facilitator of the Lake Naivasha negotiations.[13] The United States also played an active role, vigorously pressing Khartoum and the SPLA to reach agreements that would both advance peace and enable the displaced to return home. US president George W. Bush appointed Sen. John Danforth as his special envoy for the Sudan conflict. Danforth traveled to Lake Naivasha several times to intervene directly in the negotiations. In addition, Bush also dispatched his secretary of state, Colin Powell, to Lake Naivasha to add further diplomatic pressure. Other international bodies such as the African Union, the United Nations, and several European governments were also engaged in the negotiations. These international diplomatic pressures on the government in Khartoum and on its armed opponents contributed to the 2005 Comprehensive Peace Agreement that ended decades of conflict between Khartoum and the SPLA. The level of international diplomatic engagement was visible in the fact that the peace agreement was formally witnessed and signed by the presidents of Kenya and Uganda, the foreign ministers of several other African countries, US secretary of state Colin Powell, UK minister of international development Hillary Benn, and Norway minister of international development Hilde Johnson.[14]

The agreement provided that the southern region of Sudan would hold a referendum on possible independence. The vote took place in January 2011, with more than 98 percent of the people casting their ballots for independence. South Sudan became the world's newest country on July 9, 2011. The fact that the 2005 peace accord did not resolve all the issues has been painfully obvious: civil war broke out in the new country of South Sudan less than two years after its independence. Despite this further tragic conflict, however, the 2005 peace agreement shows that diplomacy can make a genuine difference in addressing massive internal displacement. The Comprehensive Peace Agreement opened the door for millions of internally displaced people to begin the process of returning home. It did this through the vigorous engagement of the countries neighboring Sudan who were members of IGAD. A troika of Western countries, the US, the UK, and Norway, were deeply involved in helping bring about the agreement and helping remove the pressures that had displaced so many people. These efforts show that vigorous efforts across borders through sustained diplomacy can make a real difference for displaced people.

The fact that less than two years after independence the new country of South Sudan fell into conflict could easily overshadow the achievements of the 2005 peace agreement between Khartoum and the SPLM. The further conflict in independent South Sudan was largely due to internal conflicts among leaders of the new South Sudan, especially between the president of the new country, Salva Kiir, and his former vice president, Riek Machar. Although tensions about borders and some other matters between the capital of the new country in Juba and the old regime in Khartoum continued after the South's independence, these were not the prime cause of the civil conflict in the newly independent country. The new leaders in South Sudan fell into personal conflict with each other due to their desire for personal power. They corruptly sought financial gain for themselves rather than the common good of the new country.[15] What has happened since 2013 in the new South Sudan, therefore, should not prevent us from learning from the success of international diplomatic efforts that led to the 2005 peace as we address IDPs in other regions today. Indeed, the intense commitment by Sudan's neighbors; by more distant countries including the US, the UK, and Norway; and by international organizations made a real difference. One can ask whether the conflict in newly independent South Sudan would have become as intense as it is if the international community were as diplomatically engaged in South Sudan as it had been in the earlier conflict between Khartoum and the SPLM. In the US, for example, the diplomacy of the government of George W. Bush that helped bring about the 2005 peace agreement was much more active than the Obama administration's efforts for peace in the new South Sudan. Although the failure of South Sudan's leaders is the chief reason there are 1.7 million IDPs in South Sudan today, the weakening of diplomatic engagement under Obama, and even more so under Trump, has been a factor as well.

The difference in US actions under Bush, on the one hand, and under Obama and Trump, on the other, is due in large part to the shifting pressures by US citizens and humanitarian agencies on the US government. The conflict between Khartoum and the SPLM attracted major attention by both religious and secular humanitarian groups in the United States. Indeed, religious agencies and secular humanitarian and human rights groups worked together to mobilize public opinion concerning this conflict. Religious communities were also very engaged within southern Sudan itself in the effort to bring peace and to enable the displaced to return home. African Americans sought to influence US diplomacy in part because of the racial aspects of the conflict. Northern Sudanese see themselves as Arab rather than African and regard southerners as black. Rumors that northerners had enslaved some southern Sudanese intensified this racial dimension. These racial dimensions mobilized black citizens and legislators in the US. In addition, evidence that the right to religious freedom and other human rights were being widely violated led to the vigorous engagement by both secular human rights groups and many Baptist Christians, who have long been vigorous advocates of religious freedom. In 2002 the United States Commission on International Religious Freedom called the government in Khartoum "the world's most violent abuser of the right to freedom of religion and belief," and Colin Powell called Sudan "the worst human rights nightmare on the planet."[16]

This extraordinarily diverse campaign in the United States put significant political pressure on the Bush administration. The campaign included leaders of evangelical churches usually regarded as on the right, the Congressional Black Caucus, the US Conference of Catholic bishops, leadership of Reform Judaism, the Southern Baptist Convention, and numerous secular human rights organizations. They exerted pressure through publicity campaigns, protests, mobilization of their members and constituencies, direct humanitarian aid to those affected in Sudan, and pressure for legislation. Allen Hertzke calls this very diverse group of actors an "unlikely coalition." Even if it was an unlikely collaboration, it was surely effective. It led the US Congress to pass the Sudan Peace Act in 2002, which in turn compelled President Bush to act. The important role the US played in the negotiations at Lake Naivasha in Kenya that led to the peace agreement was an outcome of the pressure on Bush by these many religious and secular advocates of humanitarian action. It shows that activist pressure from civil society and the religious community can exert effective influence on global politics and policy.[17]

Christian churches also played a notable role internally within the southern regions of Sudan in the pursuit of peace. Christians are a sizable part of the population in what has become the country of South Sudan. Both the Catholic and Anglican churches are important players in the social life of the region. Because the long civil war so weakened social life, the churches today are among the few functioning institutional bodies in civil society. Indeed, the churches have a stronger presence at the grassroots level of social life than did the government in Khartoum during the civil war or than the new government in Juba has since the independence of the South. At the same time, the churches also have influence at the level of national government. Therefore, the churches have been well positioned to help move the peace process forward both at the local and national levels. The Sudan Council of Churches, which includes both Protestant and Catholic communities, coordinated an effort called the People to People Peace Campaign.[18] Catholic bishop Paride Taban of Torit played an especially influential role in the pursuit of peace, and the Anglican Church was deeply involved in peacebuilding efforts as well. Southern Sudanese Christians also used their transnational links with church actors in the US, the UK, the Vatican, and elsewhere to add insights from the grass roots to the diplomatic process that was under way and to put pressure on the governments involved. The contributions of the churches reached across borders and provided important assistance to the millions of IDPs in southern Sudan.

What happened in Sudan in the run-up to the Comprehensive Peace Agreement of 2005 can serve as a model for how to address the needs of IDPs today. Countries outside Sudan, including the troika of the US, the UK, and Norway, as well as international organizations like IGAD and the African Union, played key roles in mediating the conflict. Religious and secular humanitarian organizations shaped public opinion and directly influenced government policies in very effective ways. This kind of response to the needs of the displaced in Syria, the Democratic Republic of Congo, Yemen, Central African Republic, and elsewhere could make the situation significantly different than it is. An ethical response by more people and organizations to the needs of those whose humanity is threatened can energize such action. The fate of millions of IDPs depends on action of this sort. More can and should be done. Action across borders by governments, international organizations, NGOs, and religious communities can make a real difference for the internally displaced.

THE RESPONSIBILITY TO PROTECT

A new approach to grave humanitarian and human rights abuses, called the responsibility to protect, was affirmed at the 2005 UN General Assembly World Summit. This approach can help clarify the scope of the ethical duty to take action across borders to assist people whose human dignity is gravely threatened. At this special session of the General Assembly, the heads of state of most of the nations of the world declared, "Each individual State has the responsibility to protect its populations from genocide, war crimes, ethnic cleansing and crimes against humanity."[19] The UN declaration drew the phrase "responsibility to protect" (R2P) from a 2001 report with that title prepared by the International Commission on Intervention and State Sovereignty (ICISS). The Canadian government established this commission to propose ways to prevent future tragedies like the Rwandan genocide and the Srebrenica massacres. The commission's dozen members came from all continents. Both the ICISS and the 2005 World Summit built on Francis Deng's understanding of sovereignty as responsibility and on the full body of human rights and humanitarian principles. Their central normative conclusion is that all people ought to be protected from the atrocities of genocide, war crimes, ethnic cleansing, and crimes against humanity. Such protection, of course, implies that all persons and states have a duty not to commit these atrocities. Avoiding such atrocities will not eliminate all the suffering caused by war or conflict. Nevertheless, greater adherence to the negative moral and legal norms that forbid these atrocities would significantly reduce the level of suffering.

The R2P doctrine, however, goes beyond duties not to harm. It affirms that the international community also has positive duties to prevent harm and to take positive action to stop grave abuses when they occur, even if this means acting across the border of another country. If the violation of human rights reaches the level of atrocities like genocide, ethnic cleansing, or crimes against humanity, there can be a positive duty to try to stop these crimes. In the first instance, the effort to stop the abuse should be through "diplomatic, humanitarian and other peaceful means." If such peaceful initiatives do not succeed, however, the use of armed force can become a legitimate way to carry out the duty to protect people from atrocious violations of their rights.[20]

The responsibility to protect has been the focus of heated controversy since it was endorsed in 2005. Most political realists oppose it. Realists, of course, hold that foreign policy should be determined by the interests of one's own people, not by a supposed moral responsibility to other lands. Former national security advisor and secretary of state Henry Kissinger, for example, argued that the appeals to humanitarian values that led the US and NATO to take military action in Somalia and Kosovo were a "sweeping overextension" and risked the stability of the international order.[21] Some postcolonial thinkers also oppose R2P but for quite different reasons than Kissinger's. These post-colonialists see R2P as a form of neoimperialism—a kind of twenty-first-century version of the *mission civilisatrice* that led the French to incorporate large swaths of Africa and Southeast Asia into *la plus grande France.* This colonial "mission" supposedly brought the benefits of Western civilization to the "barbarian" people who were being colonized. The Ugandan scholar Mahmood Mamdani draws on the sad history of European colonialism and the fact that much discussion of R2P has focused on crises in Africa to argue that R2P masks "a big power agenda to recolonize Africa."[22] Other Africans disagree, however. Not surprisingly, given his influence on the development of R2P, Francis Deng supports it, though he is well aware of the roles played by racism and colonialism in struggles of Sudan.[23] Deng's approach shows that some important African and postcolonial thinkers reject the claim that R2P is driven by an agenda of Western domination.

Pope Benedict XVI also supported R2P as an expression of positive moral engagement rather than a form of negative domination. In a 2008 speech at the United Nations, Pope Benedict endorsed R2P as an expression of the rising importance of efforts to protect human rights in global affairs. He reinforced his commitment to R2P in his 2009 encyclical *Caritas in veritate* by calling for the development of innovative ways to carry it out.[24] Pope Francis's ambassador to the United Nations reaffirmed the Catholic Church's support for R2P in 2017. The papal ambassador declared that this responsibility requires "meeting obligations under international human rights and international humanitarian law, and condemning deliberate attacks against civilians and civilian infrastructures. It means preventing or stopping atrocity crimes and protecting populations from them through greater legal, political and moral accountability."[25] The Catholic Church's positive endorsement of R2P is rooted in the conviction that the common humanity of all persons means that moral responsibility reaches across borders. This has direct relevance to the plight of displaced persons, both refugees and IDPs.

In fact, the responsibility to protect has been invoked on several occasions since the UN General Assembly affirmed it in 2005. Its use to support international action suggests that its acceptance as a normative standard of international affairs has been growing. R2P provided motivation and justification for several noteworthy international moves to protect people from grave rights violations over the past decade.

For example, it was the basis for international action following the 2007 election in Kenya. Because of disputes over the outcome of the election, conflict broke out between ethnic groups allied with the two chief candidates, Mwai Kibaki and Raila Odinga. The conflict led to more than one thousand deaths and the internal displacement of half a million people within Kenya. When a sizable number of persons who had sought refuge in a church were burned alive when the church was deliberately set ablaze, many people remembered similar events during the Rwandan genocide, and the fear grew that a similar disaster was in the making. Kofi Annan, who had been in charge of UN peacekeeping in Rwanda, stated that he saw the crisis in Kenya "in the R2P prism."[26] This R2P perspective led to intense diplomatic initiatives by the UN, the African Union, and a number of other governments from Africa and from around the world, including the United States.[27] Under Annan's leadership, a power-sharing agreement was reached and the downward spiral into civil war and what some observers feared might become genocide was stopped. The elections six years later in 2013 took place much more peacefully. Thus, many Kenyan people were successfully protected through international diplomatic initiatives inspired by R2P. Kenya, of course, remains very divided ethnically, and the country's political stability remains fragile, as the disputes surrounding the 2017 election have shown. International response to the conflict in Kenya after the 2007 election, however, shows that the responsibility to protect can be successfully carried out through nonviolent political and diplomatic means. The use of force, as the just war ethic affirms and as Kofi Annan subsequently put it, must be a "last resort."[28] Using force should not be considered until all peaceful ways to protect people from serious harms have been exhausted. In Kenya in 2007, creative diplomacy succeeded in averting the kind of atrocities that R2P seeks to prevent.

Despite R2P's stress on political and diplomatic initiatives, however, the possibility remains that the use of force may sometimes regrettably become necessary as a last resort to protect people effectively. The standard just/unjust war criteria governing the responsible use of force were adapted to this question by the ICISS, which first proposed the R2P doctrine. The commission concluded that military action should be "an exceptional and extraordinary measure" undertaken only when "serious and irreparable harm" is occurring or "imminently likely to occur."[29] The ICISS specifies serious harm as including genocide, ethnic cleansing, and large-scale loss of life produced by state action, state neglect, state inability to act, or failed state situations. At the UN General Assembly in 2005, the possible justifications for the use of force were set forth more narrowly. Force would be legitimate only to protect people from the atrocities of genocide, war crimes, ethnic cleansing, and crimes against humanity. These criteria were a response to the tragic failure of the international community to prevent the Rwandan genocide and the Srebrenica slaughter. Just as one deeply hopes that crises such as those in Rwanda and Srebrenica will be exceedingly rare, one should insist that military intervention to prevent or alleviate humanitarian crisis should be rare as well. Nevertheless, a sense of transnational responsibility means that force cannot be ruled out if grave atrocities are being committed.

The R2P doctrine has in fact been invoked on several occasions over the past decade to justify the use of military force when people are facing atrocious violations of their humanity. For example, in 2012 and 2013 the Security Council called on R2P when it approved the use of force to protect people in Mali from terroristic attacks on their basic rights.[30] With this UN approval, France and the Economic Community of West African States took military action in their effort to stop the atrocities and restore peace in Mali. In 2013 the Security Council supported the use of force to stop grave violations of human dignity in the Central African Republic, legitimating military action by French and African Union troops.[31] These cases suggest that the responsibility to protect continues to be relevant and that it remains a viable approach to dealing with grave crises. Those who make this argument, however, also acknowledge that two other cases—Libya and Syria—raise basic questions about the future of the doctrine of R2P.

In the Libya case, the UN authorized action to protect civilians against attacks threatened by the government of Col. Muammar Gaddafi. Gaddafi called his adversaries in Benghazi "cockroaches," using the very epithet that the Hutu had directed at the Tutsi during the Rwandan genocide.[32] This, along with other military moves, raised fears that he was about to commit grave atrocities against his opponents in Benghazi and elsewhere. These fears led the Security Council, with the notable support of the Organisation of the Islamic Conference and the League of Arab States, to call for a no-fly zone over Libya and for the use of "all necessary measures" to protect civilians.[33] NATO intervened with airpower, Gaddafi was killed, and his regime was overthrown and replaced. The longer-term effects of the removal of Gaddafi, however, were certainly not good. Libya fell into political chaos, with armed conflicts among several groups, significant violations of human rights on the basis of religion, and abuses that led many to seek refuge in unsafe ways by migrating across the Mediterranean to Europe.[34] These consequences confirmed for some the realist conviction that the pursuit of humanitarian goals not required by national self-interest is unlikely to succeed and may do more harm than good.[35]

It can be argued, however, that the negative outcome in Libya was not the result of the inadequacy of the doctrine of R2P. Rather, Libya's descent into chaos can be seen as the result of the intervening powers' failure to complete the task of protection they had begun. The 2005 ICISS report on *The Responsibility to Protect* insisted that protection includes a responsibility to help rebuild a society after a military intervention. The use of force to provide humanitarian protection not only requires observance of the traditional *jus ad bellum* norms of the just war tradition (just cause, proportionality, last resort, etc.). It also requires that one follow through with efforts to ensure that justice will be restored after the conflict has ended. *Jus post bellum* (justice after war) can be as important as the justice of initiating conflict (*jus ad bellum*) or the justice of the means used to carry it out (*jus in bello*). NATO and the US should have done much more than they did to help the post-Gaddafi transitional governments in Libya, but they effectively abandoned the country once Gaddafi was gone. Serious efforts to restore justice in Libyan society after the use of force had ended could have helped prevent the chaos that developed.[36] What happened in Libya was an imperfect and incomplete implementation of R2P, not its failure.

Opponents of R2P also cite the crisis in Syria to support their argument that R2P is a bad idea. Some even see Syria as sounding the death knell for the doctrine. The Syrian crisis has surely been a disaster. Many have died and even more have been displaced. There is little doubt that Syrian suffering gives reason to take action under R2P, even with force, if a plan of action could be developed that would do more good than harm. What action would actually advance justice, however, is far from clear. Serious violations of the ethics and law of war are being committed by most of the groups in this multisided conflict, so support for any one of them could amount to encouragement of their injustices. Identifying which military steps have a reasonable hope of success in bringing greater justice over the long haul is difficult if not impossible. It would be equally difficult to determine which action could be taken without causing disproportionate collateral harm to innocent civilians. The conflict within Syria also has significant regional dimensions, so intervention to protect Syrians could potentially end up triggering a deeper conflict involving Iran, Israel, and other Middle Eastern states. There are even global strategic risks because of the existing involvement of Russia, NATO, and the US.

The political complexities and moral ambiguities of the Syrian situation, therefore, go very deep. These complexities and ambiguities, however, do not discredit the idea that there is a responsibility to protect people in great need. Thomas Weiss has argued that three variables can determine the wisdom of the use of force in the effort to protect people from atrocities: legality, moral legitimacy, and feasibility.[37] In the case of Syria, war crimes and other atrocities have clearly violated accepted standards of legality. The moral legitimacy of efforts to stop a conflict that has displaced over half the Syrian population and killed hundreds of thousands of civilians is also evident. The feasibility of a military intervention that would alleviate the crisis, however, is far from clear. The just war tradition in its modern form sees probability of success as an essential standard for judging whether an intervention would be just. In the Syrian emergency, it is very difficult to identify a form of armed intervention that is likely to succeed.

The lack of presently feasible ways of protecting the people of Syria militarily, however, does not undermine R2P, just as the argument that the use of force is unlikely to succeed in other situations does not undermine the just war tradition. The fact that military action is unlikely to succeed does not mean that the responsibility to protect people vanishes. Rather, it implies that nonmilitary efforts should be pursued more vigorously. Intensified political and diplomatic efforts appear to be the only feasible way to halt the atrocities taking place in Syria over the longer term. This is particularly true since Russia, Iran, some Gulf states, and other international actors are playing roles in Syria that are keeping the crisis alive. The United States and others with potential political and diplomatic influence thus have a responsibility to engage these other powers in the pursuit of peace. Responsibility to protect the millions of displaced Syrians and to remember those who have perished requires continuing political and diplomatic engagement.

Effective engagement requires political wisdom and discerning insight concerning the moral outcome of the possible initiatives. Moral philosophers call such wisdom and discernment the virtue of prudence. Prudence, or practical wisdom, is the kind of moral insight that enables one to see what concrete actions will best advance the good of those affected by the action taken. It requires expertise concerning the actual workings of the political scene and sensitivity to the moral effects of possible actions on human dignity. The Kew Gardens Principle can also help form discerning concrete judgments on how to assist those whose humanity is threatened. These principles are a kind of summary of what experience has taught us about responsibilities to assist those whose suffering we have not caused. Thus, considering the needs of those in crisis will help shape wise judgment on whether action is required. Assessment of one's proximity to the crisis and especially of one's capability of action that will make a positive difference will also lead to good decisions. Also relevant is whether others are better situated to respond. Whether a concrete decision is practically wise will also depend on the proportionality of the burden of acting to the suffering of those in need. These dimensions of prudent decision-making imply that not everyone is responsible to assist all those who need help. The specific crises considered here, such as those in Libya, South Sudan, Syria, and elsewhere, indicate that positive and creative assistance is morally required today. Practical wisdom calls for a significant increase in assistance to refugees, IDPs, and others threatened by humanitarian crises. All those committed to our common humanity—and surely all faith communities—can have important influence by demonstrating that our duties do not end at the borders of our states or communities of faith. Increased action to fulfill these duties will make a real difference for the people who are facing humanitarian crises today. The very humanity of tens of millions of people is on the line.

CHAPTER 9

JUSTICE AND ROOT CAUSES

This final chapter considers the responsibility to change the social contexts and institutions that bring about emergencies and keep them going. The need to address the root causes of crises over the long term has been evident within the humanitarian movement for some time. As noted earlier, NGOs like Oxfam and faith-based agencies like Catholic Relief Services have for several decades supplemented their programs of immediate relief with more systemic efforts to address causes. They do this by working to promote development and build peace. Today the record-breaking levels of forced migration make the long-term prevention of crises more important than ever. The need to address the deeper structural issues that drive and trigger humanitarian crises is a central concern of the 2018 Global Compact on Refugees.[1]

Prevention requires addressing the institutions that either kindle or prolong emergencies. To be sure, people who are suffering will always need help through direct assistance. If someone is hungry, there is no substitute for food; if one has no shelter, at least a tent will be essential. Providing relief from the dire consequences of war, persecution, or disaster will always be necessary in humanitarian response. There is also a need, however, to take the further step of seeking to overcome the causes of these threats by changing the institutions and policies that make relief necessary.

The 2016 World Humanitarian Summit stressed the importance of prevention when it concluded that "preventing and ending conflict, including through addressing root causes, is the most important and effective way to substantially reduce risk, vulnerability and humanitarian needs for protection and assistance."[2] The summit saw "political leadership to prevent and end conflicts" as the "core responsibility" in the humanitarian movement today.[3]

Regrettably, commitment by the governments of the world to follow through on this responsibility has been less than adequate. Former UN secretary-general Ban Ki-moon declared, "This must change. Without much greater political leadership from Member States to prevent and resolve conflicts and to increase stability, we will not be able to substantially reduce the scale of humanitarian needs or the unprecedented movement of people within and across borders."[4]

The hesitancy of many governments to try to address root causes no doubt arises from the magnitude of the task proposed. It can seem utopian. Nevertheless, if prevention is understood as working to overcome the most severe threats endangering humanity rather than trying to remove all negative social forces, it is a more realistic goal. The moral standard of justice can help distinguish between fixing the world in its totality and the more modest and achievable goal of reshaping political and social institutions to prevent the major crises that are creating so much suffering today.

Justice is the appropriate guide for efforts to shape social institutions so they will support the requirements of human dignity. Here I sketch an understanding of justice that can guide efforts to make some needed institutional changes. Then I suggest implications of this understanding of justice for three aspects of the task of preventing emergencies: reducing conflict, promoting development, and addressing climate change. The approach to justice suggested here can help us redirect institutions and policies to prevent humanitarian crises over the longer term.

JUSTICE AND PREVENTION

Ensuring a basic level of justice both within and among nations is essential to preventing routine political tussles from escalating into full-fledged humanitarian crises. The meaning of justice, of course, is complex and often disputed.[5] This is true both within nations and cultures and across their boundaries. The relevance of justice to the work of humanitarian organizations is sometimes questioned as well. For example, some humanitarian NGOs see justice as an essentially political norm. They sometimes regard it as a norm governing states and legal institutions rather than NGOs. Thus, their efforts to remain independent of politics lead them to say that they do not "do" justice.[6] These same organizations, however, also say that the norms guiding their work include relief of suffering, meeting basic human needs, providing support for human dignity, and protecting a sustainable environment. These goals, of course, are requirements of justice. Developing an approach to the prevention of crisis will thus require greater clarity about the meaning of justice.

I do not aim to present a grand theory of justice like that of John Rawls; I instead sketch some of the most basic requirements of justice that are relevant to the causes of humanitarian crises. Reaching agreement on these minimal requirements of justice is less demanding than attaining consensus on all that morality requires. The humanitarian movement arose not from a grand theory but from a practical conviction that all persons ought to be treated in ways that respected at least basic or minimal requirements of their humanity. The support that the movement has gained worldwide suggests that the founders of the movement were right in taking this minimalist approach. I proceed from the presupposition that these very basic requirements of humanity are requirements of justice. The aspects of justice highlighted here, I believe, can be seen as reasonable, plausible, and useful, despite disagreements about the fuller obligations of morality.[7]

At the heart of an understanding of justice that is especially relevant to emergencies is the conviction that justice requires treating all persons with the dignity they have as members of the human community. This in turn calls for supporting people's participation as active agents in society.[8] Conversely, the injustices that very often lead to emergencies frequently take the form of exclusion—denying people the active engagement in society they need to live with dignity. The US Conference of Catholic Bishops stressed the importance of social participation for an understanding of justice. Based on their tradition's understanding of the social nature of human beings, the bishops insisted that "basic justice demands the establishment of minimum levels of participation in the life of the human community for all persons." Put negatively, "The ultimate injustice is for a person or group to be treated actively or abandoned passively as if they were non-members of the human race."[9] Other Catholic voices, such as Pope Francis, call such injustice "marginalization"— exclusion from social life and from being able to share in the common good of the human community. Pope Francis argues forcefully that justice requires that we "say no to an economy of exclusion."[10]

That justice requires at least a basic level of participation in social life for all people is supported by secular as well as religious sources. The importance of social participation for human well-being was evident to Aristotle 2,500 years ago when he affirmed that to be human is to be a social animal.[11] Or, to paraphrase John Donne, no man or woman is an island.[12] Persons can achieve their human dignity only in interaction with others in society. More recently the World Bank has emphasized that "making institutions more inclusive" is the best way to prevent societies from descending into crisis.[13] Inclusive institutions that enable people to participate in social interaction to at least a minimal level are required by justice and are a precondition for peace. Thus, the World Bank presupposes that when a society becomes deeply fractured and some of its members are excluded or marginalized, human dignity is jeopardized. In a similar way, when one group dominates another, their common humanity is undermined and the human dignity of those being dominated can be threatened or even destroyed. It is for these reasons that it makes sense to see justice as calling for social inclusion and participation for all persons and for efforts to prevent the exclusion and marginalization of anyone. Human dignity can be realized and sustained only in interaction and relationship with others. Thus, dignity will be violated and injustice done if the reciprocal bonds with others needed to sustain human dignity are weakened and destroyed.

The fragmentation of a society that leads to the exclusion and marginalization of some of its members is a form of injustice that is often at the root of humanitarian emergency. In humanitarian emergencies, the fabric of shared common life is ripped apart, leaving people isolated and vulnerable. Those who are weaker become vulnerable to manipulation and domination by the strong. They are often left with no alternative but to flee. Precisely because they are driven from their homes, displaced people are denied the social and community support needed to attain the minimal requirements of their human dignity. Displaced people are being denied two of the most basic requirements of human dignity: a relationship with others in the community they know as their home and the legal and political protection that is indispensable for personal security. Forced displacement from one's community, by its very nature, is both unjust and a violation of human rights.

These injustices have institutional dimensions that require response. Refugees and internally displaced persons are most often driven from their homes by threats from others with greater power, and this power is frequently deployed through institutions. Forced migrants face the power of states, armies, organized insurgencies, and large economic forces that leave them no alternative but to flee. The uprooting of forced migrants is both a symptom and a consequence of the way their societies have been fractured and have become exclusionary. The most basic requirement of justice therefore requires preventing this exclusion. Justice calls for changing the institutions that exert this exclusionary pressure. Put positively, justice requires developing new forms of institutional support for people's capacity to participate actively in society so they can live with dignity.

The injustices suffered by displaced people calls for institutional change. Political, social, and economic institutions must respond more adequately. Some states are failing refugees and other forcibly displaced people in important ways. Indeed, many of the displaced would never have become migrants were it not for the unjust or threatening actions of the government of their own country. In virtually all cases of forced migration, the home states of refugees and internally displaced people (IDPs) are failing to provide a minimum level of protection required by justice, even if their home state has not itself driven them from home. Regrettably, today an increasing number of states that are in a position to assist refugees by providing asylum or resettlement are seeking to avoid the responsibility to do so. In the face of the failures by states, intergovernmental agencies and NGOs can help, but they are not able to prevent forced migration from occurring in the first place. Despite their essential work, these agencies rarely have the political or financial resources needed to assist the displaced in a fully adequate way. Institutional change on the political and economic levels is needed to make relief more adequate. And it is even more essential to take the action needed to prevent the events that make relief necessary.

The effort to address these institutional dimensions of humanitarian crises and displacement is thus a requirement of justice. Justice is not only a personal virtue but a norm that should shape social institutions so that they protect the human dignity of all they affect. The following outlines several kinds of institutional reform and innovation required by the understanding of justice sketched here.

PEACEMAKING AND RECONCILIATION

Reducing the stimuli that contribute to crisis today calls for increased efforts to prevent conflict and to restore and strengthen peace. Longer-term reconciliation of adversaries is also important to keep conflict from recurring. The most common cause of emergencies today is armed conflict and more generalized violence. Reducing the antagonisms that lead to strife is thus important in preventing political or intergroup rivalries from escalating into full-scale humanitarian disasters. Peacemaking and peacebuilding efforts are important contributions to reducing the social pressures that lead to crisis. When overt conflict has been successfully halted, preventing relapse requires finding ways to pull up the roots of antagonism through some form of reconciliation among the adversaries.

Accountability is an important contribution to halting strife and preventing its return. Holding the perpetrators of war crimes accountable for what they have done can both stop them from continuing their abuses and help to deter others from committing such crimes in the future. An example of such accountability is the prosecution of Serbian leaders by the International Criminal Tribunal for the Former Yugoslavia (ICTY) for what they did in Bosnia in the 1990s. The Serbian forces committed serious acts of injustice against Bosnian Muslims in the city of Srebrenica over a period of days. They killed most of the male Muslims in the city, "ethnically cleansed" the women and children by driving them away, and raped many women as well. A number of Serbian political and military leaders were held accountable for genocide and crimes against humanity, including Serbia's president, Slobodan Milošević, who died during his trial, and the commander of the Serbian military, Ratko Mladić, who is now serving a life sentence. Once a disaster of this kind has occurred, nothing can be done to bring back those killed. However, holding those who have organized such abuses accountable for what they have done will help prevent such crises from recurring in the future. Despite the limited range of the accountability achieved for what happened in the former Yugoslavia, the work of the ICTY has made a valuable contribution to peace in the Balkans. The tribunal put those who might be considering a return to conflict on notice that, to the extent possible, the larger world will not again tolerate what was done in Srebrenica. It can be hoped, therefore, that the accountability enforced by the ICTY will contribute to peace both in the Balkans and more broadly as well.

War crimes and other legally actionable offenses have also been committed in both Syria and South Sudan, and those who have organized these crimes should be held accountable. In Syria, the government of Bashar al-Assad has used indiscriminate barrel bombs and chemical weapons against civilians. Opposition forces have attacked civilians, used torture, and committed other human rights abuses.[14] The UN's Independent Commission of Inquiry has accused virtually all groups involved in the Syrian conflict of having committed war crimes and crimes against humanity.[15] War crimes have also been frequent in South Sudan. In addition, both those supporting President Salva Kiir and those on the side of former vice president Riek Machar have corruptly enriched themselves by using public funds for their private well-being rather than for the common good of the country.[16] They, too, should be held accountable. Syria and South Sudan, however, also show the limits of what accountability can achieve.

Efforts to halt and prevent humanitarian emergencies also require strong diplomatic intervention. Action is needed now to compel those guilty of these crimes to stop. Bringing peace to Syria and South Sudan will require broad and simultaneously diplomatic, military, and economic efforts as well as legal action. The international contribution by the Intergovernmental Authority on Development and several Western countries to the 2005 Comprehensive Peace Agreement in the still-unified Sudan implies that such diplomatic efforts can make progress if there is sufficient commitment behind them. Even in Syria, a major diplomatic effort led by the great powers such as the US and Russia, along with regional powers like Iran and the Gulf states, could make a real difference.

Disarmament, demobilization, and reintegration of armed groups and reduction of arms trade could also contribute to halting ongoing conflicts and building peace. Disarmament, of course, can contribute directly to the reduction of violence. It can also demonstrate to those not presently involved in the fighting that armed self-defense is not the only way to protect their safety in the future. Moving forward on such initiatives requires leaders with both diplomatic know-how and moral commitment. Despite these high demands, however, reducing the number of soldiers and arms deployed is essential to preventing emergencies caused by war.

Building institutions of government that the people see as legitimate is also important, especially for emergencies taking place in fragile or failed states. Such legitimacy depends in part on whether the people feel they have a say about the social conditions they face. In particular, a key support for such legitimacy will be the rule of law, which requires that the same standards of justice govern everyone in society and that these standards are both publicly known and publicly accepted.[17] Such shared acceptance gives legitimacy to the way a state governs and makes an important contribution to ending and preventing crises. It helps prevent the chaos that can arise when unjust governance leads those treated unjustly to feel they have no alternative except to rise in resistance or rebellion. Establishing the rule of law is an essential institutional step in halting emergencies and preventing their recurrence.

The rule of law is a key aspect of the liberal democracy of the developed nations of the North Atlantic region. However, Western liberal democracy, in its fullness, may not always be required for legitimate governance. For people suffering under emergency conditions, a regime that treats them with at least the most basic requirements of justice may bring sufficient stability to gain legitimacy in their eyes, even if it is not fully democratic. These minimal requirements of justice include the protection of everyone's right to life and the right of all to have their voice heard in decisions about how they are governed. To borrow John Rawls's language without adopting his entire argument, a society that respects these very basic rights could be called a "decent" society even though it is not a fully democratic one.[18] Rawls asks us to recognize that even though a society may fall short of full Western-style democracy, it can gain some legitimacy in the eyes of its people. This can happen when the people compare the peace and respect that they experience in a decent society with living in the midst of civil war or with no functioning governance at all. The people may, at least implicitly, use their voice to consent to a less than fully democratic regime if it reduces conflict and increases the protection of human life. Such consent would give a government the beginnings of legitimacy, and such legitimacy could in turn enable the government to reduce conflict and take steps that lead to a stronger peace in the future.[19] This kind of minimally just but not fully democratic regime could help bring peace to a conflicted society and could be a significant step toward a more democratic polity in the future. It could make a helpful institutional contribution to halting and preventing a humanitarian emergency.

The deeper attitudes of those in humanitarian crisis also must be addressed if conflict is to be stopped and prevented from returning. Reducing the animosities that both cause conflict and result from conflict calls for both psychological and spiritual change in those involved. Efforts to prevent further conflict must work at a fairly deep level to heal the social wounds caused by conflict and to enable those involved to find a degree of reconciliation with each other. Without at least the beginnings of such reconciliation, conflict would be likely to break out once again.

Christians call such change "conversion"—a movement from animosity to respect or even to the love Jesus required when he commanded his followers to "love your neighbor as yourself" (Mark 12:31). Christians also call this kind of change "reconciliation." Thus, religious communities and religious leaders can make useful contributions to bringing about the needed change in deeper attitudes when those involved in conflict share their beliefs. In addition to these religious dimensions, it has been recognized in recent years that reconciliation has secular relevance. The prime example of its secular significance is the South African Truth and Reconciliation Commission, one of numerous similar bodies established by countries that had faced internal conflict.[20]

Several aspects of the work of these commissions can throw useful light on the prevention of humanitarian crises.

In the work of these commissions, reconciliation has social and even political dimensions. This is evident from the link between reconciliation and the idea of restorative justice. Restorative justice is a forward-looking concept that seeks to put back together a community that has been fractured by past violence or injustice. It seeks to repair relationships by reintegrating into the community those persons and groups who have been unjustly excluded. Restorative justice plays an alternative or a complementary role to retributive justice in the aftermath of conflict. Retributive justice follows the biblical injunction "an eye for an eye, a tooth for a tooth" (Lev. 24:20, Ex. 21:23, Deut. 19:21). The punishment of an injustice should be equal in weight to the harm inflicted on the victim. The call for accountability in the aftermath of grave abuses is frequently an appeal to implement retributive justice by punishing those who have committed the abuse. Ratko Mladić's life sentence for what he did in Bosnia is an example. Restorative justice, on the other hand, seeks the reunification of the community that has been fractured by injustice of conflict. Punishment may not always be necessary for such restoration if other ways to overcome division can be found. When justice is understood as requiring that all citizens share in the life of their community to the degree required for living with dignity, restoring the participation of those who have been excluded will itself bring justice. It will draw those who have been divided from each other back together, reknitting or restoring bonds of mutual respect and support.

Reconciliation is sometimes understood as not only requiring justice but even as depending on forgiveness. In the aftermath of World War II, political philosopher Hannah Arendt argued that although forgiveness is surely important in religion, especially in Christianity, it can also have an indispensable political role. Arendt argued that forgiveness brings the capacity to move beyond an ongoing cycle of tit for tat in political life. Forgiveness can set both victim and perpetrator free of this fate, enabling them to begin again in a new, more productive relationship with each other. Forgiveness can help counteract the danger that a rigorous pursuit of retributive justice will lead to a repetitive cycle of harm and revenge, making peace impossible.[21]

The political role of a kind of forgiveness was on display in the South African Truth and Reconciliation Commission (TRC). The TRC granted amnesty to those who openly acknowledged to the commission and to the public at large the abuses they had committed during the apartheid years. The work of the commission released the new, multiracial government of South Africa from the impossible task of prosecuting all who had committed injustices under apartheid. It freed those who had committed these abuses from the fear that they might suffer such grave penalties under the new regime being established by Nelson Mandela that they should oppose the creation of a new South Africa, even forcefully. At the same time, the requirement that crimes be truthfully acknowledged meant the past was not buried in ways that could lead to a later irruption of angry, unhealed memories into future conflict. Amnesty became a way of giving the new South Africa a fresh start that could help it begin to move beyond the conflicts and injustices of apartheid. Many other countries that have faced serious emergencies have adopted similar commissions as ways of seeking a new start.

Despite the admiration that many rightly have for the TRC, the relation between accountability and forgiveness amid conflict or its aftermath is not a simple affair. In South Africa, for example, the amnesty granted to the worst offenders of the apartheid regime helped bring about peaceful transition to multiracial democracy. However, some who have carefully studied the process have concluded that the spirit of this amnesty gradually evolved from being a tool for obtaining the full truth under the TRC into a spirit that supported impunity, making it possible for some leaders in the post-Mandela governments to become and remain quite corrupt.[22]

Similar concerns about the relation of justice and reconciliation emerged in Uganda when the International Criminal Court (ICC) issued a warrant in 2005 for the arrest of Joseph Kony and other leaders of the Lord's Resistance Army (LRA) who had been wreaking havoc in the north of that country. The ICC wanted to bring the LRA leaders to justice for crimes such as the abduction of children as child soldiers and sex slaves, grotesque murders, and numerous rapes. Following the warrant for his arrest, however, Kony declared that he would not participate in peace negotiations. Thus, some came to see the pursuit of justice through the prosecution of Kony as an obstacle to peace. For example, Archbishop John Baptist Odama of Gulu stated that the ICC indictment "directly works against efforts to end [the] war peacefully."[23] The Ugandan situation raises the question of whether advancing reconciliation may sometimes call for delaying the pursuit of justice, at least for a time. On the other hand, the amnesties granted to political and military leaders in El Salvador following their massive human rights violations delivered neither reconciliation nor justice.

The tension between accountability and reconciliation is very real, and it can call for compromises that might seem morally unacceptable. Nevertheless, the moral virtue of prudence is again essential here. In a prudential perspective, it was appropriate to grant amnesty to those who spoke the truth to the TRC, for this helped South Africa move beyond apartheid peacefully. Subsequently, however, prudence also required holding accountable those officials in the post-Mandela governments who behaved corruptly, even at the highest levels such as that held by President Jacob Zuma. Retributive justice and forgiveness or amnesty do not need to stand in contradiction to each other. Justice and forgiveness can require different actions, at different times, in relation to different persons. Practical wisdom will be essential to judging when full accountability is required and when forgiveness is appropriate. Finding the appropriate balance between the two approaches under the concrete circumstances and at a specific moment is not easy. It is essential, however, in the effort to overcome crisis and to prevent its return. Prudence is the virtue that guides the way.

DEVELOPMENT AND THE ROOTS OF CRISIS

Poverty is one of the root causes of humanitarian crisis. Because of this, preventing humanitarian emergencies calls for efforts to overcome poverty by advancing development. Poverty is also an outcome of humanitarian crisis. Thus, efforts to alleviate poverty must address the harms brought by humanitarian emergencies.

To clarify the relation between development, conflict, and humanitarian relief, it is important to indicate how the term "development" is used here. I follow Amartya Sen in using the term "development" to indicate the expansion of a set of substantive freedoms and values, including attaining enough nutrition to avoid starvation and undernourishment, having resources and health care sufficient to escape premature death, obtaining a level of education at least adequate for literacy and numeracy, and enjoying a level of political participation sufficient to a life of basic freedom.[24] Development, as used here, includes overcoming poverty measured in terms of monetary income. But it also includes more than raising dollar incomes or gross domestic product per capita. The UN Development Programme describes human development as the advancement of "an environment for people, individually and collectively, to develop to their full potential and to have a reasonable chance of leading productive and creative lives that they value."[25] Pope Paul VI's understanding of "integral development" was similar to that of Sen and the UN Development Programme. In Pope Paul's approach, development includes overcoming poverty, but it should not be restricted to economic growth alone. It is the "integral" advancement of "each person and of the whole person."[26] Such advancement includes overcoming poverty, political oppression, and lack of education. At a deeper level, human development is a moral reality; it includes the growth of people's moral commitment to the common good. At its deepest level, Pope Paul's understanding of human development includes growth in love of one's fellow humans and of God.[27] These religious dimensions are centrally important for Christians in their work for development, but in an approach relevant to our pluralistic context, Sen's approach is a helpful guide.

Drawing on these understandings reveals a reciprocal relation between low levels of development and humanitarian crises. Poverty often contributes to the political conflicts that generate humanitarian emergencies, and such emergencies almost always drive more people into poverty. This has led to an increased recognition of the need for coordination between development programs and efforts to bring relief to those suffering in emergencies.

The desirability of linking development and relief is evident from some figures on refugee displacement. Just ten conflicts, taken together, caused more than 50 percent of the forced migration in every year since 1991. Many of these conflicts are in very poor countries, including Afghanistan, Sudan, South Sudan, Somalia, the Democratic Republic of Congo, Nigeria, Pakistan, and Myanmar. In 2016 developing countries were hosting a disproportionate share of the world's refugees—89 percent of the world's total. The six richest nations, however, were hosting only 9 percent of the worldwide number of refugees.[28]

These realities have led the World Bank to recognize that its efforts to alleviate poverty and advance development now need to include programs specifically designed to assist forcibly displaced persons. People who have been driven from their homes have experienced catastrophic losses and very often have no economic resources at all. Frequently they have been traumatized. These losses can affect their ability to take advantage of the opportunities available in their new homes, making them further vulnerable to poverty. Standard development efforts are often not adequate to address the poverty of the displaced. Forced migrants may need special forms of health services due to the trauma they have faced. They frequently need special educational assistance for their children, such as teaching them a new language. In contexts where there are many refugees and IDPs, development efforts should include targeted efforts to help them escape poverty.[29]

Because most refugees and IDPs are in countries that are themselves very poor, their hosts rarely have the resources to respond adequately to their needs. Development assistance, therefore, should directly assist displaced people through health care, education, and other programs targeted on the special needs of the displaced. Such assistance should also aim to enable displaced people to use their initiative and skills to help themselves and move toward self-reliance. Since freedom and agency are essential aspects of full human development, programs should support the self-reliance of those they assist, not reduce them to passive recipients of aid. This means both development and relief efforts should facilitate access to the labor market and foster economic inclusion.[30] This, in turn, helps the displaced get jobs and supports their freedom of movement to go where the jobs are. This both reduces poverty among the displaced and advances the development of the communities where they are present.

Such efforts are called for by the moral requirements of justice. As I have argued earlier, justice requires enabling all persons to attain at least the minimal level of participation in social life required to sustain their human dignity. Many refugees and internally displaced lack the resources needed for such participation. They are in danger of falling through the cracks of communities fractured by conflict. Enabling the displaced to participate in social life through work and active engagement in public life is essential to restoring their dignity. Such increased public participation by refugees also benefits host communities, for it enables the displaced to contribute to the common good of the communities where they reside.

The countries surrounding Syria and South Sudan are particularly in need of assistance due to the huge numbers of refugees they have received. In mid-2018 Jordan was hosting 666,000 Syrian refugees, and the very poor country of Uganda had received over a million displaced South Sudanese. Jordan has been remarkably open to receiving the Syrians in flight, and Uganda has been particularly ready to allow South Sudanese refugees to work and acquire land. Both countries have responded generously to the requirements of justice by welcoming so many displaced people. But there are limits to how far this can go. Both host countries surely need help if they are to remain open to those fleeing disastrous conditions. The World Bank recognizes this and is providing some of the assistance needed.

In Uganda, however, the current Yoweri Museveni government often restricts the human rights of its political opponents. These restrictions impede the integral development advocated by both Sen and Pope Paul VI. This has led the World Bank and other agencies to ask whether assistance to Uganda through its government will really promote development. Thus, the World

Bank has been pressing the Ugandan regime to clean up its act by showing greater respect for human rights of all its citizens. The Uganda case shows that political repression can impede efforts both to promote development and to respond to humanitarian needs. Nevertheless, the needs are so great that these political challenges must be grappled with, which the World Bank is seeking to do. It is pressing the government in Kampala to change so that its restrictions on human rights do not short-circuit the response to the needs of the poor in Uganda, including the refugees from South Sudan. Thus, the link between development and relief can be complicated. This linkage calls for economic initiatives that respond to poverty in effective ways and for political wisdom concerning how to respond to a government whose human rights policies are inadequate. Assisting the displaced requires practical wisdom or prudence, the virtue that synthesizes political insight into what will work with moral devotion to human dignity and well-being. This is a daunting challenge. Nevertheless, with the needed commitment to justice and the required practical wisdom, development policies that relieve the suffering of the displaced are possible.

An additional aspect of the link between development and prevention of humanitarian crisis arises from the fact that poverty can be not only a result of conflict but, in some circumstances, one of the causes of conflict. Paul Collier, a specialist on African economies, has concluded that a country with low income, low growth, and high economic dependence on primary commodities like oil or diamonds is more likely to fall into civil war than are better off countries. Since war is the most common cause of humanitarian emergencies and displacement, Collier's data suggest that poverty also brings about crisis and displacement. Low or declining economic growth also increases the chance of civil war. If the initial income of a developing country is cut in half, its risk of civil war will be doubled. Put positively, each percentage point of growth reduces a developing country's chance of civil war by 1 percent. Thus, if a country's economy grows by 3 percent over five years, the likelihood that it will experience civil war during that period declines from 14 to 11 percent, and if its economy declines by 3 percent, the chance of war increases to 16 percent. The chance of war is further increased by the so-called resource curse, the dependence of the economy on the lucrative export of resources like oil or diamonds, where profits can easily be used by those in power to keep themselves there—by force, if necessary.[31]

War consumes resources and impedes growth, of course, creating a vicious circle where conflict leads to deeper poverty and poverty in turn stimulates further war. Collier calls this the "conflict trap."[32] He is careful to point out that the existence of poverty does not tell us if a particular country will experience war at any particular moment. But he is convinced that the overall structural pattern in poor countries leads to a reciprocal relation between poverty and conflict, and he backs up his conclusion with empirical data. Collier's argument suggests that reducing the number and intensity of the humanitarian emergencies can be helped by reducing the poverty of the countries where they occur.

Consider the situation of El Salvador today. As noted in chapter 7, there has been strong controversy about the United States' responsibility to admit migrants from El Salvador who are claiming the right to asylum because of gang violence in their country. The Trump administration has denied these asylum claims and has taken the extraordinary step of separating children from their parents at the US border to deter additional Salvadorans from seeking asylum in the US. The US government also decided that beginning on September 9, 2019, it would begin deporting the 195,000 Salvadorans already admitted to the US with "temporary protected status" after the 2001 earthquake in their country.[33] In announcing the withdrawal of temporary protected status, the Secretary of Homeland Security Kirstjen Nielsen stated that the conditions caused by the earthquake that justified admitting Salvadorans no longer existed. Thus, the US both denied that the danger of gang warfare was serious enough to justify granting Salvadorans asylum as refugees and maintained that the country is safe enough to send home a very large number of Salvadorans previously granted protection.

An excellent study by Micaela Sviatschi, of both the International Crisis Group and Princeton University, has challenged the presuppositions of these changes in US policy. Quantitative analysis of official statistics on violence and migration and fieldwork across the country lead Sviatschi to conclude that El Salvador is in a state of humanitarian crisis.[34] She argues that conflict has created large numbers of internally displaced persons within El Salvador and is leading many refugees and asylum seekers to flee the country and head north. The violence has several causes. It is partly the result of the failure of the United States to help El Salvador recover from the 1980–92 civil war that the US had helped to fund. The civil war led to the deaths of more than 75,000 people and displaced about 25 percent of the population, many to the United States. Putting the country back together after the war required more resources than were available within El Salvador itself. El Salvador's poverty thus kept crisis conditions going. The crisis is also partly due to the deportation back to El Salvador of Salvadoran youths who came to the US with their families seeking security and who became part of gangs while in the US. These deportees took gang conflict back to El Salvador with them, causing much of the conflict there today. Finally, El Salvador has not received the development support needed to address the gang conflict that today makes the country one of the most dangerous places on earth. Reducing the gang warfare will depend in part on reducing poverty, improving education, and increasing opportunities for productive work. Regrettably, the US plan to deport nearly two hundred thousand additional Salvadoran immigrants back to their home country goes in the opposite direction of what is needed. Such deportations will intensify the humanitarian crisis in the country, for youth deported to El Salvador will be prime candidates for recruitment by the gangs.

What is needed to address El Salvador's humanitarian crisis over the longer term is quite similar to what both Sen and the Catholic tradition see as essential dimensions of integral development. Donor countries, international organizations, and NGOs should support development programs that generate jobs and improve education, especially for marginalized groups. Such actions can help reduce the poverty and lack of education that often lead young males to join gangs. The government of El Salvador should also undertake programs to provide job skills and employment opportunities to youth. Such programs should work with NGOs and the church to reintegrate members of gangs into society. The Salvadoran government should commit resources to strengthening police training and to ensuring that those suspected of abuse or corruption are held accountable. Both the government and international agencies should invest in strengthening institutions of law enforcement and violence prevention. These steps will increase the possibility that present gang members will see they can improve their lives by moving from gang activity to economically productive work. These steps will help violent youth gain new hope and lead them to work that will improve both their own lives and the life of their communities.

El Salvador thus illustrates some of the ways that development can address the roots of humanitarian crises. Development-oriented efforts can help reduce the gang strife that is creating so many IDPs in El Salvador and leading so many to flee the country as refugees and asylum seekers. If the United States wants fewer Salvadoran asylum seekers at its border, it should address the reasons they migrate. This will take time, of course, as do most efforts for social change that are based on commitment to moral values. If Collier is right, however, the commitment can be expected to have a positive payoff. For the United States, development efforts in El Salvador will help reduce the migratory pressure on its southern border.

CLIMATE CHANGE AND FORCED MIGRATION

An additional structural pressure that is having increasing humanitarian effects is climate change. There is a scientific consensus that climate change is occurring and is due to human activity. The conclusions of the Intergovernmental Panel on Climate Change are representative of this consensus. Its *2014 Synthetic Report* highlights several points as particularly relevant for policy-makers.[35] The warming of the climate system is unequivocally real, and many of the changes observed since the 1950s are unprecedented. These changes are creating new risks for both natural and human systems and are amplifying existing risks that already endanger human and natural systems. Some of the risks arise from slowly occurring changes, such as increasing temperatures on the earth's surface, melting glaciers, and rising sea levels. Rapid-onset events, such as hurricanes and floods, bring on other emergencies. Climate change will intensify the pressures that lead to massive human displacement. Thus, the 2015 Paris Agreement on climate change highlights the need for "integrated approaches to avert, minimize and address displacement related to the adverse impacts of climate change."[36]

The harmful effects of environmental changes are usually distributed unevenly, with more harmful effects very often falling on disadvantaged people.[37] In his influential encyclical on environmental justice, Pope Francis has pointed out that developing countries face the most harmful effects of climate change. Poorer countries lack the financial resources to adapt to climate change and to address harmful effects of climate change on the physical environment and on human well-being. Francis insists, therefore, that we "must integrate questions of justice in debates on the environment, so as to hear both the cry of the earth and the cry of the poor."[38] The pope calls this integration of duties of justice with responsibilities to protect the earth "integral ecology."[39] Such an integrated approach is indispensable in addressing the way climate change increases the pressures forcing people from their homes. To be sure, the broader effects of climate change on the nonhuman world, such as the extinction of many living species, are ethically and religiously important in themselves and must be addressed. The specific concern of this study, however, is response to humanity in crisis, so the focus here is the effects of climate change on human well-being. This narrower focus is justified by its relevance to emergencies in which millions of human lives are at stake.

There are two main ways that climate change can influence the occurrence of humanitarian crises. The first is through direct impact that compels people to move to protect their own physical safety or to sustain their capacity to be economically productive. For example, climate change is accompanied by droughts, floods, and rising sea levels that threaten people in very immediate ways. The second way climate change contributes to emergencies is indirect, such as when environmental problems lead to conflict over land, water, or other resources, and these conflicts in turn harm human communities.

A notable example of climate change directly endangering people is on several small, low-lying islands in the south Pacific region.[40] Island states such as Kiribati and Tuvalu face a "disproportionately high disaster risk" because their coastal populations are exposed to a range of hazards increased by climate change.[41] Rising sea levels are putting pressure on a significant part of their populations to migrate. Most of the islands of Kiribati are less than three meters above sea level, and there is no high ground to which people can move. In Tuvalu the 2015 cyclone Pam displaced half of the population.[42] These island communities are among the least developed in the world. They have among the lowest carbon emissions rates in the world. Thus, the actions of other nations, especially rich, highly developed countries, are the source of most of the danger these islands face from rising seas.

Protection of the island people requires humanitarian support that enables them to relocate in ways that preserve their dignity. The desire of the residents to keep their dignity alive amid their necessary movement is clear from their objections to being called refugees.[43] Jane McAdam and Maryanne Loughry report that the islanders think of refugees as people victimized by their own government and as somehow reduced to passivity. They do not see themselves as victims of their own governments since the island governments are not persecuting them. Neither are they passive since they are working vigorously to deal with the environmental challenges they face.

Nevertheless, the people of Kiribati and Tuvalu are facing a genuine crisis brought on by multiple pressures, including lack of education, unemployment, and low economic development. There is no doubt, however, that climate change is one of the important sources of the crisis. Climate change has been a trigger that has sent the other pressures past a tipping point.[44] Due to climate change, the effects of other sources of crisis have been magnified. Although climate change is not the sole cause of the crisis on the islands, the crisis would very likely not be happening in its absence. What is happening on these small islands thus points to the kind of humanitarian challenge raised by climate change in many other settings.

The government in Kiribati recognizes that migration is necessary, perhaps eventually for the whole population, so it is undertaking programs that will prepare the people to move in a gradual way and at the same time keep their culture alive. Island leaders are urging other nations to become ready to receive them. They are also advocating worldwide reduction in carbon emissions, for these emissions are key sources of their plight. Reducing these emissions will require real change in economic and industrial activities worldwide, including changes in ways of life that have become routine in rich, highly developed nations. The plight of the islands indicates that the rich have a stringent responsibility to make the changes needed to protect the dignity and well-being of those most affected by climate change—namely, the economically, politically, and environmentally disadvantaged.

Other much larger countries are facing direct challenges from climate change that are similar to those affecting these small Pacific islands. Bangladesh, for example, is highly vulnerable to climate change. It is a large country with a population of over 160 million people, many of whom live in low-lying, flood-prone coastal areas. The effects of climate change are already magnifying the hazards Bangladesh has faced in the past, such as floods and cyclones. The rise of sea levels due to climate change in future decades will likely put up to 30 percent of Bangladesh's coastal land under water by 2080. If this happens, it will displace up to 18 million people—more than 10 percent of the population of Bangladesh—over the next forty years, chiefly within the country itself. Displacement of this magnitude will reverse the development progress Bangladesh has made over the past several decades. It will also require significantly increased humanitarian assistance for these displaced people.[45] The Pacific islands, therefore, are far from alone as they grapple with the destructive effects of climate change. These small islands and large countries like Bangladesh indicate that ethically responsible humanitarian action requires addressing the causes of climate change.

A second way climate change contributes to humanitarian crises is by stimulating conflict and war, which in turn lead to emergency conditions. A case of such indirect linkage between climate change and humanitarian emergency occurred in the Darfur region of Sudan in 2003 when a conflict broke out between black African farmers in the southern part of Darfur and Arab-identified, cattle-herding pastoralists in the north of Darfur. The herders were supported by a militia known as Janjaweed, which was itself backed by Sudan's government in Khartoum. The Janjaweed attacked civilians indiscriminately in an ethnically targeted campaign with racial overtones that produced high levels of forced displacement, taking 300,000 lives and creating 2.7 million IDPs and 250,000 refugees.[46] Because of the savagery and indiscriminate nature of the conflict, the International Criminal Court charged Omar al-Bashir, the president of Sudan, with war crimes, crimes against humanity, and genocide. This was the first time the ICC sought the arrest of a sitting head of state.

Climate change played a role in the occurrence of this tragic conflict. Ban Ki-moon, who as secretary-general of the United Nations worked to mediate peace in Darfur, wrote that the Darfur conflict arose at least partly from climate change. He noted that since the early 1980s rainfall had declined in Darfur by 40 percent. The drop in the rains coincided with the rising temperature of the Indian Ocean and the disruption of seasonal monsoons, which had been brought about by larger ecological changes.[47] The decline of rain in Darfur reduced plant growth and led the farmers to fence their land to protect it from the cattle of the pastoralists. This brought about conflict between the northern pastoralists and the southern farmers.

A recent study published by the National Academy of Sciences of the US makes this argument more systematically and extends it to conflict across Africa as a whole.[48] Through quantitative studies of changes in temperature and of the occurrence of war in African countries between 1981 and 2002, the study concluded that an increase in temperature of 1°C over a year led to a 4.5 percent increase in the likelihood of civil war in the same year and a 0.9 percent increase in the following year. When these results were combined with existing forecasts of temperature increases, the study projected that there would be an increase in African armed conflict of roughly 54 percent by 2030, with an additional 393,000 battle deaths if the future wars remain as deadly as those of recent years. The authors conclude that there are significant links between the warming brought about by global climate change and rising risk of civil war in Africa.

An analogous study argues that the ongoing conflict in Syria has been intensified by climate change. There has been a simultaneous rise of the conflict in Syria and a decline in Syria's water supply due to global warming.[49] Water scientist Peter Gleick notes that Syria is known as a "climate change hot spot," where consequences of climate change are particularly intense.[50] In 2006 the region experienced a drought that was one of its worst in almost one thousand years. The drought brought evaporation from reservoirs and loss of water needed for agricultural production. This decline in agricultural and economic productivity inflamed social and political unrest in Syria. Gleick does not maintain that climate change was the sole cause of the

Syrian conflict. He knows that political, religious, and ethnic forces played very important roles in bringing on the crisis. Gleick insists, however, that climate change and the diminishment of the water supply are "influencing factors that contributed to the conflict in Syria."[51] The harshness of drought reduced agricultural and economic productivity, which in turn added to the social and political pressures leading to conflict. Although not the sole cause of the Syrian emergency, climate change has been an important contributing factor.[52]

Darfur, Syria, the Pacific Islands, and Bangladesh all point to ways that climate change intensifies humanitarian crises even if it is not the sole cause. Response to the suffering brought by these emergencies must pay serious attention to ways that environmental factors contribute to them. Some of these responses will be more local and rise from the grass roots, while others will be more at the level of global institutions.

An example of a grassroots environmental movement to reduce conflict is the Green Belt Movement founded by Wangari Maathai in Kenya. The movement aimed to prevent the deforestation that was threatening to bring about the expansion of deserts and reduce agricultural production in Kenya. Maathai saw desertification and the decline of agriculture as leading to conflicts in Africa that are driving many from their homes. In her words, "If we are serious about engendering cultures of peace in Africa, protection and rehabilitation of the environment must be a priority."[53] Maathai translated this into action through the Green Belt Movement's tree-planting campaign. By planting trees, the movement sought to reduce the expansion of the Sahara desert, thus improving agricultural possibilities and decreasing conflict over water and fertile land. Maathai's efforts began in Kenya, spread to other African countries, and led to the planting of over 30 million trees. Maathai won the Nobel Peace Prize for this work and for her other efforts for peace.

It is important to note that while Maathai stresses the contribution of environmental protection to peace, she also insists that environmental responsibility should be linked with the reduction of poverty, the protection of human rights, and the advancement of democracy. In her speech accepting the Nobel Peace Prize, she insisted on the "indivisibility" of sustainable development, democracy, and peace.[54] The Green Belt Movement continues her advocacy on all these fronts.[55] Maathai's work is guided by a vision of what the UN and the World Bank today call "sustainable development" and what the Catholic tradition calls "integral development." Although no one person can effectively overcome the way climate change contributes to humanitarian problems, Maathai's influence has been significant.[56] It indicates that efforts that begin at the grass roots can have some real influence on the causes and contexts that shape humanitarian crises and displacement.

On the global level, the 2015 Paris Agreement on climate change, though far from perfect, is a major achievement in seeking the needed global response to the challenges of climate change. The agreement draws all nations into a common effort. Its central goal is keeping global temperature from rising more than 2 degrees Celsius above preindustrial levels and to work further to keep temperature increase below 1.5 degrees Celsius. It promises increased support for developing countries to assist them in making the needed adaptations. The agreement charts a new course in the global climate effort.[57]

The agreement's goals were not created from above nor were they to be coercively enforced from above. The states party to the agreement committed themselves to their own "nationally determined contributions" to greenhouse gas reductions.[58] Numerous civil society groups from both the Global North and Global South also helped shape the agreement. The Paris Agreement, therefore, has been a promising example of local, regional, and global cooperation for the common good of all peoples. Achieving the needed cooperation, of course, made significant moral demands, so the Paris Agreement is both an important political accomplishment and a moral achievement as well. It promises to reduce some of the environmental pressures that are at the root of many humanitarian emergencies and much of the displacement occurring today. This is why President Donald Trump's decision to withdraw the United States from the agreement is so morally objectionable.

Despite US withdrawal, the agreement remains an important contribution not only to the protection of the environment but also indirectly to the reduction of humanitarian emergencies and displacement. In addition, a significant number of US cities, states, corporations, universities, and faith communities have joined together in a bottom-up movement calling itself We Are Still In.[59] The name signals their desire to counter the decision by the US to pull out of the Paris accord. Members of the movement have pledged to reduce their carbon emissions so that the US meets the Paris Agreement's emission standards despite Trump's withdrawal on the federal level. This movement surely can have significant effect, for the signers of the "We Are Still In" declaration represent agencies with budgets totaling $6.2 trillion, a larger amount than the total economy of any nation other than the US or China. Because of their moral conviction that climate change must be combated, these agencies are making valuable contributions to environmental protection and to humanitarian efforts as well. They are addressing the deeper sources of humanitarian crises and are doing so in a way that promises to have positive effect over the long term.

*　*　*

This book discusses events that have caused much human suffering. The conflicts discussed here have taken millions of human lives and driven many millions of people from their homes. These happenings surely deserve to be called humanitarian crises, for they have put the humanity of huge numbers of people at risk. They gravely threaten the bonds of moral concern among persons, so they put the bond of common humanity that links all people in crisis as well. The suffering addressed here gives us reasons to wonder whether the ethical and religious responsibilities proposed are so idealistic as to be illusory.

History, however, gives us good reason to hope that political realism and power politics do not have the last word on humanity in crisis today. The efforts of faith communities like those mobilized by Bartolomé de las Casas and his Dominican companions helped give rise to the modern humanitarian movement. This humanitarian movement itself has had some remarkable successes despite the incompleteness of its work. Over the past century, normative advocacy by groups like the International Committee of the Red Cross have reduced human suffering by helping to create the standards of the international humanitarian law. Even though the law of war is too frequently violated, the work of the founders of the Red Cross has made a real difference. More recently, the effort to hold nations and their leaders accountable for violating these normative standards has led to the creation of the International Criminal Court. The ICC is still a developing institution, but its very existence puts people on notice that they can be held accountable for abuse of human dignity, especially for humanitarian atrocity.

These historical achievements suggest that ethical and religious standards can have real influence in the effort to help human beings in crisis situations.[60] There are good historical and secular reasons to hope that ethical action and advocacy can help us move in the direction proposed in this book. There are also strong religious reasons for such hope. Religious communities and their members are at work around the world, actively responding to the needs of people facing crisis and seeking to prevent such crises in the future. Religious faith strengthens the hope that change is possible.

Christians know that God's grace and compassionate love have empowered members of their community to address humanitarian crises with effectiveness in the past. That grace and compassionate love are continuing to do so today. By cooperating together, all those who want to overcome the crises that humanity faces today can make a difference.

ENDNOTES

1. THREATS TO HUMANITY

1. For a similar sketch of the threats leading to humanitarian crises, see the United Nations Secretary-General, *One Humanity*, I:3, p. 2.
2. Martin, Weerasinghe, and Taylor, *Humanitarian Crises and Migration*, 5.
3. The International Rescue Committee put the number of deaths in the DRC from 1998 to 2007 at over 5 million, although estimates of the number of fatalities vary. See "Measuring Mortality in the Democratic Republic of Congo," International Rescue Committee, May 1, 2007, https://www.rescue.org/report/mortality-democratic-republic-congo-ongoing-crisis. The UN Office for the Coordination of Humanitarian Affairs (OCHA) estimated that 6.9 million Congolese were in grave need in 2017. See OCHA, *Aperçu des Besoins Humanitaire 2017: République Démocratique du Congo*," December 2016, http://reliefweb.int/sites/reliefweb.int/files/resources/drc_hno_2017.pdf, 4. On the political situation in the DRC today, see Council on Foreign Relations, Global Conflict Tracker, "Violence in the Democratic Republic of Congo," n.d., accessed July 25, 2017, https://www.cfr.org/global/global-conflict-tracker/p32137#!/conflict/violence-in-the-democratic-republic-of-congo.
4. The legal definition of genocide includes all acts "committed with intent to destroy, in whole or in part, a national, ethnical, racial or religious group." See the "Convention on the Prevention and Punishment of the Crime of Genocide," adopted by the UN General Assembly, December 9, 1948, https://treaties.un.org/doc/Publication/UNTS/Volume%2078/volume-78-I-1021-English.pdf. For argument that the Srebrenica massacre met this definition, see the judgment of the International Court of Justice, "Application of the Convention on the Prevention and Punishment of the Crime of Genocide (Bosnia and Herzegovina v. Serbia and Montenegro)," February 26, 2007, https://www.icj-cij.org/en/case/91.
5. For major international assessments of the Rwandan genocide, see United Nations, *Report of the Independent Inquiry*; also the study of the Rwandan genocide prepared by Alison Liebhafsky Des Forges for Human Rights Watch, *Leave None*

to *Tell the Story*, and the report of the organization African Rights, *Rwanda: Death, Despair and Defiance*. For a UN assessment of the Srebrenica massacre, see United Nations Secretary-General, *Report of the Secretary-General pursuant to General Assembly Resolution 53/35*.

6. UN High Commissioner for Human Rights, "Zeid Urges Creation of Hybrid Special Court in Sri Lanka as UN Report Confirms Patterns of Grave Violations," September 16, 2015, http://ohchr.org/EN/NewsEvents/Pages/DisplayNews.aspx?NewsID=16432&LangID=E. See also the UN Secretary-General, *Report of the Secretary-General's Internal Review Panel on United Nations Actions in Sri Lanka*. For a further study that sees Sri Lanka as a failure in protection, see Niland, *Inhumanity and Humanitarian Action*.

7. UN High Commissioner for Refugees, "Syria Emergency," n.d., accessed July 2018, http://www.unhcr.org/en-us/syria-emergency.html.

8. Independent International Commission of Inquiry on the Syrian Arab Republic, *Report of the Independent International Commission of Inquiry on the Syrian Arab Republic*, submitted to the UN Human Rights Council, February 5, 2015, UN document A/HRC/28/69, https://www.refworld.org/docid/54e74b777.html, Conclusions, p. 138.

9. Panel of Experts on South Sudan, "Letter Dated 22 January 2016."

10. Food and Agriculture Organization, "As South Sudan Conflict Escalates, 4.6 Million People at Risk of Severe Food Insecurity," May 29, 2015, http://www.fao.org/news/story/en/item/287907/icode/.

11. United Nations High Commissioner for Refugees (UNHCR), "South Sudan Emergency," n.d., accessed July 2018, http://www.unhcr.org/en-us/south-sudan-emergency.html; and UN OCHA, "UN Humanitarian Chief Urges Parties to Cease Hostilities," 1.

12. UNHCR, *Global Trends: Forced Displacement in 2017*, 1 and 4.

13. Mark Leon Goldberg, "Haiti Three Years On: Facts and Figures from the Earthquake Recovery," *UN Dispatch*, January 11, 2013, http://www.undispatch.com/haiti-three-years-on-facts-and-figures-from-the-earthquake-recovery.

14. For a careful treatment of the relation between environmental issues and migration, see IOM, *IOM Outlook on Migration, Environment, and Climate Change*.

15. See *Foreign Affairs* 96, no. 1 (January/February 2017), issue titled "Out of Order? The Future of the International System," https://www.foreignaffairs.com/issues/2017/96/1, cover and table of contents.

16. Zeid Ra'ad Al Hussein, "The Impossible Diplomacy of Human Rights," lecture given on the occasion of receiving the 2017 Raymond "Jit" Trainor Award for Excellence in the Conduct of Diplomacy, Georgetown University and United States Institute of Peace, February 16, 2017. Both video and text versions of this lecture are at https://isd.georgetown.edu/trainor2017.

17. For a useful overview of these and similar movements, see Judis, *Populist Explosion*.

18. See Mamdani, *Saviors and Survivors*. Mamdani states this charge in his conclusion: "In its present form, the call for justice is really a slogan that masks a big power agenda to recolonize Africa" (300).

19. Donald J. Trump, Inaugural Address, January 20, 2017, Washington, DC, https://www.whitehouse.gov/inaugural-address. For populism in US history, see Kazin, *Populist Persuasion*; and Gerstle, "Contradictory Character of American Nationality," 33–58. For analyses of recent populist movements in other parts of the world, see *Foreign Affairs* 95, no. 6 (November/December 2016), issue titled "The Power of Populism: Marine Le Pen, Fareed Zakaria, Michael Kazin, and Much More," https://www.foreignaffairs.com/issues/2016/95/6.

20. Inglehart and Norris, "Trump, Brexit, and the Rise of Populism."

21. Naomi Klein, "It Was the Democrats' Embrace of Neoliberalism That Won It for Trump," *Guardian*, November 9, 2016, http://www.naomiklein.org/articles/2016/11/it-was-democrats-embrace-neoliberalism-won-it-trump. For a similar analysis, see Frank, *Listen, Liberal*. For a disturbing picture of the economic diminishment of working-class whites in the United States, see Case and Deaton, "Mortality and Morbidity in the 21st Century."

22. Haass, *World in Disarray*, 233.

23. Haass, 227.

24. UN General Assembly, *Report of the United Nations High Commissioner for Refugees: Part II, Global Compact on Refugees*, UN Doc. A/73/12 (Part II), approved December 17, 2018, no. 7, https://www.unhcr.org/gcr/GCR_English.pdf.

25. *Global Compact on Refugees*, no. 4.

2. HUMANITY AS MORAL STANDARD

1. Marx and Engels, *Manifesto of the Communist Party*, Part III, 2, in Marx and Engels, *Basic Writings on Politics and Philosophy*, 35. See also *Oxford English Dictionary*, "humanitarian," meaning 3, http://www.oed.com/view/Entry/89276.

2. Chesterton, *Everlasting Man*, 84, cited in the *Oxford English Dictionary* entry for "humanitarian," cited above, at 3B.

3. Barnett and Weiss, *Humanitarianism Contested*, 9.

4. See "The Fundamental Principles of the International Red Cross and Red Crescent Movement," proclaimed 1965, revised October 31, 1986, on the ICRC website, http://www.icrc.org/eng/resources/documents/red-cross-crescent-movement/fundamental-principles-movement-1986-10-31.htm.

5. See ICRC, "E-briefing: Principles Guiding Humanitarian Action," May 25, 2016, https://www.icrc.org/en/document/e-briefing-principles-guiding-humanitarian-action.

6. Pictet, *Fundamental Principles of the Red Cross: Commentary*, 14.

7. "Fundamental Principles of the International Red Cross and Red Crescent Movement," II, Impartiality.

8. Pictet, "Humanitarian Law," 53.

9. This twofold meaning of humanity is referred to by Didier Fassin and others. See Fassin, *Humanitarian Reason*, 2.

10. Pictet, *Fundamental Principles*, 15.

11. Pictet, 17.

12. See Kant, *Grounding for the Metaphysics of Morals*, 36.
13. United Nations, Universal Declaration of Human Rights, preamble.
14. See article 3 of all four Geneva Conventions (called Common Article 3 because of its appearance in all four conventions), available on the ICRC website: http://www.icrc.org/eng/assets/files/publications/icrc-002-0173.pdf.
15. United Nations, Universal Declaration of Human Rights, Preamble.
16. "Oxfam Purpose and Beliefs," esp. the third and last under "Our Beliefs," on the Oxfam website: http://www.oxfam.org/en/about/what/purpose-and-beliefs.
17. See Slim, "Not Philanthropy but Rights." For an application of a rights-based philosophy at Oxfam, see Offenheiser and Holcombe, "Challenges and Opportunities."
18. "CRS Guiding Principles," http://www.catholicrelief.org/about/guiding-principles.cfm.
19. "CRS Guiding Principles," second principle, "Rights and Responsibilities."
20. "CRS Guiding Principles," preamble.
21. United Nations, Universal Declaration of Human Rights, Art. 2.
22. See UN Human Rights Office of the High Commissioner, International Covenant on Economic, Social and Cultural Rights.
23. "The Fundamental Principles of the Red Cross and Red Crescent," ICRC publication 1996, ref. 0513, p. 2, http://www.icrc.org/eng/assets/files/other/icrc_002_0513.pdf.
24. See "On the Obsolescence of the Concept of Honor," in Berger, Berger, and Kellner, *Homeless Mind*, 83–96.
25. Waldron, *Dignity, Rank, and Rights*, 33.
26. Thomas Aquinas, *Summa theologica*, IIa–IIae, q. 26, On the Order of Love.
27. Pope John XXIII, Radio Television Address of September 11, 1962, cited in Vatican Council II, *Gaudium et spes: Pastoral Constitution on the Church in the Modern World*, no. 69, note 10.
28. Vatican Council II, *Gaudium et spes*, no. 26.
29. Waldron, *Dignity, Rank, and Rights*, 34–35.
30. Pinker, *Better Angels of Our Nature*, chap. 4, esp. 132.
31. For a discussion of these two revolutions, see Pinker, chaps. 4 and 7.
32. Jonathan Glover presents a stark picture of the continuing reality of the suffering of war, oppression, and genocide in the twentieth century in his *Humanity: A Moral History of the 20th Century*.

3. RELIGIOUS TRADITIONS AND HUMANITARIAN RESPONSE

1. Pinker, *Better Angels of Our Nature*, 183.
2. Pinker, 676.
3. Pinker, 677.
4. Stamatov, *Origins of Global Humanitarianism*, esp. chaps. 1 and 2.
5. Stamatov, chaps. 3–5.

6. Montesino's sermon, recorded by Bartolomé de las Casas, *Historia de Las Indias*, in *Obras escogidas*, studio critico y edición por Juan Perez de Tudela Buesco, Madrid: Atlas, 1957–58, vol. 2., col. 176. Cited in Ruston, *Human Rights and the Image of God*, 67.

7. Francisco Vitoria, "On the American Indians," in *Vitoria: Political Writings*, 231–92; and Las Casas, *In Defense of the Indians*.

8. Text recorded by Bartolomé de Las Casas in his *Historia de Las Indias*, translated and quoted in Ruston, *Human Rights and the Image of God*, 67.

9. See Vitoria, "Lectures on Thomas Aquinas," which treats a classic articulation of natural law, Thomas Aquinas's *Treatise on Law* in *Summa Theologiae* I-II, 90–105, in *Vitoria: Political Writings*, 155–204.

10. For a persuasive argument that the sixteenth-century writing of Vitoria, with its appeal to natural law, anticipates modern, universalist ideas of human rights, see Ruston, *Human Rights and the Image of God*, esp. parts 2 and 3, esp. 76–77.

11. Vatican Council II, *Gaudium et Spes*, no. 41.

12. See Huntington, "Religion and the Third Wave."

13. Toft, Philpott, and Shah, *God's Century*, chap. 4, esp. tables 4.1–4.4.

14. See "Our Mission," on the Caritas Internationalis website: http://www.caritas.org/who-we-are/mission/.

15. See "Conflicts and Disasters," on the Caritas Internationalis website: http://www.caritas.org/what-we-do/conflicts-and-disasters/caritas-emergencies/.

16. Vatican Council II, *Dignitatis humanae*, no. 1.

17. Vatican Council II, *Dignitatis humanae*, no. 1.

18. John XXIII, *Pacem in terris*, no. 10; and Vatican Council II, *Gaudium et spes*, no. 22.

19. Aquinas, *Summa contra gentiles*, 116, emphasis added.

20. Vatican Council II, *Dignitatis humanae*, no. 2.

21. Vatican Council II, *Gaudium et spes*, no. 25.

22. Vatican Council II, *Gaudium et spes*, no. 12; see also International Theological Commission, *Communion and Stewardship: Human Persons Created in the Image of God* (2004), www.vatican.va/roman_curia/congregations/cfaith/cti_documents/rc_con_cfaith_doc_20040723_communion-stewardship_en.html.

23. See Christiansen, "Movement, Asylum, Borders"; and Dulles, "Christianity and Humanitarian Action."

24. For reflection on the frequency of the command to love the stranger in normative text of the Hebrew Bible, see Sacks, *Dignity of Difference*, 58–60, and chap. 6.

25. See Plaut, "Jewish Ethics and International Migrations"; and Wechsler, "For the Sake of My Kin and Friends."

26. Sacks, *Dignity of Difference*, 45–66.

27. Sacks, 53.

28. For an excellent treatment of the significance of borders for an Islamic approach to humanitarian intervention, see Hashmi, "Is There an Islamic Ethic of Humanitarian Intervention?"

29. Casewit, "Hijra as History and Metaphor."

30. See Organization of the Islamic Conference, "Enhancing Refugee Protection in the Muslim World."

31. On these practices and the duty of Muslims to perform them, see Krafess, "Influence of Muslim Religion on Humanitarian Aid."

32. Zaat, *Protection of Forced Migrants in Islamic Law*.

33. See Kelsay, *Arguing the Just War in Islam*.

34. See Masud, "Obligation to Migrate."

35. The term "engaged Buddhism" is from Nhất Hạnh, *Interbeing*.

36. *Mahabharata* XX: 113, 8, cited in Sharma, *Hinduism and Human Rights*, 5.

37. See Juergensmeyer, "Hindu Nationalism and Human Rights"; and Mehta, "Hinduism and the Politics of Rights in India."

38. See Queen and King, *Engaged Buddhism*.

39. King, *Socially Engaged Buddhism*, 22–24.

40. See Queen and King, *Engaged Buddhism*; and Appleby, *Ambivalence of the Sacred*, 121–43.

41. "Master Cheng Yen's Jing Si Aphorisms," December 14, 2009, on the Tzu Chi website: http://www.tw.tzuchi.org/en/index.php, under the link "Our Founder."

42. Jing Si Abode English Editorial Team, "The Great Things Love Can Achieve: Typhoon Haiyan (Yolanda) Relief," January 22, 2014, based on Dharma Master Cheng Yen's conversations with visitors in Chinese, on the Tzu Chi website: http://www.tw.tzuchi.org/en/index.php?option=com_content&view=article&id=1191%3Athe-great-things-love-can-achieve-typhoon-haiyan-yolanda-relief&catid=82%3Amiscellaneous&Itemid=326&lang=en.

43. Albuja et al., *Global Overview 2012*, 72. There has also been evidence that Buddhists have initiated conflict with Muslims in Myanmar and that these conflicts have created humanitarian issues. See "Top UN Officials Call for Probe into Latest Violence in Myanmar's Rakhine State," *UN News*, January 23, 2014, http://www.un.org/apps/news/story.asp?NewsID=46987&Cr=myanmar&Cr1=#.UuKEB7ROkdU. The BBC provides some background in "What Is behind Burma's Wave of Religious Violence?" *BBC*, April 4, 2013, http://www.bbc.co.uk/news/world-asia-22023830.

44. King, *Socially Engaged Buddhism*, 83–90.

45. See Walton, *Buddhism, Politics and Political Thought in Myanmar*; and Matthew J. Walton, "Religion and Violence in Myanmar: Sitagu Sayadaw's Case for Mass Killing," *Foreign Affairs*, November 6, 2017, https://www.foreignaffairs.com/articles/burma-myanmar/2017-11-06/religion-and-violence-myanmar.

4. RELIGIOUS ACTION TODAY

1. For a summary of the scriptural texts of the major world religions that affirm the "golden rule" as a key moral norm, see Küng, *Global Ethic*, 98–99.

2. See Barnett, *Empire of Humanity*, 79.

3. Pictet, *Fundamental Principles*, 14.

4. Barnett, *Empire of Humanity*, 49.

5. Ager and Ager, "Faith and the Discourse," 457.

6. See Ferris, "Faith and Humanitarianism," 610–12.

7. McCleary and Barro, "Private Voluntary Organizations," 533.

8. Barnett, *Empire of Humanity*, 17. For helpful studies of some practical ways religion influences engagement in humanitarian action today, see Barnett and Stein, *Sacred Aid*.

9. For a classic presentation of the secularization hypothesis, see Luckmann, *Invisible Religion*.

10. Kepel, *Revenge of God*; Berger, *Desecularization of the World*; and Toft, Philpott, and Shah, *God's Century*.

11. Casanova, *Public Religions in the Modern World*, 5.

12. See Huntington, "Religion and the Third Wave"; and Toft, Philpott, and Shah, *God's Century*, chap. 4.

13. Grim and Finke, *Price of Freedom Denied*, 18–21.

14. See Deng, "Sudan—Civil War and Genocide," 13–21.

15. Two studies of such nonviolent movements in recent politics are Roberts and Ash, *Civil Resistance and Power Politics*; and Chenoweth and Stephan, *Why Civil Resistance Works*.

16. See Appleby, *Ambivalence of the Sacred*.

17. UNHCR, *Partnership Note: On Faith-Based Organizations, Local Faith Communities, and Faith Leaders* (2014), http://www.unhcr.org/en-us/protection/hcdialogue%20/539ef28b9/partnership-note-faith-based-organizations-local-faith-communities-faith.html?query=Affirmations%20for%20Faith%20Leaders, nos. 1.1–1.3.

18. UNHCR, *Welcoming the Stranger: Affirmations for Faith Leaders*, 2013, https://www.unhcr.org/51b6de419.html. This edition of the "affirmations" is in multiple languages.

19. Crisp, "25 Years of Forced Migration," 4–5.

20. Sobrino, *Where Is God?*, 138–41.

21. See Sobrino, 144–46; and Sobrino, *Principle of Mercy*, esp. chap. 3, "The Crucified Peoples." For my own development of this understanding of the cross and its relevance for social struggles today, see my "Social Ethics under the Sign of the Cross," Presidential Address to the Society of Christian Ethics, *Annual of the Society of Christian Ethics* 16 (1996): 3–18.

22. See Walker et al., "Role of Spirituality," 121–23. In addition to providing meaning and the communal support discussed below, Walker and colleagues also see reduction in anxiety and enhancement of resilience through the support provided by communion with the sacred as consequences of faith that are relevant to humanitarian needs. See also Goździak, "Spiritual Emergency Room."

23. Walker et al., "Role of Spirituality," 122–23.

24. See Joseph Hampson, "JRS Accompaniment—A New Way of Being Present?" Thailand: Jesuit Refugee Services, December 6, 2009, https://jrsap.org/Assets/Pray/File/a_new_way_of_being_present.pdf. For a somber warning about how bureaucratic contexts can sometimes distort assistance to displaced people, see Harrell-Bond, "Can Humanitarian Work with Refugees Be Humane?"

25. See Jesuit Refugee Service, *Annual Report* 2017, https://jrs.net/wp-content/uploads/2018/10/AR2017_EN.pdf, 3 and 17.

26. "Mission Statement," on the Catholic Relief Services website, http://crs.org/about/mission-statement/.

27. Kirmani and Khan, "Does Faith Matter?," 1 and 9–10.

28. See Islamic Relief Worldwide's website under Policy, Research and Publications, https://www.islamic-relief.org/publications/.

29. See Cornille, *Im-Possibility of Interreligious Dialogue*, 4–5.

30. See Slim, "Not Philanthropy but Rights."

31. The following discussion of the ethical requirements of love of neighbor is based on the important work of the specialist in Christian ethics, Gene Outka. See his *Agape*, esp. chap. 1 and 8.

32. Outka, *Agape*, 20.

33. Outka, 91 and 309–12. This overlap of egalitarian justice and Christian love is also discussed in illuminating ways by Reinhold Niebuhr, *Nature and Destiny of Man*, chap. 9.

34. For an illuminating discussion of how love can be developmentally awakened to the importance of justice and social structures, based on reflection on response to the apartheid regime in pre-1994 South Africa, see Nolan, *Hope in an Age of Despair*, chap. 4.

5. BORDERS AND SHARED HUMANITY

1. Carens, "Aliens and Citizens"; and Marfleet, *Refugees in a Global Era*, 288–90.

2. Nussbaum, *For Love of Country*, 5. Nussbaum subsequently changed her view on the importance of nation-states, as I note later.

3. Vatican Council II, *Gaudium et spes*, no. 24.

4. Pope Francis, "Visit to Refugees," Mòria Refugee Camp, Lesvos, Greece, April 16, 2016, http://w2.vatican.va/content/francesco/en/speeches/2016/april/documents/papa-francesco_20160416_lesvos-rifugiati.html; and Pope Francis, "Meeting with the People of Lesvos and with the Catholic Community: A Remembering of the Victims of Migration," Lesvos, Greece, April 16, 2016, http://w2.vatican.va/content/francesco/en/speeches/2016/april/documents/papa-francesco_20160416_lesvos-cittadinanza.html. For a fuller record of Pope Francis's teachings on refugees, see Pope Francis, *Stranger and You Welcomed Me*.

5. John XXIII, *Pacem in terris*, no. 25.

6. John XXIII, no. 105.

7. Philpott, *Revolutions in Sovereignty*, esp. chap. 1.

8. UN General Assembly, "Declaration on the Granting of Independence to Colonial Countries and Peoples," General Assembly Resolution 1514 (XV), December 14, 1960. http://www.un.org/en/decolonization/declaration.shtml.

9. Philpott, *Revolutions in Sovereignty*, 41.

10. The phrase is taken from the title of Stanley Hoffmann's fine book, *Duties beyond Borders*.

11. John XXIII, *Pacem in terris*, nos. 135 and 138.

12. Benedict XVI, *Caritas in veritate*, no. 67.

13. John Paul II, *Sollicitudo rei socialis*, no. 26.

14. Kofi A. Annan, "Two Concepts of Sovereignty," *Economist*, September 18, 1999, 49. Annan used virtually the same words in his annual report to the General Assembly on September 20, 1999, press release, SG/SM/7136, https://www.un.org/press/en/1999/19990920.sgsm7136.html.

15. John Paul II, *Centesimus annus*, no. 51.

16. John XXIII, *Pacem in terris*, no. 25.

17. This condemnation is in the Bull issued by Pope Innocent X, *Zelo domus Dei*, November 20, 1648, in Ehler and Morall, *Church and State through the Centuries*, 196. The condemnation is cited in Philpott, *Revolutions in Sovereignty*, 87 and 261. Aspects of the Catholic response to the Westphalian treaties are explored in Ryan, "Catholics and the Peace of Westphalia."

18. For a post–World War II Catholic discussion of the limits on sovereignty, see Maritain, *Man and the State*, esp., chap. 2, "The Concept of Sovereignty," which rejects the idea of state sovereignty altogether (p. 53). For an overview of recent Catholic efforts to hold states accountable to the human rights of their citizens, see Huntington, "Religion and the Third Wave."

19. See Appiah, *Cosmopolitanism*, xiv–xviii.

20. Nussbaum, *Frontiers of Justice*, 255–62. For a similar argument, see Benhabib, *Rights of Others*.

21. Sacks, *Dignity of Difference*, 45–66. See also Uriel Tal, "Structures of Fellowship and Community in Judaism," in *Jewish-Christian Dialogue: Six Years of Christian-Jewish Consultations: The Quest for World Community, Jewish and Christian Perspectives* (Geneva: International Jewish Committee on Interreligious Dialogue and World Council of Churches' Subunit on Dialogue with People of Living Faiths and Ideologies, 1975), 32 and 35.

22. Sacks, *Dignity of Difference*, chap. 3.

23. Pius XI, *Quadragesimo anno*, nos. 79–80.

24. See Coleman, *American Strategic Theology*, 226.

25. John XXIII, *Pacem in terris*, no. 139.

26. John XXIII, nos. 140–41.

27. Consolidated versions of the Treaty on European Union and the Treaty on the Functioning of the European Union, 2012/C 326/01, Title I, art. 5, no. 3, and Protocol no. 2, http://eur-lex.europa.eu/legal-content/EN/TXT/HTML/?uri=CELEX:12012M/TXT&from=EN.

28. See "The Sveriges Riksbank Prize in Economic Sciences in Memory of Alfred Nobel 2009," https://www.nobelprize.org/prizes/economic-sciences/2009/summary/.

29. See Ostrom's speech accepting the Nobel Prize, "Beyond Markets and States," esp. 412–13. Ostrom's major work on these matters is *Governing the Commons*.

30. Ostrom, "Challenge of Common-Pool Resources."
31. See Ostrom, 11.
32. For a classic statement of this development, see Nye and Keohane, "Transnational Relations and World Politics."
33. Slaughter, *New World Order*.
34. Slaughter, *Chessboard and the Web*. I have called the emerging global scene "a network of crisscrossing communities" in my *The Common Good and Christian Ethics*, 229.
35. Slaughter, *New World Order*, 268.

6. RIGHTS AND NEGATIVE DUTIES

1. Office of the High Commissioner for Human Rights, "Zeid Urges Creation of Hybrid Special Court in Sri Lanka as UN report Confirms Patterns of Grave Violations," September 16, 2015, http://ohchr.org/EN/NewsEvents/Pages/DisplayNews.aspx?NewsID=16432&LangID=E. See also the UN Secretary-General, *Report of the Secretary-General's Internal Review Panel*, 35. For a further study that sees Sri Lanka as a failure in protection, see Niland, *Inhumanity and Humanitarian Action*.

2. Simon Adams, *Failure to Protect: Syria and the UN Security Council*, Global Center for the Responsibility to Protect, Occasional Paper Series, no. 5, March 2015, http://www.globalr2p.org/media/files/syriapaper_final.pdf.

3. Report of the Independent International Commission of Inquiry on the Syrian Arab Republic to the UN Human Rights Council, Thirty-Sixth Session, September 11–29, 2017, advance edited version released September 6, 2017, A/HRC/36/55, https://www.ohchr.org/Documents/HRBodies/HRCouncil/CoISyria/A_HRC_36_55_EN.docx.

4. Statement by UN High Commissioner for Human Rights Zeid Ra'ad Al Hussein, "The Syrian Crisis Is Breaking Our World," March 19, 2018, http://www.ohchr.org/EN/NewsEvents/Pages/DisplayNews.aspx?NewsID=22851&LangID=E.

5. UNHCR, Rohingya Emergency, n.d., accessed July 15, 2018, http://www.unhcr.org/en-us/rohingya-emergency.html. See also UNHCR, "100 Days of Horror and Hope: A Timeline of the Rohingya Crisis," December 1, 2017, http://www.unhcr.org/news/stories/2017/12/5a1c313a4/100-days-horror-hope-timeline-rohingya-crisis.html.

6. Statement by Adama Dieng, "United Nations Special Adviser on the Prevention of Genocide, on His Visit to Bangladesh to Assess the Situation of Rohingya Refugees from Myanmar," Dhaka, Bangladesh, March 12, 2018, https://www.un.org/sg/en/content/sg/note-correspondents/2018-03-12/note-correspondents-statement-adama-dieng-united-nations.

7. Interagency Standing Committee Principals, "The Centrality of Protection in Humanitarian Action," December 17, 2013, http://www.refworld.org/docid/52d7915e4.html.

8. "The Protection of Human Rights in Humanitarian Crises: A Joint Background Paper by OHCHR and UNHCR IASC Principals," May 8, 2013, http://www.refworld

.org/docid/537f08744.html. This definition was originally developed by the ICRC. See Sylvie Giossi Caverzasio, *Strengthening Protection in War*.

9. These dimensions of protection are included in the 1951 Convention Relating to the Status of Refugees and Its 1967 Protocol. See articles 17, 21, 22, 26, 33. http://www.unhcr.org/4ec262df9.html.

10. 1951 Convention Relating to the Status of Refugees, Article 1, A (2), http://www.unhcr.org/4ec262df9.html.

11. 1967 Protocol Relating to the Status of Refugees, http://www.unhcr.org/en-us/3b66c2aa10.

12. See Goodwin-Gill and McAdam, *Refugee in International Law*, 49. For a careful overview of the developing legal understanding of refugee status, see 15–47.

13. UNHCR, *World at War*.

14. IDPs have been internationally defined as those "who have been forced or obliged to flee or to leave their homes ... and who have not crossed an internationally recognized State border." OCHA, *Guiding Principles on Internal Displacement*, p. 1, http://www.unhcr.org/43ce1cff2.html.

15. UNHCR, *Global Trends*, 2.

16. Martin, Weerasinghe, and Taylor, *Humanitarian Crises and Migration*, 3.

17. Martin, Weerasinghe, and Taylor, 5.

18. Betts, *Survival Migration*, 23.

19. Zetter, *Protecting Forced Migrants*, sec. 4.1.

20. Zetter, sec. 4.3.

21. Zetter, sec. 4.3.

22. See Luijpen, "Justice as an Anthropological Form of Co-Existence," esp. 180. For approaches that are both similar and interestingly different from this, see also Lyotard, "The Other's Rights"; and Derrida and Dufourmantelle, *Of Hospitality*.

23. This phrase, and some of the analysis that follows, is drawn from Farley, "Feminist Version of Respect for Persons."

24. Farley, 187, 189.

25. That human beings are neither beasts nor gods and should be treated accordingly is a presupposition of ethical politics. See Aristotle, *Politics*, book I, ch. 3 (1253a). Martha Nussbaum takes this as a fundamental presupposition of the "capabilities approach" to ethics in social and economic life that she has developed with Amartya Sen. See, for example, Nussbaum, "Human Capabilities, Female Human Beings," 73.

26. Betts, *Survival Migration*, 23.

27. Shue, *Basic Rights*, 18.

28. Shue, 21, 24, and 71.

29. Guterres, "Global Conflicts and Human Displacement."

30. Duties to refrain from causing serious rights violations can be called negative duties, and duties to protect or assist can be called positive duties. Henry Shue has shown, however, that positive duties should not be understood as less stringent than negative duties. Negative and positive duties are often equally stringent. See Shue, *Basic Rights*, 51–60.

31. This is the implication of the title of Michael Walzer's *Just and Unjust Wars: A Moral Argument with Historical Illustrations*.

32. For overviews of the development of the just war ethic in Christianity, see LeRoy Walters, "Five Classic Just War Theories;" and Hehir, "Just War Ethic and Catholic Theology." For the secular relevance of the ethic today, see Walzer, *Just and Unjust Wars*. For a discussion of whether analogies to just war thought can be found in Islam, see the essays by Tibi, "War and Peace in Islam"; and Hashmi, "Interpreting the Islamic Ethics of War and Peace."

33. See Walzer, *Just and Unjust Wars*, xxx.

34. Walzer, 58–59; and Aquinas, *Summa theologica*, IIa-IIae, q. 64, art. 7.

35. UN General Assembly, Convention on the Prevention and Punishment of the Crime of Genocide, December 9, 1948.

36. See Protocol I, Additional to the Geneva Conventions of August 12, 1949, available through website of the International Committee of the Red Cross, https://www.icrc.org/en/doc/war-and-law/treaties-customary-law/geneva-conventions/overview-geneva-conventions.htm, relating to the Protection of Victims of International Armed Conflicts, June 8, 1977, art. 48, which states that parties to a conflict "shall at all times distinguish between the civilian population and combatants and between civilian objects and military objectives and accordingly shall direct their operations only against military objectives."

37. The language is from Article 7 of the Rome Statute of the International Criminal Court. See also Robertson, *Crimes against Humanity*, 430–39.

38. Human Rights Watch, *South Sudan's New War*, 1, 82, and 83.

39. "Interim Report of the Panel of Experts on South Sudan established pursuant to Security Council resolution 2206 (2015)," November 15, 2016, https://documents-dds-ny.un.org/doc/UNDOC/GEN/N16/350/68/pdf/N1635068.pdf?OpenElement.

40. International Criminal Court, *Rome Statute of the International Criminal Court*, Art. 8, 2, b, xxii.

41. UNHCR, South Sudan Emergency, December 11, 2018, http://www.unhcr.org/en-us/south-sudan-emergency.html.

42. Independent International Commission of Inquiry on the Syrian Arab Republic, *Report of the Independent International Commission of Inquiry on the Syrian Arab Republic*, submitted to the UN Human Rights Council, February 5, 2015, V, Conclusions, no. 135, UN doc no. A/HRC/28/69, https://www.ohchr.org/EN/HRBodies/HRC/RegularSessions/Session28/Documents/A.HRC.28.69_E.doc.

43. International Criminal Court, *Rome Statute of the International Criminal Court*, arts. 5–8.

44. For a discussion of the promising though less-than-perfect record of the ICC, see Bosco, *Rough Justice*.

45. On the relation between the moral and legal norms of armed conflict and the reality of displacement, see Hehir, "Ethics and Policy of War in Light of Displacement."

7. POSITIVE DUTIES AND SHARED RESPONSIBILITY

1. This discussion of the Kew Gardens Principle draws on Simon, Powers, and Gunnemann, *Ethical Investor*, 22–25.

2. For an overview of what has been subsequently been learned about the facts of the case, see Nicolas Lemann, "A Call for Help: What the Kitty Genovese Story Really Means," *New Yorker*, March 10, 2014, https://www.newyorker.com/magazine/2014/03/10/a-call-for-help.

3. This argument has some similarities to Kant's discussion of the relation between perfect and imperfect duties. One has a perfect or precisely specified duty not to kill a nearby innocent person for no good reason. There can also be a duty to come to the aid of a person threatened by circumstances one did not cause. This latter obligation Kant call an imperfect duty—imperfect because its scope and object are not precisely specified and because the person or institution who has the duty to respond needs further specification. See Immanuel Kant, *Grounding for the Metaphysics of Morals*, 30. Amartya Sen draws on both Kant and the Kew Gardens Principle in his discussion of perfect and imperfect obligations to protect rights, in *Idea of Justice*, 372–76.

4. The roles of Belgium and France are more complex. It can be argued that Belgium's colonial role in Rwanda contributed to the ethnic animosities that irrupted in the 1994 genocide, and that France's relation with Juvénal Habyarimana's regime, both before and after it orchestrated the genocide, was a kind of remote and indirect cooperation in the evil that occurred. It is not necessary here to settle the question of Belgian and French complicity.

5. "We Could Have Saved 300,000 Lives in Rwanda," CNBC, July 29, 2013, https://www.cnbc.com/id/100546207.

6. Clinton is quoted in David Remnick, "The Wanderer: Bill Clinton's Quest to Save the World, Reclaim His Legacy—and Elect His Wife," *New Yorker*, September 18, 2006, https://www.newyorker.com/magazine/2006/09/18/the-wanderer-3.

7. Simon, Powers, and Gunnemann, *Ethical Investor*, 23–25.

8. For a helpful discussion of the movement of responsibility from national communities and home governments to more regional or international actors, see Martin, "Rethinking the International Refugee Regime," 28–30. The movement of responsibility from local to international or global actors is governed by the principle of subsidiarity, as discussed in chapter 5 of this book.

9. See the web page of the IGAD Special Envoys for South Sudan: http://southsudan.igad.int/. For a discussion of some of the regional tensions among members of IGAD and possible contributions by the members of IGAD Plus from outside the region, see the International Crisis Group Report, *South Sudan: Keeping Faith with the IGAD Peace Process*, Africa Report No. 228, July 27, 2015, https://d2071andvip0wj.cloudfront.net/228-south-sudan-keeping-faith-with-the-igad-peace-process.pdf.

10. See Kant, *Critique of Pure Reason*, A548/B576, p. 473.

11. Aristotle, *Nicomachean Ethics*, book 6, 1140 a 25–1140 b 30, pp. 152–54.

12. US Customs and Border Protection website, data on Southwest Border Migration FY2018, https://www.cbp.gov/newsroom/stats/sw-border-migration/fy-2018.

13. See Cantor, "Gang Violence as a Cause of Forced Migration."

14. US Department of Justice, "Attorney General Jeff Sessions Delivers Remarks Discussing the Immigration Enforcement Actions of the Trump Administration," San Diego, CA, May 7, 2018, https://www.justice.gov/opa/speech/attorney-general-sessions-delivers-remarks-discussing-immigration-enforcement-actions.

15. See "Transcript: White House Chief of Staff John Kelly's Interview with NPR," *NPR*, May 11, 2018, https://www.npr.org/2018/05/11/610116389/transcript-white-house-chief-of-staff-john-kellys-interview-with-npr.

16. Robert Muggah, "How to Fix Latin America's Homicide Problem," *Conversation*, June 28, 2017, https://theconversation.com/how-to-fix-latin-americas-homicide-problem-79731; see also Robert Muggah, "It's Official: San Salvador Is the Murder Capital of the World," *Los Angeles Times*, March 2, 2016, http://www.latimes.com/opinion/op-ed/la-oe-0302-muggah-el-salvador-crime-20160302-story.html. For an overview of flight from the Northern Triangle to the United States, see Cantor, "Gang Violence as a Cause of Forced Migration," 27–45.

17. "Shining Light on Latin America's Homicide Epidemic," *Economist*, April 5, 2018, https://www.economist.com/briefing/2018/04/05/shining-light-on-latin-americas-homicide-epidemic.

18. Betts, *Survival Migration*.

19. On the right of refugees and asylum seekers to family unity, see Jastram and Newland, "Family Unity and Refugee Protection"; and Nicholson, "Right to Family Life and Family Unity."

20. Anthony Faiola and Nick Miroff, "As Trump Tightens Asylum Rules, Thousands of Venezuelans Find a Warm Welcome in Miami," *Washington Post*, May 18, 20128, https://www.washingtonpost.com/world/national-security/even-as-trump-tightens-asylum-rules-thousands-of-venezuelans-find-a-warm-welcome-in-miami/2018/05/15/5e747fec-52cf-11e8-a551-5b648abe29ef_story.html?utm_term=.2ae59e9885b8.

21. On the legal issues, see Reynolds, "Persecution, Politics and Protection in the United States."

22. Universal Declaration of Human Rights, Art. 14, 1.

23. For discussion of the right to asylum in international legal conventions, see Goodwin-Gill and McAdam, *Refugee in International Law*, 358–65.

24. 1951 Convention Relating to the Status of Refugees, Art. 31, http://www.unhcr.org/en-us/3b66c2aa10. See also Goodwin-Gill and McAdam, *Refugee in International Law*, 384–85.

25. 1951 Convention Relating to the Status of Refugees, Art. 33, 1.

26. 1951 Convention Relating to the Status of Refugees, introductory note, p. 5. See also Goodwin-Gill and McAdam, *Refugee in International Law*, 204.

27. UNHCR, *Global Trends: Forced Displacement 2017*, 2, 3, 13, and 17.

28. UNHCR, Rohingya Emergency, n.d., http://www.unhcr.org/en-us/rohingya-emergency.html.

29. UN General Assembly, New York Declaration for Refugees and Migrants, A/RES/71/1, September 19, 2016, http://www.unhcr.org/57e39d987, 2/24–3/24.

30. United Nations, *Report of the United Nations High Commissioner for Refugees*, para. 14, p. 4.

31. Von Gunter Bannas, "Merkel: 'Wir schaffen das,'" *Frankfurter Allgemeine*, August 31, 2015, http://www.faz.net/aktuell/politik/angela-merkels-sommerpressekonferenz-13778484.html.

32. UNHCR, "Operational Portal, Refugee Situations: Lebanon," n.d., https://data2.unhcr.org/en/situations/syria/location/71; and Oxfam International, "Making Aid Work in Lebanon," April 4, 2018, https://www.oxfam.org/en/research/making-aid-work-lebanon.

33. See UNHCR, *Vulnerability Assessment for Syrian Refugees*.

34. UNHCR, "Operational Portal, Refugee Situations: Syria Regional Refugee Response," https://data2.unhcr.org/en/situations/syria.

35. UNHCR, "South Sudan: Regional Refugee Response Plan," January–December 2018, https://data2.unhcr.org/en/documents/download/63469.

36. Stephen M. Walt, "Don't Give ISIS What It Wants," *Foreign Policy*, November 16, 2015, http://foreignpolicy.com/2015/11/16/dont-give-isis-what-it-wants-united-states-reaction/.

37. Ariane Rummery, "Greater Support in Countries of First Asylum Needed to Stem Refugee Outflows," UNHCR, August 26, 2015, http://www.unhcr.org/55ddd2c86.html.

8. ACTING ACROSS BORDERS

1. *Guiding Principles on Internal Displacement*, 1, "Scope and Purpose," no. 2, http://www.unhcr.org/43ce1cff2.html. The *Guiding Principles* were prepared under the guidance of the representative of the secretary-general on internal displacement, Francis Deng, and were presented to the UN Commission on Human Rights in 1998.

2. Richard Holbrooke, "A Borderline Difference," *Washington Post*, May 8, 2000, http://www.washingtonpost.com/wp-dyn/content/article/2010/12/13/AR2010121305364.html.

3. Internal Displacement Monitoring Centre, *Global Report on Internal Displacement 2018*, esp. v, 5, and 9, http://internal-displacement.org/global-report/grid2018/.

4. World Bank, *Forcibly Displaced*, 18.

5. Internal Displacement Monitoring Centre, *Global Report on Internal Displacement 2018*, v and 17.

6. Stephen O'Brien, Helen Clark, David Miliband, Jan Egeland, and Chaloka Beyani, "Open Letter by the Emergency Relief Coordinator and Co-signatories: 'The Invisible Majority: Helping Internally Displaced People,'" September 22, 2016, https://interagencystandingcommittee.org/system/files/open_letter_the_invisible_majority_helping_idp.pdf.

7. *Guiding Principles on Internal Displacement*, Principle 1.

8. *Guiding Principles on Internal Displacement*, Principle 3.

9. On this conflict, see Goodwin-Gill and McAdam, *Refugee in International Law*, 32–35.

10. Deng has written extensively on the concept of sovereignty as responsibility. See, for example, Deng et al., *Sovereignty as Responsibility*, xvii–xviii.

11. The 2018 Plan of Action, issued to commemorate the twentieth anniversary of the *Guiding Principles*, rightly states that these principles embody the normative emphases of "sovereignty as responsibility." See UNHCR, *20th Anniversary of the Guiding Principles on Internal Displacement: A Plan of Action for Advancing Prevention, Protection and Solutions for Internally Displaced People 2018–2020*, May 23, 2018, http://www.globalprotectioncluster.org/_assets/files/20180523-gp20-plan-of-action-final.pdf, 2.

12. UNHCR, *20th Anniversary of the Guiding Principles*.

13. Mohamed el-Mukhtar Hussein, "Negotiating Peace: The Road to Naivasha," Conciliation Services, *Accord*, no. 18 (2006), http://www.c-r.org/accord/sudan/negotiating-peace-road-naivasha.

14. For an overview of the international diplomacy, see Norwegian minister of international development Hilde F. Johnson's firsthand account of what transpired at Naivasha and elsewhere, *Waging Peace in Sudan*.

15. See Katherine Noel, "Understanding the Roots of Conflict in South Sudan: Interview with Alex de Waal," Council on Foreign Relations, September 14, 2016, https://www.cfr.org/interview/understanding-roots-conflict-south-sudan.

16. Cited in Hertzke, *Freeing God's Children*, 239.

17. See Finnemore and Sikkink, "International Norm Dynamics and Political Change."

18. Agwanda and Harris, "People-to-People Peacemaking and Peacebuilding."

19. United Nations General Assembly, *2005 World Summit Outcome Document*, September 16, 2005, nos. 138–39, https://www.unsystem.org/content/2005-world-summit-outcome-document-16-september-2005.

20. UN General Assembly, *2005 World Summit Outcome Document*, nos. 138–39.

21. Kissinger, *Does America Need a Foreign Policy?*, 271.

22. Mamdani, *Saviors and Survivors*, 300.

23. See Cohen and Deng, "Sovereignty as Responsibility."

24. Benedict XVI, "Address of the Holy Father"; and *Caritas in veritate*, no. 67.

25. Bernardito Auza, *The Responsibility to Protect and Accountability for Prevention*, September 6, 2017, https://holyseemission.org/contents/statements/59b07e40cc3c3.php.

26. Quoted in Roger Cohen, "How Kofi Annan Rescued Kenya," *New York Review of Books* 55, no. 13, August 14, 2008, https://www.nybooks.com/articles/2008/08/14/how-kofi-annan-rescued-kenya/.

27. The International Coalition for the Responsibility to Protect, "II. International Response to Halt the Spread of Violence," http://www.responsibilitytoprotect.org/index.php/crises/crisis-in-kenya.

28. Cohen, "How Kofi Annan Rescued Kenya."

29. See ICISS, *The Responsibility to Protect*, 36–37.
30. UN Security Council, "Resolution 2085 (2012) Stresses Need to Further Refine Military Planning," December 20, 2012, SC/10870, http://www.un.org/press/en/2012/sc10870.doc.htm; and UN Security Council, "Security Council Establishes Peacekeeping Force for Mali Effective 1 July, Unanimously Adopting Resolution 2100 (2013)," April 25, 2013, SC/10987, http://www.un.org/press/en/2013/sc10987.doc.htm.
31. UN Security Council Resolution 2127 (December 5, 2013), http://www.un.org/en/ga/search/view_doc.asp?symbol=S/RES/2127(2013)&referer=.
32. Jon Leyne, "Libya Protests: Defiant Gaddafi Refuses to Quit," *BBC*, February 22, 2011, http://www.bbc.com/news/world-middle-east-12544624.
33. UN Security Council, Resolution 1973 (March 17, 2011), nos. 4 and 6, http://www.un.org/en/ga/search/view_doc.asp?symbol=S/RES/1973%282011%29.
34. Amnesty International, "*Libya Is Full of Cruelty*," 5–6, http://www.amnestyusa.org/research/reports/libya-is-full-of-cruelty-stories-of-abduction-sexual-violence-and-abuse-from-migrants-and-refugees.
35. See Kuperman, "Obama's Libya Debacle."
36. See Chollet and Fishman, "Who Lost Libya."
37. Weiss, "Military Humanitarianism."

9. JUSTICE AND ROOT CAUSES

1. UN General Assembly, *Report of the United Nations High Commissioner for Refugees: Part II, Global Compact on Refugees*, UN Doc. A/73/12 (Part II), approved December 17, 2018, no. 8–9. https://www.unhcr.org/gcr/GCR_English.pdf.
2. UN Secretary-General, *Outcome of the World Humanitarian Summit*, no. 15.
3. World Humanitarian Summit, Core Commitment One, https://www.agendaforhumanity.org/sites/default/files/resources/2018/Jan/core_ommitment_afh.pdf.
4. UN Secretary-General, *Outcome of the World Humanitarian Summit*, no. 17.
5. See, for example, MacIntyre, *Whose Justice?*
6. Rubenstein, *Between Samaritans and States*, 16–17.
7. I have elsewhere presented a more fully developed account of the standards of justice suggested in outline here. See Hollenbach, *Common Good and Christian Ethics*, esp. chap. 6, 7, and 8; Hollenbach, *Global Face of Public Faith*, esp. part 3.
8. For a relational understanding of human dignity relevant to humanitarian action that is similar to that adopted here, see Fast, "Unpacking the Principle of Humanity." Fast's relational approach could be extended to include a more universal solidarity and relationality that ought to exist in the human community as a whole.
9. US Conference of Catholic Bishops, "Economic Justice for All, Pastoral Letter on Catholic Social Teaching and the US Economy," November 1986, in O'Brien and Shannon, *Catholic Social Thought*, no. 77, p. 715.
10. Francis, *Joy of the Gospel*, no. 53.
11. Aristotle, *Politics*, 1.1253a.

12. In John Donne's original words, "No Man is an *Iland*, intire of it selfe; every man is a peece of the *Continent*, a part of the *maine*," in *Devotions upon Emergent Occasions*, 87.

13. World Bank, *Pathways for Peace*, xviii.

14. Ferris and Kirişci, *Consequences of Chaos*, 117–18.

15. See, for example, UN Human Rights Council, "UN Commission of Inquiry on Syria: The Siege and Recapture of Eastern Ghouta Marked by War Crimes, Crimes against Humanity," Geneva, June 20, 2018, https://www.ohchr.org/EN/HRBodies/HRC/Pages/NewsDetail.aspx?NewsID=23226&LangID=E.

16. See Enough Project and Not on Our Watch (NOOW), "Fueling Atrocities: Oil and War in South Sudan," *Sentry*, March 2018, https://thesentry.org/reports/fueling-atrocities/.

17. For fuller discussions of the meaning of the rule of law, see the World Justice Project's discussion of its four principles of the rule of law: accountability, just laws, open government, and accessible and impartial dispute resolution, in "What Is the Rule of Law?" https://worldjusticeproject.org/about-us/overview/what-rule-law.

18. See Rawls, *Law of Peoples*, esp. 64–67.

19. For background to some aspects of the argument suggested here, see Doyle, "The John W. Holmes Lecture." This lecture by Doyle summarizes the fuller study of Doyle and Sambanis, *Making War and Building Peace*.

20. For a helpful study of the achievements of these commissions, see Bakiner, *Truth Commissions*.

21. Arendt, *Human Condition*, 212–19.

22. See Merwe and Lykes, "Transitional Justice Processes," 363.

23. Archbishop Odama is quoted in Apuuli, "The ICC Arrest Warrants," 185.

24. See Sen, *Development as Freedom*, 36. This is a paraphrase of what Sen calls the substantive freedoms that are the end or goal of development.

25. UN Development Programme, "What Is Human Development?" http://hdr.undp.org/en/content/what-human-development.

26. Paul VI, *Populorum progressio*, no. 14. The translation of the original Latin used here is more helpful than the English on the Vatican site.

27. Paul VI, nos. 21 and 22.

28. See UN Development Programme, *Human Development Report 2016*, box 1.5, p. 36; and World Bank, *Forcibly Displaced*, figs. 1.6 and 1.7, p. 21–23. This study by the World Bank was conducted in cooperation with the UN High Commissioner for Refugees.

29. World Bank, *Forcibly Displaced*, 1.

30. Verme et al., *Welfare of Syrian Refugees*, xi. See also Betts and Collier, *Refuge*, chap. 6, "Rethinking Assistance: Restoring Autonomy."

31. Collier, *Bottom Billion*, 19–22. For additional work by Collier on the relation between poverty and civil war, see his *Wars, Guns, and Votes*; and *Conflict, Political Accountability, and Aid*.

32. Collier, *The Bottom Billion*, chap. 2.

33. "Secretary of Homeland Security Kirstjen M. Nielsen Announcement on Temporary Protected Status for El Salvador," January 8, 2018, https://www.dhs.gov/news/2018/01/08/secretary-homeland-security-kirstjen-m-nielsen-announcement-temporary-protected.

34. Sviatschi, *El Salvador's Politics of Perpetual Violence*; and Micaela Sviatschi, "By Deporting 200,000 Salvadorans, Trump May Be Boosting Gang Recruitment," *Washington Post*, February 12, 2018, https://www.washingtonpost.com/news/monkey-cage/wp/2018/02/12/by-deporting-200000-salvadorans-trump-may-be-boosting-gang-recruitment/?utm_term=.74ae03c2f758.

35. Intergovernmental Panel on Climate Change, *Climate Change 2014 Synthesis Report: Summary for Policymakers*, https://www.ipcc.ch/site/assets/uploads/2018/02/AR5_SYR_FINAL_SPM.pdf.

36. United Nations, "Report of the Conference of the Parties on Its Twenty-First Session (COP 21), Held in Paris from 30 November to 13 December 2015," Addendum, part 2, Action Taken by the Conference of the Parties, no. 49, https://unfccc.int/resource/docs/2015/cop21/eng/10a01.pdf.

37. These points are highlighted in Intergovernmental Panel on Climate Change, *Climate Change 2014 Synthesis Report*.

38. Francis, *Laudato si'*, no. 49. See also no. 25.

39. Francis, esp. chap. 4.

40. For an overview of the situation in the low areas of the Asia Pacific region, see Burkett, "In Search of Refuge."

41. Internal Displacement Monitoring Centre and Norwegian Refugee Council, *Global Report on Internal Displacement 2016*, 19.

42. International Organization for Migration, *IOM Strategy in Asia and the Pacific 2017–2020* (Bangkok: IOM, 2017), https://www.iom.int/sites/default/files/country/AP/IOM-Strategy-in-Asia-and-the-Pacific-2017-2020.pdf, 13.

43. See Jane McAdam and Maryanne Loughry, "We Aren't Refugees," *Inside Story: Current Affairs and Culture from Australia and Beyond*, June 30, 2009, http://insidestory.org.au/we-arent-refugees.

44. McAdam and Loughry.

45. For helpful overviews of the threats brought to Bangladesh by climate change, see McAdam, *Climate Change, Forced Migration, and International Law*, chap. 6, "Moving with Dignity: Responding to Climate Change-Related Mobility in Bangladesh," 161–85; and Radelet, *Great Surge*, esp. 270–75.

46. See International Coalition for the Responsibility to Protect, *Crisis in Darfur*, http://www.responsibilitytoprotect.org/index.php/crises/crisis-in-darfur.

47. Ban Ki-moon, "A Climate Culprit in Darfur," *Washington Post*, op-ed, June 16, 2007.

48. Burke et al., "Warming Increases the Risk of Civil War in Africa."

49. See the report on Peter Gleick's presentation at a symposium titled "The Role of Science Diplomacy in International Crises: Syria as a Case Study," organized by the American Association for the Advancement of Science, in Juan David Romero,

"Climate Change Hits Conflict Zones Harder: Syria Case Study," June 10, 2016, on the AAAS website: https://www.aaas.org/news/climate-change-hits-conflict-zones-harder-syria-case-study.

50. Quoted in Romero, "Climate Change Hits Conflict Zones Harder."

51. Quoted in Romero.

52. The contribution of climate change to the Syrian conflict is acknowledged by some of those who have argued against climate change as the sole cause of the conflict. Alex de Waal argues that the Darfur conflict erupted because of political factors, particularly the Sudan government's support of militia groups as proxies to suppress resistance. Nevertheless, he notes that "drought, famine and the social disruptions they brought about made it easier for the government to pursue this strategy." See Alex de Waal, "Is Climate Change the Culprit for Darfur?," *African Arguments* (blog), June 25, 2007, http://africanarguments.org/2007/06/25/is-climate-change-the-culprit-for-darfur.

53. Maathai, *Challenge for Africa*, 249.

54. Maathai, Nobel Lecture.

55. See "Mainstream Advocacy" on website of the Green Belt Movement, http://www.greenbeltmovement.org/what-we-do/advocacy.

56. Her influence is indicated by her many awards, which include being named to the United Nations Environment Programme's Global 500 Hall of Fame and being elected by *Earth Times* as one of one hundred persons in the world who have made a difference in the environmental arena. See Maathai's biography on the Nobel Prize website, https://www.nobelprize.org/nobel_prizes/peace/laureates/2004/maathai-bio.html.

57. The text of the Paris Agreement is available on the website of the United Nations Framework Convention on Climate Change (UNFCCC), https://unfccc.int/sites/default/files/english_paris_agreement.pdf.

58. Paris Agreement, art. 4, para. 2.

59. See the We Are Still In website: https://www.wearestillin.com/.

60. On the effective influence of "normative entrepreneurs" on human rights and other normative dimensions of international affairs, see Finnemore and Sikkink, "International Norm Dynamics and Political Change"; and Sikkink, *Evidence for Hope*.

BIBLIOGRAPHY

African Rights. *Rwanda: Death, Despair, Defiance*. 2nd ed. London: African Rights, 1995.

Ager, Alastair, and Joey Ager. "Faith and the Discourse of Secular Humanitarianism." *Journal of Refugee Studies* 24, no. 3 (September 1, 2011): 456–72.

Agwanda, Titus, and Geoff Harris. "People-to-People Peacemaking and Peacebuilding: A Review of the Work of the New Sudan Council of Churches." *African Security Review* 18, no. 2 (June 1, 2009): 42–52.

Albuja, Sebastian, Emilie Arnaud, Fran Beytrison, Martina Caterina, Guillaume Charron, Urs Fruehauf, Anne-Kathrin Glatz, et al. *Global Overview 2012: People Internally Displaced by Violence and Conflict*. Internal Displacement Monitoring Center, April 2013. http://www.internal-displacement.org/sites/default/files/publications/documents/2012-global-overview-corporate-en.pdf.

Amnesty International. *"Libya Is Full of Cruelty": Stories of Abductions, Sexual Violence and Abuse from Migrants and Refugees*. London: Amnesty International, 2015: 5–6, http://www.amnestyusa.org/research/reports/libya-is-full-of-cruelty-stories-of-abduction-sexual-violence-and-abuse-from-migrants-and-refugees.

Appiah, Anthony. *Cosmopolitanism: Ethics in a World of Strangers*. Issues of Our Time. New York: Norton, 2006.

Appleby, R. Scott. *The Ambivalence of the Sacred: Religion, Violence, and Reconciliation*. Lanham, MD: Rowman & Littlefield, 2000.

Apuuli, Kasaija Phillip. "The ICC Arrest Warrants for the Lord's Resistance Army Leaders and Peace Prospects in Northern Uganda." *Journal of International Criminal Justice* 4 (2006): 179–87.

Aquinas, Thomas. *Summa contra gentiles*. Translated by Vernon J. Bourke. Notre Dame, IN: University of Notre Dame Press, 1975.

Arendt, Hannah. *The Human Condition*. 2nd ed. Chicago: University of Chicago Press, 1998.

Aristotle. *Nicomachean Ethics*, translated by Martin Ostwald. Indianapolis: Bobbs-Merrill, 1962.

———. *Politics*. Trans. Benjamin Jowett. In *The Basic Works of Aristotle*, ed. Richard McKeon. New York: Random House, 1941.

Bakiner, Onur. *Truth Commissions: Memory, Power, and Legitimacy*. Pennsylvania Studies in Human Rights. Philadelphia: University of Pennsylvania Press, 2016.

Banchoff, Thomas F., and Robert Wuthnow, eds. *Religion and the Global Politics of Human Rights*. New York: Oxford University Press, 2011.

Barnett, Michael N. *Empire of Humanity: A History of Humanitarianism*. Ithaca, NY: Cornell University Press, 2013.

Barnett, Michael N., and Janice Gross Stein, eds. *Sacred Aid: Faith and Humanitarianism*. New York: Oxford University Press, 2012.

Barnett, Michael N., and Thomas G. Weiss. *Humanitarianism Contested: Where Angels Fear to Tread*. New York: Routledge, 2011.

Benedict XVI. "Address of the Holy Father to the General Assembly of the United Nations Organization in New York." April 18, 2008. Libreria Editrice Vaticana. http://w2.vatican.va/content/benedict-xvi/en/speeches/2008/april/documents/hf_ben-xvi_spe_20080418_un-visit.html.

———. *Caritas in veritate*. Encyclical of June 29, 2009. Libreria Editrice Vaticana. http://w2.vatican.va/content/benedict-xvi/en/encyclicals/documents/hf_ben-xvi_enc_20090629_caritas-in-veritate.html.

Benhabib, Seyla. *The Rights of Others: Aliens, Residents and Citizens*. New York: Cambridge University Press, 2004.

Berger, Peter L., ed. *The Desecularization of the World: Resurgent Religion and World Politics*. Washington, DC: Ethics and Public Policy Center; Grand Rapids, MI: Eerdmans, 1999.

Berger, Peter L., Brigitte Berger, and Hansfried Kellner. *The Homeless Mind: Modernization and Consciousness*. New York: Vintage, 1974.

Betts, Alexander. *Survival Migration: Failed Governance and the Crisis of Displacement*. Ithaca, NY: Cornell University Press, 2013.

Betts, Alexander, and Paul Collier. *Refuge: Rethinking Refugee Policy in a Changing World*. New York: Oxford University Press, 2017.

Bosco, David L. *Rough Justice: The International Criminal Court in a World of Power Politics*. Oxford: Oxford University Press, 2014.

Burke, Marshall B., Edward Miguel, Shanker Satyanath, John A. Dykema, and David B. Lobell. "Warming Increases the Risk of Civil War in Africa." *Proceedings of the National Academy of Sciences* 106, no. 49 (December 8, 2009): 20670–74.

Burkett, Maxine. "In Search of Refuge: Pacific Islands, Climate-Induced Migration, and the Legal Frontier." *Asia Pacific Issues*, Analysis from the East-West Center, no. 98 (January 2011): 1–8. https://ssrn.com/abstract=1754222.

Cantor, David James. "Gang Violence as a Cause of Forced Migration in the Northern Triangle of Central America." In *The New Refugees: Crime and Displacement in Latin America*, edited by David James Cantor and Serna N. Rodriguez, 27–45. London: University of London, 2016.

Carens, Joseph H. "Aliens and Citizens: The Case for Open Borders." *Review of Politics* 49, no. 2 (March 1987): 251–73.

Casanova, José. *Public Religions in the Modern World.* Chicago: University of Chicago Press, 1994.
Case, Anne, and Angus Deaton. "Mortality and Morbidity in the 21st Century." *Brookings Papers on Economic Activity,* no. 1 (Spring 2017): 397–476.
Casewit, Daoud S. "Hijra as History and Metaphor: A Survey of Qur'anic and Hadith Sources." *Muslim World* 88, no. 2 (1998): 105–28.
Caverzasio, Sylvie Giossi. *Strengthening Protection in War: A Search of Professional Standards.* Geneva: ICRC, 2001.
Chenoweth, Erica, and Maria J. Stephan. *Why Civil Resistance Works: The Strategic Logic of Nonviolent Conflict.* New York: Columbia University Press, 2013.
Chesterton, G. K. *The Everlasting Man.* New York: Dodd, Mead & Co., 1925. Reprint, Westport, CT: Greenwood Press, 1974.
Chollet, Derek, and Ben Fishman. "Who Lost Libya: Obama's Intervention in Retrospect, a Close Call." *Foreign Affairs* 94, no. 3 (May–June 2015): 154–57.
Christiansen, Drew. "Movement, Asylum, Borders: Christian Perspectives." *International Migration Review* 30, no. 1 (1996): 7–11.
Cohen, Roberta, and Francis M. Deng. "Sovereignty as Responsibility: Building Block for R2P." In *The Oxford Handbook of the Responsibility to Protect,* edited by Alex J. Bellamy and Tim Dunne, 74–93. Oxford: Oxford University Press, 2016.
Coleman, John Aloysius. *An American Strategic Theology.* Eugene, OR: Wipf and Stock, 2005.
Collier, Paul. *The Bottom Billion: Why the Poorest Countries Are Failing and What Can Be Done about It.* New York: Oxford University Press, 2008.
———. *Conflict, Political Accountability, and Aid.* New York: Routledge, 2011.
———. *Wars, Guns and Votes: Democracy in Dangerous Places.* New York: Harper Perennial, 2010.
Cornille, Catherine. *The Im-Possibility of Interreligious Dialogue.* New York: Crossroad, 2008.
Crisp, Jeff. "25 Years of Forced Migration." *Forced Migration Review,* 25th Anniversary Collection, November 2012. https://www.fmreview.org/sites/fmr/files/FMRdownloads/en/25th-anniversary/crisp.pdf.
de Waal, Alex. "Is Climate Change the Culprit for Darfur?" *African Arguments* (blog), June 25, 2007. https://africanarguments.org/2007/06/25/is-climate-change-the-culprit-for-darfur/.
Deng, Francis Mading. "Sudan—Civil War and Genocide." *Middle East Quarterly* 8, no. 1 (Winter 2001): 13–21.
Deng, Francis M., Sadikiel Kimaro, Terrence Lyons, Donald Rothchild, and I. William Zartman. *Sovereignty as Responsibility: Conflict Management in Africa.* Washington, DC: Brookings Institution, 1996.
Derrida, Jacques, and Anne Dufourmantelle. *Of Hospitality: Anne Dufourmantelle Invites Jacques Derrida to Respond,* translated by Rachel Bowlby. Cultural Memory in the Present. Stanford, CA: Stanford University Press, 2000.
Des Forges, Alison Liebhafsky. *Leave None to Tell the Story: Genocide in Rwanda.* New York: Human Rights Watch, March 1999. https://www.hrw.org/reports/1999/rwanda/.

Donne, John. *Devotions upon Emergent Occasions, and Death's Duel*. Vintage Spiritual Classics. New York: Vintage, 1999.

Doyle, Michael W. "The John W. Holmes Lecture: Building Peace." *Global Governance* 13, no. 1 (January–March 2007): 1–15.

Doyle, Michael W., and Nicholas Sambanis. *Making War and Building Peace: United Nations Peace Operations*. Princeton, NJ: Princeton University Press, 2006.

Dulles, Avery. "Christianity and Humanitarian Action." In *Traditions, Values, and Humanitarian Action*, edited by Kevin Cahill, 5–20. New York: Fordham University Press and Center for International Health and Cooperation, 2003.

Ehler, Sidney Zdeneck, and John Brimyard Morrall. *Church and State through the Centuries: A Collection of Historic Documents with Commentaries*. New York: Biblio and Tannen, 1988.

Farley, Margaret A. "A Feminist Version of Respect for Persons." *Journal of Feminist Studies in Religion* 9, no. 1–2 (Spring–Fall 1993): 183–98.

Fassin, Didier. *Humanitarian Reason: A Moral History of the Present Times*. Berkeley: University of California Press, 2012.

Fast, Larissa. "Unpacking the Principle of Humanity: Tensions and Implications." *International Review of the Red Cross* 97, no. 897–898 (June 2015): 111–31.

Ferris, Elizabeth. "Faith and Humanitarianism: It's Complicated." *Journal of Refugee Studies* 24, no. 3 (2011): 606–25.

Ferris, Elizabeth G., and Kemal Kirişci. *The Consequences of Chaos: Syria's Humanitarian Crisis and the Failure to Protect*. Washington, DC: Brookings Institution Press, 2016.

Finnemore, Martha, and Kathryn Sikkink. "International Norm Dynamics and Political Change." *International Organization* 52, no. 4 (October 1, 1998): 887–917.

Francis. "Meeting with the People of Lesvos and with the Catholic Community: A Remembering of the Victims of Migration." April 16, 2016. http://w2.vatican.va/content/francesco/en/speeches/2016/april/documents/papa-francesco_20160416_lesvos-cittadinanza.html.

———. *The Joy of the Gospel: Evangelii Gaudium: Apostolic Exhortation*. Vatican City: Libreria Editrice Vaticana, 2013.

———. *Laudato si.'* Encyclical of May 24, 2015. http://w2.vatican.va/content/francesco/en/encyclicals/documents/papa-francesco_20150524_enciclica-laudato-si.html.

———. *A Stranger and You Welcomed Me: A Call to Mercy and Solidarity with Migrants and Refugees*. Edited by Robert Ellsberg. Maryknoll, NY: Orbis Books, 2018.

Frank, Thomas. *Listen, Liberal, or, What Ever Happened to the Party of the People?* New York: Metropolitan, 2016.

Gerstle, Gary. "The Contradictory Character of American Nationality: A Historical Perspective." In *Fear, Anxiety, and National Identity: Immigration and Belonging in North America and Western Europe*. Edited by Nancy Foner and Patrick Simon. New York: Russell Sage Foundation, 2015. e-book.

Glover, Jonathan. *Humanity: A Moral History of the Twentieth Century*. 2nd ed. New Haven, CT: Yale University Press, 2012.

Goodwin-Gill, Guy S., and Jane McAdam. *The Refugee in International Law*. 3rd ed. New York: Oxford University Press, 2007.

Goździak, Elżbieta M. "Spiritual Emergency Room: The Role of Spirituality and Religion in the Resettlement of Kosovar Albanians." *Journal of Refugee Studies* 15, no. 2 (2002): 136–52.

Grim, Brian J., and Roger Finke. *The Price of Freedom Denied: Religious Persecution and Conflict in the Twenty-First Century*. Cambridge: Cambridge University Press, 2011.

Guterres, António. "Global Conflicts and Human Displacement: 21st Century Challenges." Speech delivered July 11, 2015. https://www.unhcr.org/admin/hcspeeches/55ba370f9/global-conflicts-human-displacement-21st-century-challenges-delivered-antonio.html.

Haass, Richard. *A World in Disarray: American Foreign Policy and the Crisis of the Old Order*. New York: Penguin, 2018.

Harrell-Bond, Barbara E. "Can Humanitarian Work with Refugees Be Humane?" *Human Rights Quarterly* 24, no. 1 (2002): 51–85.

Hashmi, Sohail H. "Interpreting the Islamic Ethics of War and Peace." In *Islamic Political Ethics: Civil Society, Pluralism, and Conflict*, edited by Sohail Hashmi, 194–216. Ethikon Series in Comparative Ethics. Princeton, NJ: Princeton University Press, 2002.

———. "Is There an Islamic Ethic of Humanitarian Intervention?" *Ethics and International Affairs* 7 (1993): 55–73.

Hehir, J. Bryan. "The Ethics and Policy of War in Light of Displacement." In *Driven from Home: Protecting the Rights of Forced Migrants*, edited by David Hollenbach, 185–205. Washington, DC: Georgetown University Press, 2010.

———. "The Just War Ethic and Catholic Theology: Dynamics of Change and Continuity." In *War or Peace? The Search for New Answers*, ed. Thomas A. Shannon, 15–39. Maryknoll, NY: Orbis Books, 1980.

Hertzke, Allen D. *Freeing God's Children: The Unlikely Alliance for Global Human Rights*. Lanham, MD: Rowman & Littlefield, 2004.

Hoffmann, Stanley. *Duties beyond Borders: On the Limits and Possibilities of Ethical International Politics*. Syracuse, NY: Syracuse University Press, 1981.

Hollenbach, David. *The Common Good and Christian Ethics*. New York: Cambridge University Press, 2002.

———, ed. *Driven from Home: Protecting the Rights of Forced Migrants*. Washington, DC: Georgetown University Press, 2010.

———. *The Global Face of Public Faith: Politics, Human Rights, and Christian Ethics*. Washington, DC: Georgetown University Press, 2003.

———. "Social Ethics under the Sign of the Cross." Presidential Address to the Society of Christian Ethics. *Annual of the Society of Christian Ethics* 16 (1996): 3–18.

Human Rights Watch. *South Sudan's New War: Abuses by Government and Opposition Forces*. New York: Human Rights Watch, August 7, 2014. https://www.hrw.org/report/2014/08/07/south-sudans-new-war/abuses-government-and-opposition-forces.

Huntington, Samuel. "Religion and the Third Wave." *National Interest*, no. 24 (Summer 1991): 29–42.

Independent International Commission of Inquiry on the Syrian Arab Republic. *Report of the Independent International Commission of Inquiry on the Syrian Arab Republic*. Submitted to the U.N. Human Rights Council, February 5, 2015. https://documents-dds-ny.un.org/doc/UNDOC/GEN/G15/019/37/PDF/G1501937.pdf?OpenElement.

Inglehart, Ronald F., and Pippa Norris. "Trump, Brexit, and the Rise of Populism: Economic Have-Nots and Cultural Backlash." Harvard Kennedy School Faculty Research Working Paper series, RWP16-026, August 2016. https://research.hks.harvard.edu/publications/workingpapers/citation.aspx?PubId=11325&type=FN&PersonId=83.

Internal Displacement Monitoring Centre and Norwegian Refugee Council. *Global Report on Internal Displacement 2016*. http://www.internal-displacement.org/sites/default/files/publications/documents/2016-global-report-internal-displacement-IDMC.pdf.

———. *Global Report on Internal Displacement 2018*. http://www.internal-displacement.org/global-report/grid2018/.

International Commission on Intervention and State Sovereignty (ICISS). *The Responsibility to Protect: Report of the International Commission on Intervention and State Sovereignty*. Ottawa: International Development Research Center, December 2001. http://responsibilitytoprotect.org/ICISS%20Report.pdf.

International Criminal Court. *Rome Statute of the International Criminal Court*. July 1, 2002. https://www.icc-cpi.int/nr/rdonlyres/ea9aeff7-5752-4f84-be94-0a655eb30e16/0/rome_statute_english.pdf.

International Organization for Migration (IOM). *IOM Outlook on Migration, Environment, and Climate Change*. Geneva: International Organization for Migration, 2014. https://publications.iom.int/system/files/pdf/mecc_outlook.pdf.

Jastram, Kate, and Kathleen Newland. "Family Unity and Refugee Protection." In *Refugee Protection in International Law: UNHCR's Global Consultations on International Protection*, edited by Erika Feller, Volker Turk, and Frances Nicholson, 555–603 (Cambridge: Cambridge University Press, 2003). http://www.refworld.org/docid/470a33be0.html.

John Paul II. *Centesimus annus*. Encyclical of May 1, 1991. http://w2.vatican.va/content/john-paul-ii/en/encyclicals/documents/hf_jp-ii_enc_01051991_centesimus-annus.html.

———. *Sollicitudo rei socialis*. Encyclical of December 30, 1987. http://w2.vatican.va/content/john-paul-ii/en/encyclicals/documents/hf_jp-ii_enc_30121987_sollicitudo-rei-socialis.html.

John XXIII. *Pacem in terris*. Encyclical of April 11, 1963. http://w2.vatican.va/content/john-xxiii/en/encyclicals/documents/hf_j-xxiii_enc_11041963_pacem.html.

Johnson, Hilde F. *Waging Peace in Sudan: The Inside Story of the Negotiations That Ended Africa's Longest Civil War*. Portland, OR: Sussex Academic, 2011.

Judis, John B. *The Populist Explosion: How the Great Recession Transformed American and European Politics*. New York: Columbia Global Reports, 2016.

Juergensmeyer, Mark. "Hindu Nationalism and Human Rights." In *Religious Diversity and Human Rights*, edited by Irene Bloom, J. Paul Martin, and Wayne Proudfoot, 243–61. New York: Columbia University Press, 1996.

Kant, Immanuel. *Critique of Pure Reason*, translated by Norman Kemp Smith. New York: St. Martin's Press, 1965.

———. *Grounding for the Metaphysics of Morals*. Translated by James W. Ellington. 3rd edition. Indianapolis: Hackett, 1993.

Kazin, Michael. *The Populist Persuasion: An American History*. Rev. ed. with a new preface. Ithaca, NY: Cornell University Press, 2017.

Kelsay, John. *Arguing the Just War in Islam*. Cambridge, MA: Harvard University Press, 2009.

Kepel, Gilles. *The Revenge of God: The Resurgence of Islam, Christianity, and Judaism in the Modern World*. University Park: Pennsylvania State University Press, 1994.

King, Sallie B. *Socially Engaged Buddhism*. Honolulu: University of Hawai'i Press, 2009.

Kirmani, Nida, and Ajaz Ahmed Khan. "Does Faith Matter: An Examination of Islamic Relief's Work with Refugees and Internally Displaced Persons," *Refugee Survey Quarterly* 27, no. 2 (January 1, 2008): 41–50.

Kissinger, Henry. *Does America Need a Foreign Policy? Toward a Diplomacy for the 21st Century*. New York: Simon & Schuster, 2002.

Krafess, Jamal. "The Influence of the Muslim Religion in Humanitarian Aid." *International Review of the Red Cross* 87, no. 858 (June 2005): 327–42.

Küng, Hans. *A Global Ethic for Global Politics and Economics*. New York: Oxford University Press, 1998.

Kuperman, Alan J. "Obama's Libya Debacle: How a Well-Meaning Intervention Ended in Failure." *Foreign Affairs* 94, no. 2 (March–April 2015): 66–77.

Las Casas, Bartolomé de. *In Defense of the Indians: The Defense of the Most Reverend Lord, Don Fray Bartolomé de Las Casas, of the Order of Preachers, Late Bishop of Chiapa, against the Persecutors and Slanderers of the Peoples of the New World Discovered across the Seas*. Translated by Stafford Poole. DeKalb: Northern Illinois University Press, 1992.

Luckmann, Thomas. *The Invisible Religion: The Problem of Religion in Modern Society*. Translated from the German. New York: Macmillan, 1967.

Luijpen, William. "Justice as an Anthropological Form of Co-Existence." Chap. 6 in *Phenomenology of Natural Law*. Pittsburgh: Duquesne University Press, 1967.

Lyotard, Jean-François. "The Other's Rights." In *On Human Rights: The Oxford Amnesty Lectures 1993*, edited by Stephen Shute and Susan Hurley, 135–47. New York: Basic Books, 1993.

Maathai, Wangari. *The Challenge for Africa*. New York: Anchor Books, 2010.

———. Nobel Lecture. December 10, 2004. https://www.nobelprize.org/prizes/peace/2004/maathai/26050-wangari-maathai-nobel-lecture-2004/.

MacIntyre, Alasdair. *Whose Justice? Which Rationality?* Notre Dame, IN: University of Notre Dame Press, 1988.
Mamdani, Mahmood. *Saviors and Survivors: Darfur, Politics, and the War on Terror.* New York: Pantheon Books, 2009.
Marfleet, Philip. *Refugees in a Global Era.* New York: Palgrave Macmillan, 2006.
Maritain, Jacques. *Man and the State.* Washington, DC: Catholic University of America Press, 1998.
Martin, Susan F. "Rethinking the International Refugee Regime in Light of Human Rights and the Global Common Good." In *Driven from Home: Protecting the Rights of Forced Migrants*, edited by David Hollenbach, 15–33. Washington, DC: Georgetown University Press, 2010.
Martin, Susan Forbes, Sanjula S. Weerasinghe, and Abbie Taylor, eds. *Humanitarian Crises and Migration: Causes, Consequences and Responses.* New York: Routledge, 2014.
Marx, Karl, and Friedrich Engels. *Basic Writings on Politics and Philosophy by Karl Marx & Friedrich Engels.* Edited by Lewis S. Feuer. London: Fontana, 1969.
Masud, Muhammad Khalid. "The Obligation to Migrate: The Doctrine of Hijra in Islamic Law." In *Muslim Travellers: Pilgrimage, Migration, and the Religious Imagination*, edited by Dale F. Eickelman and James Piscatori, 29–49. Berkeley: University of California Press, 1990.
McAdam, Jane. *Climate Change, Forced Migration, and International Law.* Oxford: Oxford University Press, 2012.
McCleary, Rachel M., and Robert J. Barro. "Private Voluntary Organizations Engaged in International Assistance, 1939–2004." *Nonprofit and Voluntary Sector Quarterly* 37, no. 3 (2008): 512–36.
Mehta, Pratap Bhanu. "Hinduism and the Politics of Rights in India." In *Religion and the Global Politics of Human Rights*, edited by Thomas Banchoff and Robert Wuthnow, 193–212. Oxford: Oxford University Press, 2011.
Merwe, Hugo van der, and M. Brinton Lykes. "Transitional Justice Processes as Teachable Moments." *International Journal of Transitional Justice* 10, no. 3 (November 2016): 361–65.
Nhất Hạnh, Thich. *Interbeing: Fourteen Guidelines for Engaged Buddhism.* 3rd ed. Berkeley, CA: Parallax Press, 1998.
Nicholson, Frances. *The Right to Family Life and Family Unity of Refugees and Others in Need of International Protection and the Family Definition Applied.* UNHCR, Division of International Protection. PPLA/2018/01, January 2018. https://www.unhcr.org/en-us/5a8c40ba1.pdf.
Niebuhr, Reinhold. *The Nature and Destiny of Man: A Christian Interpretation.* 2 vols. Louisville, KY: Westminster John Knox, 1996.
Niland, Norah. *Inhumanity and Humanitarian Action: Protection Failures in Sri Lanka.* Tufts University. Feinstein International Center, September 2014. http://fic.tufts.edu/assets/Inhumanity-and-Humanitarian-Action_9-15-2014.pdf.
Nolan, Albert. *Hope in an Age of Despair.* Maryknoll, NY: Orbis Books, 2009.
Nussbaum, Martha Craven. *For Love of Country?* Boston: Beacon Press, 2002.

———. *Frontiers of Justice: Disability, Nationality, Species Membership*. Cambridge, MA: Belknap Press of Harvard University Press, 2007.

———. "Human Capabilities, Female Human Beings." In *Women, Culture, and Development: A Study of Human Capabilities*, edited by Martha Nussbaum and Jonathan Glover, 61–104. Oxford: Oxford University Press, 1995.

Nye, Joseph S., and Robert O. Keohane. "Transnational Relations and World Politics: An Introduction." *International Organization* 25, no. 3 (Summer 1971): 329–49. https://doi.org/10.1017/S0020818300026187.

O'Brien, David J., and Thomas A. Shannon, eds. *Catholic Social Thought: The Documentary Heritage*. Maryknoll, NY: Orbis Books, 1992.

Offenheiser, Raymond C., and Susan H. Holcombe. "Challenges and Opportunities in Implementing a Rights-Based Approach to Development: An Oxfam America Perspective." *Nonprofit and Voluntary Sector Quarterly* 32, no. 2 (June 2003): 268–301.

Ostrom, Elinor. "Beyond Markets and States: Polycentric Governance of Complex Economic Systems," Noble Prize lecture, delivered December 8, 2009, Stockholm University, https://www.nobelprize.org/uploads/2018/06/ostrom_lecture.pdf.

———. "The Challenge of Common Pool Resources." *Environment* 50, no. 4 (August 2008): 8–20.

———. *Governing the Commons: The Evolution of Institutions for Collective Action* (Cambridge, UK: Cambridge University Press, 1990).

Outka, Gene H. *Agape: An Ethical Analysis*. Yale Publications in Religion 17. New Haven, CT: Yale University Press, 1972.

Panel of Experts on South Sudan. "Letter Dated 22 January 2016 from the Panel of Experts on South Sudan Established Pursuant to Security Council Resolution 2206 (2015) Addressed to the President of the Security Council." UN Security Council, January 22, 2016. https://reliefweb.int/sites/reliefweb.int/files/resources/N1543824.pdf.

Paul VI. *Populorum progressio*. Encyclical of March 26, 1967, http://w2.vatican.va/content/paul-vi/en/encyclicals/documents/hf_p-vi_enc_26031967_populorum.html.

Philpott, Daniel. *Revolutions in Sovereignty: How Ideas Shaped Modern International Relations*. Princeton, NJ: Princeton University Press, 2001.

Pictet, Jean. *The Fundamental Principles of the Red Cross: Commentary*. January 1, 1979. https://www.icrc.org/en/doc/resources/documents/misc/fundamental-principles-commentary-010179.htm.

———. "Humanitarian Law and the Protection of War Victims." *International Review of the Red Cross* 15 (1975): 312–13.

Pinker, Steven. *The Better Angels of Our Nature: Why Violence Has Declined*. New York: Penguin Books, 2012.

Pius XI. *Quadragesimo anno*. Encyclical of May 15, 1931. http://w2.vatican.va/content/pius-xi/en/encyclicals/documents/hf_p-xi_enc_19310515_quadragesimo-anno.html.

Plaut, W. Gunther. "Jewish Ethics and International Migrations." *International Migration Review* 30, no. 1 (1996): 18–26.

Queen, Christopher S., and Sallie B. King, eds. *Engaged Buddhism: Buddhist Liberation Movements in Asia*. Albany: State University of New York Press, 1996.

Radelet, Steven C. *The Great Surge: The Ascent of the Developing World*. New York: Simon & Schuster, 2015.

Rawls, John. *The Law of Peoples*. Cambridge, MA: Harvard University Press, 2003.

Reynolds, Sarnata. "Persecution, Politics and Protection in the United States: Finding Refuge from Organized Crime in the Americas." In *The New Refugees: Crime and Forced Displacement in Latin America*, edited by David James Cantor and Nicolás Rodríguez Serna, 129–46. London: Institute of Latin American Studies, 2016.

Roberts, Adam, and Timothy Garton Ash, eds. *Civil Resistance and Power Politics: The Experience of Non-Violent Action from Gandhi to the Present*. New York: Oxford University Press, 2009.

Robertson, Geoffrey. *Crimes against Humanity: The Struggle for Global Justice*. New York: New Press, 2013.

Rubenstein, Jennifer C. *Between Samaritans and States: The Political Ethics of Humanitarian INGOs*. Oxford: Oxford University Press, 2015.

Ruston, Roger. *Human Rights and the Image of God*. London: SCM Press, 2004.

Ryan, E. A. "Catholics and the Peace of Westphalia." *Theological Studies* 9, no. 4 (1948): 590–99.

Sacks, Jonathan. *The Dignity of Difference: How to Avoid the Clash of Civilizations*. Rev. ed. New York: Continuum, 2003.

Sen, Amartya. *Development as Freedom*. New York: Anchor, 2000.

———. *The Idea of Justice*. Cambridge, MA: Belknap Press of Harvard University Press, 2011.

Sharma, Arvind. *Hinduism and Human Rights: A Conceptual Approach*. New Delhi: Oxford University Press, 2004.

Shue, Henry. *Basic Rights: Subsistence, Affluence, and US Foreign Policy*. 2nd. ed. Princeton, NJ: Princeton University Press, 1996.

Sikkink, Kathryn. *Evidence for Hope: Making Human Rights Work in the 21st Century*. Princeton, NJ: Princeton University Press, 2017.

Simon, John G., Charles W. Powers, and Jon P. Gunnemann. *The Ethical Investor: Universities and Corporate Responsibility*. New Haven, CT: Yale University Press, 1972.

Slaughter, Anne-Marie. *The Chessboard and the Web: Strategies of Connection in a Networked World*. New Haven, CT: Yale University Press, 2017.

———. *A New World Order*. Princeton, NJ: Princeton University Press, 2005.

Slim, Hugo. "Not Philanthropy but Rights: The Proper Politicisation of Humanitarian Philosophy." *International Journal of Human Rights* 6, no. 2 (June 2002): 1–22.

Sobrino, Jon. *The Principle of Mercy: Taking the Crucified People from the Cross*. Maryknoll, NY: Orbis Books, 1994.

———. *Where Is God? Earthquake, Terrorism, Barbarity, and Hope*. Maryknoll, NY: Orbis Books, 2004.

Stamatov, Peter. *The Origins of Global Humanitarianism: Religion, Empires, and Advocacy*. New York: Cambridge University Press, 2013.

Sviatschi, Micaela. *El Salvador's Politics of Perpetual Violence*. International Crisis Group, Latin America Report, no. 64, December 19, 2017. https://www.crisisgroup.org/latin-america-caribbean/central-america/el-salvador/64-el-salvadors-politics-perpetual-violence.

———. *Summa theologica*. 5 vols. Translated by the Fathers of the English Dominican Province. Allen, TX: Christian Classics, 1981.

Tibi, Bassam. "War and Peace in Islam." In *Islamic Political Ethics: Civil Society, Pluralism, and Conflict*, edited by Sohail Hashmi, 175–93. Ethikon Series in Comparative Ethics. Princeton, NJ: Princeton University Press, 2002.

Toft, Monica Duffy, Daniel Philpott, and Timothy Samuel Shah. *God's Century: Resurgent Religion and Global Politics*. New York: Norton, 2011.

UN Development Programme. *Human Development Report 2016: Human Development for Everyone*. New York: United Nations, 2017. http://hdr.undp.org/sites/default/files/2016_human_development_report.pdf.

UN General Assembly. Convention on the Prevention and Punishment of the Crime of Genocide. Approved December 9, 1948. http://www.hrweb.org/legal/genocide.html.

UN High Commissioner for Refugees (UNHCR). *Global Trends: Forced Displacement 2017*. https://www.unhcr.org/5b27be547.pdf.

———. *Vulnerability Assessment of Syrian Refugees in Lebanon*. 2017. https://data2.unhcr.org/en/documents/download/61312.

———. *World at War: Global Trends: Forced Displacement in 2014*. June 18, 2015. http://www.unhcr.org/en-us/statistics/country/556725e69/unhcr-global-trends-2014.html.

UN Human Rights Office of the High Commissioner. International Covenant on Economic, Social and Cultural Rights. December 16, 1966. https://www.ohchr.org/EN/ProfessionalInterest/Pages/CESCR.aspx.

UN Office for the Coordination of Humanitarian Affairs (OCHA). "UN Humanitarian Chief Urges Parties to Cease Hostilities, Protect Civilians and Aid Workers." *Humanitarian Bulletin, South Sudan*, no. 5 (May 23, 2018): 1, https://reliefweb.int/sites/reliefweb.int/files/resources/20180523_OCHA_SouthSudan_Humanitarian_Bulletin%235.pdf.

———. *Guiding Principles on Internal Displacement*. New York: United Nations, 2001: 1, http://www.unhcr.org/43ce1cff2.html.

UN Secretary-General. *One Humanity: Shared Responsibility, Report of the Secretary-General for the World Humanitarian Summit*. February 2, 2016. https://reliefweb.int/report/world/one-humanity-shared-responsibility-report-secretary-general-world-humanitarian-summit.

———. *Outcome of the World Humanitarian Summit: Report of the Secretary-General*. UN General Assembly, August 23, 2016. https://reliefweb.int/report/world/outcome-world-humanitarian-summit-report-secretary-general-a71353.

———. *Report of the Secretary-General Pursuant to General Assembly Resolution 53/35: The Fall of Srebrenica*. Submitted to UN General Assembly, November 15, 1999. https://undocs.org/A/54/549.

———. *Report of the Secretary-General's Internal Review Panel on United Nations Actions in Sri Lanka.* November 2012. http://www.un.org/News/dh/infocus/Sri_Lanka/The_Internal_Review_Panel_report_on_Sri_Lanka.pdf.

United Nations. *Report of the Independent Inquiry into the Actions of the United Nations during the 1994 Genocide in Rwanda.* December 15, 1999. http://www.un.org/en/ga/search/view_doc.asp?symbol=S/1999/1257.

———. *Report of the United Nations High Commissioner for Refugees, Part II: Global Compact on Refugees.* September 13, 2018, A/73/12. https://www.unhcr.org/gcr/GCR_English.pdf.

———. Universal Declaration of Human Rights. Proclaimed by United Nations General Assembly December 10, 1948. http://www.un.org/en/universal-declaration-human-rights/index.html.

Vatican Council II. *Dignitatis humanae, Declaration on Religious Freedom.* December 7, 1965. http://www.vatican.va/archive/hist_councils/ii_vatican_council/documents/vat-ii_decl_19651207_dignitatis-humanae_en.html.

———. *Gaudium et spes: Pastoral Constitution on the Church in the Modern Word.* December 7, 1965. http://www.vatican.va/archive/hist_councils/ii_vatican_council/documents/vat-ii_cons_19651207_gaudium-et-spes_en.html.

Verme, Paolo, Chiara Gigliarano, Christina Wieser, Kerren Hedlund, Marc Petzoldt, and Marco Santacroce. *The Welfare of Syrian Refugees: Evidence from Jordan and Lebanon.* Washington, DC: World Bank and UNHCR, 2016. https://openknowledge.worldbank.org/handle/10986/23228.

Vitoria, Francisco de. *Vitoria: Political Writings.* Edited by Anthony Pagden, and Jeremy Lawrance. New York: Cambridge University Press, 1991.

Waldron, Jeremy. *Dignity, Rank, and Rights.* New York: Oxford University Press, 2012.

Walker, Peter, Dyan Mazurana, Amy Warren, George Scarlett, and Henry Lewis. "The Role of Spirituality in Humanitarian Crisis Survival and Recovery." In *Sacred Aid: Faith and Humanitarianism*, edited by Michael N. Barnett and Janice Gross Stein, 115–39. New York: Oxford University Press, 2012.

Walters, LeRoy. "Five Classic Just War Theories: A Study of the Thought of Thomas Aquinas, Vitoria, Suarez, Gentili, and Grotius." Ph.D. diss., Yale University, 1971.

Walton, Matthew J. *Buddhism, Politics and Political Thought in Myanmar.* New York: Cambridge University Press, 2017.

Walzer, Michael. *Just and Unjust Wars: A Moral Argument with Historical Illustrations.* New York: Basic Books, 1977.

Wechsler, Harlan J. "For the Sake of My Kin and Friends: Traditions, Values, and Humanitarian Action in Judaism." In *Traditions, Values, and Humanitarian Action*, edited by Kevin Cahill, 21–40. New York: Fordham University Press and Center for International Health and Cooperation, 2003.

Weiss, Thomas G. "Military Humanitarianism: Syria Hasn't Killed It." *Washington Quarterly* 37, no. 1 (Spring 2014): 7–20.

World Bank. *Forcibly Displaced: Toward a Development Approach Supporting Refugees, the Internally Displaced, and Their Hosts.* 2017. https://openknowledge.worldbank.org/handle/10986/25016.

———. *Pathways for Peace: Inclusive Approaches to Preventing Violent Conflict*. Washington, DC: World Bank, 2018.

Zaat, Kirsten. *The Protection of Forced Migrants in Islamic Law*. Research Paper no. 146. Policy Development and Evaluation Service, United Nations High Commissioner for Refugees. December 2007. https://www.unhcr.org/research/working/476652cb2/protection-forced-migrants-islamic-law-kirsten-zaat.html.

Zetter, Roger. *Protecting Forced Migrants: A State of the Art Report of Concepts, Challenges and Ways Forward*. Bern: Swiss Federal Commission on Migration (FCM), 2014. http://www.ekm.admin.ch/content/dam/data/ekm/dokumentation/materialien/mat_schutz_e.pdf.

INDEX

Information in tables is indicated by *t* after the page number.

abolition of slavery, 23, 26
Abraham, 37–38, 40
accompaniment, 56–60
accountability, 70, 93–95, 135–36, 138–40, 152, 163n18
Acts, Book of, 36, 65
Afghanistan, 141
African Union, 99–100, 119, 122, 125–26
Ager, Alastair, 47
Ager, Joey, 47
al-Assad, Bashir, 135
al-Bashir, Omar, 94, 149
Al Hussein, Zeid Ra'ad, 6, 80–81
"America first," 7. *See also* Trump, Donald
Annan, Kofi, 68, 125
Appiah, Kwame Anthony, 70
Appleby, Scott, 52
Aquinas, Thomas of, 22, 28–29, 34–35, 72
Arendt, Hannah, 138
Aristotle, 35, 87, 102, 132, 165n25
Assad, Bashir al-, 135
asylum, 40–41, 63, 103–7, 144–45
Augustine, 72–73
autonomy, 86–87

Bangladesh, 43–44, 50, 81, 108, 148, 150
Ban Ki-moon, 130–31, 149
Barnett, Michael, 47–48
Bashir, Omar al-, 94, 149
Battle of Solferino, 13–14
Belgium, 2, 26–27, 167n4
Benedict XVI, Pope, 68, 124
Benn, Hillary, 119
Berlin Wall, 51
Betts, Alexander, 84, 88–89, 105
borders, duties across, 64–65
Bosnia-Herzegovina, 51, 80, 138. *See also* Srebrenica massacre
Brexit, 5–6
Buddhism, 43–46, 55, 58–59, 160n43
Bush, George W., 119–20

Cambodia, 44
Cameron, David, 109
Canada, 123
capability, to assist, 107–13
Care USA, 48*t*
Caribbean, 26–27
Caritas Internationalis, 33
Caritas in veritate (Benedict XVI), 124
Casanova, José, 49
Catholic Relief Services (CRS), 18–19, 33, 48, 49*t*, 57, 130
Central African Republic, 1, 6, 115–16, 122, 126
Cheng Yen, 44

189

Chesterton, G. K., 13
child separation policy, of United States, 105. *See also* asylum; Trump, Donald
China, 43, 51, 99–101
climate change, 1, 8, 83–84, 131, 146–52, 174n52
Clinton, Bill, 98–99
Collier, Paul, 143–44
Colombia, 1, 37
colonialism, 26–29, 41, 68, 124
Communist Manifesto (Marx and Engels), 13
compassion: in Buddhism, 43–44, 46, 55; from, to justice, 59–62; and humanity, 15; in Judaism, 38; problems with aid as result of, 18; and secularization, 47
condescension, 18, 59–60
"conflict trap," 144
Congo Free State, 26–27. *See also* Democratic Republic of Congo (DRC)
Convention on the Status of Refugees, 82, 89, 106–7
Cornille, Catherine, 58
cosmopolitanism, 70
crisis migrants, 84. *See also* forced migrants; internally displaced persons (IDPs); refugees
Croatia, 51
CRS (Catholic Relief Services), 18–19, 33, 48, 49t, 57, 130
"cultural backlash," 7

Dalai Lama, 51
Danforth, John, 119
Darfur, 94, 148–50, 174n52
Defense of the Indians (Las Casas), 28
De Indis (Vitoria), 27, 29
democracy: Catholicism and, 33, 49; legitimate governance and, 136–37; secularism and, 31–32; in South Africa, 139
Democratic Republic of Congo (DRC), 1–2, 115, 141, 155n3
Deng, Francis Mading, 116–17, 124
development: and climate change, 148; and displaced persons, 141–42, 145, 148; and humanitarian crises, 140, 145; and rights-based humanitarianism, 17, 142–43; sustainable, 150–51
de Waal, Alex, 174n52

Dieng, Adama, 81
dignity, human. *See* human dignity
disarmament, 136
Djibouti, 100
Doctors without Borders, 48, 48t
Dominican Republic, 27
Donne, John, 132
DRC (Democratic Republic of Congo), 1–2, 115, 141, 155n3
Dunant, Henri, 13, 47
duties across borders, 64–65
duties to internally displaced people, 115–22. *See also* internally displaced persons (IDPs); refugees
duty not to harm, 90–95
duty of asylum, 103–7
duty of refuge, 103–7
duty to protect: and human dignity, 86–88; and human rights, 79–82; and refugees, 82–85; and vulnerability, 84
duty to respond, 5–11, 99–100

earthquake, Haitian (2010), 4
Economic Community of West African States (ECOWAS), 126
El Salvador, 54, 103–5, 144–45
Engels, Friedrich, 13
Eritrea, 100
Ethiopia, 100, 108, 115
European Union, 5–6, 74, 94, 99–100
Exodus, Book of, 38, 72

faith, 27, 34–35, 54–56, 58
faith-based organizations: and accompaniment, 56–59; actions of, 46–50, 48t–49t expenditures of, 49t and humanitarian crises, 51–52; and justice, 59–62; and long-term response, 59–62; motivations of, 52; and negative effects of religion, 50–51; and people from other religious traditions, 57–58; and positive effects of religion, 51; recognition of, 52–53
Farley, Margaret, 86
Finke, Roger, 50
forced migrants, 84–85, 146–52. *See also* internally displaced persons (IDPs); refugees
France, 2, 7, 111, 124, 126, 167n4

Francis, Pope, 65, 132, 146
freedom: of conscience, 32; and human dignity, 86–87; religious, 32, 121

Gaddafi, Muammar, 126
Gandhi, Mohandas, 51
Genesis, Book of, 34, 39, 65, 71
Geneva Conventions, 17, 19, 23, 34, 92
genocide: defined, 155n4; in Myanmar, 81; Rwandan, 2, 91–92, 98–99; Srebrenica massacre, 2–3, 92, 135, 155n4
Genovese, Kitty, 98
Ghosananda, Maha, 44
Gleick, Peter, 149–50
Global Compact on Refugees, 9, 109, 130
globalization, 7–8, 22–23
God: doubting goodness of, 54; and human dignity, 26, 35; image and likeness of, 19, 34–35, 39, 65, 71; in Islam, 39–40; in Judaism, 71–72; love of, and suffering, 36, 54–55
"golden rule," 46
Good Samaritan parable, 35–36
Goodwin-Gill, Guy, 83
Green Belt Movement, 150–51
Grim, Brian, 50
Guatemala, 103–5
Guterres, António, 52, 90

Haas, Richard, 7–8
Haitian earthquake (2010), 4
harm, duty not to, 90–95
Hebrew Immigrant Aid Society, 49t
Hertzke, Allen, 121
hijra, 40–41
Hinduism, 31, 37, 42–43, 50
Hispaniola, 27
Holbrooke, Richard, 115
Honduras, 103–5
human dignity, 22; and autonomy, 86; and duty to protect, 86–88; egalitarian understanding of, 26; and freedom, 86–87; and humanitarian crises, 88; and human rights, 16–19; and justice, 131, 142; and relationality, 86; secularism and, 26; and state self-determination, 70
humanitarian crisis(es): in Buddhism, 43–45; challenge of, 2–5; Christianity and response to, 31–37; defined, 2; and development, 140, 145duty to respond to, 5–11; and faith-based organizations, 51–52; in Hinduism, 42–43; and human dignity, 88; "humanitarian" as concept in, 13–16; and humanity, 12; in Islam, 39–42; in Judaism, 37–39; and poverty, 140–45
humanitarianism: religious traditions and, in history, 25–31; rights-based, 17–20
human rights: basic, 88–89; Catholic commitment to, 33–34, 37, 69; centrality of 85–90; and creation, 39; and faith communities, 49; and Hinduism, 42; and human dignity, 16–19; and humanitarian crises, 12; and love, 60–61; protection of, 79–82; and religious leaders, 51; and Second Vatican Council, 32–33; and sovereignty, 67; and subsidiarity principle, 73–74; and Universal Declaration of Human Rights, 16, 19–20, 23, 34, 79–80
humility, 58–59
Huntington, Samuel, 32–33
Hurricane Katrina, 77

ICC (International Criminal Court), 6, 94–95, 139, 152
ICISS (International Commission on Intervention and State Sovereignty), 123, 125, 127
ICRC (International Committee of the Red Cross), 13–16, 19, 35, 46–47, 64
ICTY (International Criminal Tribunal for the Former Yugoslavia), 135
IDPs. *See* internally displaced persons (IDPs)
IGAD (Intergovernmental Authority on Development), 100, 119
immigration, backlash against, 7
India, 43, 50–51
in-group/out-group divisions, 21
Innocent X, Pope, 69, 163n17
Interagency Standing Committee, 81–82
Intergovernmental Authority on Development (IGAD), 100, 119
internally displaced persons (IDPs), 82–84, 115–22, 141–42. *See also* refugees

International Commission on Intervention and State Sovereignty (ICISS), 123, 125, 127
International Committee of the Red Cross (ICRC), 13–16, 19, 35, 46–47, 64
International Criminal Court (ICC), 6, 94–95, 139, 152
International Criminal Tribunal for the Former Yugoslavia (ICTY), 135
International Justice Mission, 48
International Rescue Committee, 48*t*
interreligious understanding, 57–58
Iran, 127–28, 136
Iraq, 37, 111–12, 115
Iraq War, 111–12
Islam, 26, 39–42, 46, 50, 58. See also *hijra*
Islamic Relief, 48, 57
Islamic Relief USA, 49*t*
Islamic State in Syria (ISIS), 80–81
Israel, 38, 50

Jesuit Refugee Service (JRS), 10, 56–58
John Paul II, Pope, 51, 68–69
Johnson, Hilde, 119
John XXIII, Pope, 22, 32–33, 65, 67–69
Jordan, 93, 110, 112, 142
Judaism, 34, 37–39, 71–72, 121
jus ad bellum, 91, 127. See also just war ethic
jus in bello, 91–92. See also just war ethic
jus post bellum, 127
justice: and reconciliation, 138–39; and climate change, 146; from compassion to, 59–62; in Hinduism, 42; and human dignity, 131, 142; in Judaism, 38; love and, 61–62; moral standard of, 131; and prevention, 131–34; and refugees, 5; and religious leaders, 51; restorative, 138; retributive, 138, 140; in Second Vatican Council, 34; and shared responsibility, 112
just war ethic, 42, 90–92, 94, 125, 127–28

Kabila, Joseph, 2
Kant, Immanuel, 16, 64, 167n3
Kelly, John, 104
Kenya, 94, 100, 119, 124–25
Kenyatta, Uhuru, 94
Kew Gardens Principle, 98, 128, 167n3

Khmer Rouge, 44
Kibaki, Mwai, 125
Kiir, Salva, 3–4, 135
King, Martin Luther, Jr., 26, 51
Kiribati, 147–48
Kissinger, Henry, 123
Kony, Joseph, 139
Kosovo, 123. See also Srebrenica massacre

Las Casas, Bartolomé de, 28
Lashkar-e-Taiba, 50
League of Arab States, 126
Lebanon, 93, 108–10, 112
Leopold II of Belgium, 26–27
Le Pen, Marine, 7
Leviticus, Book of, 72, 138
Libya, 126–27
lobsters, 75
long-distance advocacy, 26
Lord's Resistance Army (LRA), 139
Loughry, Maryanne, 147
Louisiana, 77
love: accompaniment and, 56–57; as equal regard, 60–61; and humanity, 15; justice and, 61–62; justice *vs.*, 60; and mutuality, 60; of neighbor, 27, 72–73, 137; ordering of, for different persons, 22; as self-sacrifice, 60
LRA (Lord's Resistance Army), 139
Luke, Gospel of, 35–36

Maathai, Wangari, 150–51, 174n56
Machar, Riek, 4, 135
Mahabharata, 42
Maine, 75
Mali, 126
Mamdani, Mahmood, 124, 156n18
Mandela, Nelson, 51, 139
Mark, Gospel of, 137
Marx, Karl, 13
Matthew, Gospel of, 36
McAdam, Jane, 83, 147
meaning, in face of suffering, 53–56
Médecins sans Frontières (Doctors without Borders), 48, 48*t*
Memory of Solferino, A (Dunant), 14
Mercy Corps, 48*t*
Merkel, Angela, 109

Mexico, 27–28
Milošević, Slobodan, 135
Mladić, Ratko, 135, 138
Montesino, Antonio, 27, 29–30
Mumbai terror attacks (2008), 50
Museveni, Yoweri, 142–43
mutuality, 59–60
Myanmar, 1, 6, 44, 58–59, 81, 141, 160n43

nationalism, 5–7, 43–44
Native Americans, 28–29
neighbor love, 27, 72–73, 137
New Orleans, Louisiana, 77
New York Declaration, 108–9
NGOs (non-governmental organizations), 47–48, 76–78, 131–34
Nhất Hạnh, Thích, 44
Nielsen, Kirstjen, 144
Nigeria, 141
Noah, 39
non-governmental organizations (NGOs), 47–48, 76–78, 131–34
Northern Triangle, of Central America, 103–5
Norway, 99–100
Nussbaum, Martha, 64, 70

Obama, Barack, 101
O'Brien, Stephen, 116
Odama, John Baptist, 139
Odinga, Raila, 125
On the Law of War (Vitoria), 29
oppressive states, 1
Organisation of Islamic Cooperation, 41
Organisation of the Islamic Conference (Organisation of Islamic Cooperation), 41, 126
Ostrom, Elinor, 75
Oxfam International, 17–19, 48t, 130

Pacem in terris (John XXIII), 33
Pakistan, 43, 50, 107–8, 141
Palestinians, 38, 50, 109
Paris Agreement, 151–52. *See also* climate change
paternalism, 18, 59–60
Paul, 36
Paul VI, Pope, 140–42

peacemaking, 134–40
Peace of Westphalia, 66, 69
People to People Peace Campaign, 122
Peru, 27–28
Philippines, 32, 44
Philpott, Daniel, 33, 66
physical security, as right, 89
Pictet, Jean, 14–15, 47
Pinker, Steven, 23–26, 31
Pius XI, Pope, 73
polycentric responsibility, 75–78
Pope Benedict XVI, 68, 124
Pope Francis, 65, 132, 146
Pope Innocent X, 69, 163n17
Pope John Paul II, 51, 68–69
Pope John XXIII, 22, 32–33, 65, 67–69
Pope Paul VI, 140–42
Pope Pius XI, 73
populism, 5–7, 77, 90
Portugal, 32
poverty, 1, 4, 33, 107, 140–45, 150
Powell, Colin, 119
Protestant Reformation, 66, 69
Protocol Relating to the Status of Refugees, 82–83

Quadragesimo anno (Pius XI), 73
Quakers, 26
Qur'an, 39–41

R2P (responsibility to protect), 122–28
Rakhine State, 81
Rawls, John, 137
reconciliation, 51–52, 134–40
Red Cross, 13–16, 19, 35, 46–47, 64
Reformation, 66, 69
refugees, 64–65; and climate change, 146–52; and Convention on Status of Refugees, 82, 89, 106–7; and duty of refuge, 103–7; and duty to protect, 82–85; and Global Compact on Refugees, 9, 109, 130; and poverty, 141–42; and Protocol Relating to the Status of Refugees, 82–83; and Rwandan genocide, 2; and South Sudan civil war, 4; Syrian, 3, 77, 93–94, 108–10. *See also* asylum; Jesuit Refugee Service (JRS); UN High Commissioner for Refugees (UNHCR)

relationality, 86–87, 171n8
Religions for Peace 9th World Assembly, 53
responsibility: criteria for, 97–102; in New York Declaration, 108–9; polycentric, 75–78; shared, 107–13; sovereignty as, 118
responsibility to protect (R2P), 122–28
restorative justice, 138
retributive justice, 138, 140
rights-based humanitarianism, 17–20
Rohingya refugees, 44, 50, 81, 108. *See also* Myanmar
Russia, 127–28, 136. *See also* Soviet Union
Rwandan genocide, 2, 80, 91–92, 98–99
Rwandan Patriotic Front, 2

Sacks, Jonathan, 38–39
Samaritan's Purse, 48, 49*t*
Save the Children, 48*t*
Second Vatican Council, 32, 35, 49, 65, 69
secularism, 10–11; and human dignity, 26; and humanitarianism, 13, 24, 47–49; and just war ethic, 90–91; and meaning in face of suffering, 53–54; and nondiscrimination, 57–58; and Peace of Westphalia, 69
self-sacrifice, 60, 102
Sen, Amartya, 140, 142, 167n3
Serbia, 51, 135. *See also* Srebrenica massacre
Sessions, Jeff, 104
Shah, Timothy, 33
Shue, Henry, 88–89, 165n30
Sivaraksa, Sulak, 44
Slaughter, Anne-Marie, 76–77
slavery, 23, 26–28
Sobrino, John, 54
Solferino, Battle of, 13–14
Somalia, 100, 123, 141
South Africa, 51, 97–98, 139
South African Truth and Reconciliation Commission, 137–40
South Korea, 32
South Sudan, 1, 3–4, 50, 77, 92–93, 99–100, 115, 135. *See also* Sudan
sovereignty, 65–70, 77, 117–18
Soviet Union, 51, 83
Spain, 26–27, 29, 32

SPLM/A (Sudan Peoples' Liberation Movement/Army), 118–19
Srebrenica massacre, 2–3, 92, 135, 155n4. *See also* Bosnia-Herzegovina; Yugoslavia
Sri Lanka, 3, 44, 50, 80
Stalin, Joseph, 32
Stamatov, Peter, 26–27
subsidiarity principle, 73–74
subsistence, as right, 89
Sudan, 50, 100, 108, 117–21, 141. *See also* Darfur; South Sudan
Sudan Council of Churches, 122
Sudan Peoples' Liberation Movement/Army (SPLM/A), 118–19
Sumbeiywo, Lazaro, 119
survival migrants, 84–85, 105
Sviatschi, Micaela, 144
Syrian crisis, 1, 3, 10, 50, 58, 65, 77, 80–81; and basic rights, 93–94; and climate change, 149–50, 174n52; and duty to respond, 99; and Germany, 109; internally displaced persons in, 115; and Iraq War, 111–12; and refugees, 93–94, 108–10; and responsibility to protect, 128; war crimes in, 135

Thailand, 58–59
Thomas Aquinas, 22, 28–29, 34–35, 72
Tibet, 51
Tolstoy, Leo, 51
Trump, Donald, 6; asylum seekers and, 103–4, 144; and child separation policy, 105; and climate change, 151; nationalism of, 7; as populist, 7; and South Sudan, 101
Turkey, 93, 108, 110
Tutu, Desmond, 51
Tuvalu, 147
Tzu Chi organization, 44

Uganda, 100, 108, 110, 119, 139, 142–43
UN High Commissioner for Refugees (UNHCR), 47, 52
United Kingdom: Brexit in, 5–6; Rwandan genocide and, 2, 98–99; South Africa and, 97; Syrian refugees and, 109–10
United Nations: Global Compact on Refugees, 9; Rwandan genocide and, 2;

Srebrenica massacre and, 3; Universal Declaration of Human Rights, 16
United States: asylum seekers to, 103–6, 144–45; child separation policy of, 105; Rwandan genocide and, 2; South Africa and, 97; Sudan and, 119–21
Universal Declaration of Human Rights, 16, 19–20, 23, 34, 79–80

Vatican II, 32, 35, 49, 65, 69
Venezuela, 105–6
Vitoria, Francisco, 27–29

Waldron, Jeremy, 22–23
Walker, Peter, 161n22
Walt, Stephen, 111
We Are Still In, 151–52

Weiss, Thomas, 128
Welcoming the Stranger: Affirmations for Faith Leaders, 52–53
World Bank, 133
World Humanitarian Summit, 130–31
World Vision International, 48, 49t
World War II, 66

Yale University, 97–98
Yemen, 1, 6, 122
Yugoslavia, 3, 50–51, 135

Zaire, 2
zakat, 41
Zetter, Roger, 84
Zuma, Jacob, 140

ABOUT THE AUTHOR

David Hollenbach, SJ, is Pedro Arrupe Distinguished Research Professor in the Walsh School of Foreign Service and Senior Fellow of the Berkley Center for Religion, Peace and World Affairs at Georgetown University. His teaching and research deal with human rights, religious and ethical responses to humanitarian crises, and religion in political life from the standpoint of Catholic social thought, theology, and the social sciences. His books include *Driven from Home: Protecting the Rights of Forced Migrants* and *The Common Good and Christian Ethics*. He has taught often at Hekima University College in Nairobi, Kenya.